THE CHANGING CHARACTER OF WAR AND PEACEMAKING

THE CHANGING CHARACTER OF WAR AND PEACEMAKING

Papers from the 2023 Conference on the
Resolution of Intractable Conflict (CRIC 2023)
held at Harris Manchester College,
University of Oxford from 18th – 20th September 2023

JOHN ALDERDICE AND
PADRAIG O'MALLEY

Published in the New England Journal of Public Policy, Volume 36, Issue 1, 2024

ARTIS
EUROPE

In September during each of the last ten years, John Alderdice (https://lordalderdice.com) has organized and hosted a **Conference on the Resolution of Intractable Conflict (CRIC)** at Harris Manchester College, University of Oxford. In recent times many of the papers presented at these annual conferences have been published in the New England Journal of Public Policy. In 2023, to celebrate the tenth anniversary conference, Professor Padraig O'Malley, the Editor-in-Chief of the NEJPP invited Lord Alderdice to join him as Guest Editor for a Special Issue devoted to papers from CRIC 2023. The CRIC theme for 2023 was **The Changing Character of War and Peacemaking.**

The original published digital version of this NEJPP Special Issue is available without charge at https://scholarworks.umb.edu/nejpp/vol36/iss1/

This hard copy format is produced by ARTIS Europe Ltd (https://artiseurope.com) and they hold the copyright for the cover design © 2024.

The cover designer was Irena Czaplicka-Laskowska - irena.laskowska@gmail.com

We are especially grateful to Dr Moisés and Mrs Mimi Lemlij and their family foundation for their generous financial support that made CRIC 2023 and this hard copy publication possible.

ISBN:
978-1-80541-637-1 - eBook
978-1-80541-638-8 - paperback

NEW ENGLAND JOURNAL OF PUBLIC POLICY, VOLUME 36, ISSUE 1, 2024

Special Issue: The Changing Character of War and Peacemaking

EDITOR'S NOTE

Padraig O'Malley

University of Massachusetts Boston, padraig.omalley@umb.edu

After the fall of the Berlin Wall in 1991 and the dissolution of the Soviet Union, Francis Fukuyama wrote *The End of History and the Last Man*. He argued that the evolution of humanity had reached an end point with the triumph of Western liberal democracy, anchored in the Bretton Woods Agreement post WWII, as the final form of government. A rules-based order was in place and in the process of being universally accepted and being adhered to.[1]

History, however, has had the last laugh.

Liberal democracies are under siege. In this upheaval of the world order—the old order is frayed and flagging, what will replace it has yet to emerge. The unipolar world of the 1990s where the United States was the single hegemonic power has been replaced by a multipolar world in which China is competing with the United States to become *pari passu*.

David Sanger's book *New Cold Wars* explores the resurgence of great power rivalries and the simultaneous confrontations between the United States, China, and Russia and how the assumptions of the post-Cold War era, where economic globalization and the expansion of free markets were expected to foster stability and American hegemony, have proven to be flawed.[2] Sanger delves into the erosion of the "Washington Consensus" and the failure of multiple US administrations to recognize the looming threats posed by an increasingly assertive China and a resurgent Russia.

Sanger poses critical questions: Will Vladimir Putin's mistakes in Ukraine lead to his downfall or prompt him to resort to nuclear weapons? Will China invade Taiwan, the semiconductor capital? Will China and Russia deepen their partnership to

Padraig O'Malley is the John Joseph Moakley Professor of Peace and Reconciliation at the John W. McCormack Graduate School of Policy and Global Studies, University of Massachusetts Boston.

undermine American dominance? And can a politically divided America still lead the world in this new era of great power competition?

What was heralded as a forthcoming age of democracy on the rise across the globe has proved otherwise. The number of liberal democracies has declined from a peak of forty-four in 2009 to only thirty-two in 2022, while the number of closed autocracies has increased from twenty-two in 2012 to thirty-three in 2022. According to the V-Dem Institute's 2024 Democracy Report, democracy declined or "autocratization" was ongoing in forty-two countries in 2023, home to thirty-five percent of the world's population, while democratization was taking place in eighteen countries hosting only five percent. Autocracies are becoming bolder and less concerned about international opinion. Indicators of liberal democracy, such as high court independence and executive oversight, have declined in twenty-five to thirty-two countries in recent years, as autocratization intensifies.[3] In the June 2024 European elections, the far right made huge gains, especially in France and Germany, threatening the centrist consensus at the heart of the Union.

The Republican Party in the United States has veered sharply to the right, to a more authoritarian mode. Donald Trump has vowed, if he is elected to the presidency again, to do away with many of the checks and balances that underline its institutions and expand the power of the president. Loyalty to the president will take precedence over loyalty to the constitution, the Department of Justice will become a personal fiefdom.

An unrestrained Trump, possibly withdrawing the US from NATO, ending financial aid and military hardware shipments to Ukraine, giving Vladmir Putin free rein in Ukraine, and imposing prohibitive tariffs on China would redraw the global geopolitical map overnight.[4] Europe is undergoing its own transformation: deep internal divisions within EU member countries grow as once marginal right-wing parties in Italy, Hungary, France, Germany, the Netherlands, Hungary, Spain, Poland, and Finland have either gained a foothold in government or may be on their way to doing so.[5]

Meanwhile, military alliances and strategic partnerships are multiplying—NATO, including new members Finland and Sweden; the US, Japan, South Korea, and the Philippines, in the Asia Pacific; and the Quad, a loose strategic relationship between the US, India, Australia, and Japan—while some partners such as Singapore, Vietnam, and Indonesia are deepening security ties with the US to hedge against China's rise. In the Middle East, the Axis of Resistance—a loose coalition of groups—Iran, Hezbollah in Lebanon, Syria, and peripherally Hamas and the Houthi in Yemen, and various Shiite militias in Iraq, such as those under the umbrella of the Popular Mobilization Forces (PMF) pose an ongoing threat to Israel and Western interests in the region. China and Russia have deepened their strategic partnership. China is a pivotal conduit for goods for Russia's defense industry and their two economies have become interconnected.[6]

In 2003 and 2005 the journal published two volumes on war. A selection of the articles became the book, *Sticks & Stones: Living with Uncertain Wars.* "Sticks and Stones," of course, refers to Albert Einstein's response when he was asked what would be used to prosecute wars in a post nuclear exchange world.[7]

Twenty years on, we are not yet at that point, but warnings about the use of tactical nuclear weapons (with an explosive reach approaching the atomic bomb in Hiroshima in 1945) have entered the conversation in a troubling way, especially Vladimir Putin's threats over Ukraine.[8] We are getting used to hearing about circumstances in which they might be used. What was once verboten has become normalized.[9] The Doomsday Clock is set at ninety seconds to midnight, the closest to midnight since its inception in 1947. Geopolitical and technological factors are intertwined, creating different and often unforeseeable consequences. Among these factors are a) the collapse of the WWII rules-based world order and no agreement on what should take its place, b) the proliferation of military alliances, c) tensions between the United States and China over Taiwan and the South China Sea, d) an untamed nuclear North Korea, e) Israel-Iran confrontations in the Middle East with the US committed to Israel's defense, f) the evolution of drone warfare, with some drones programmed to hit specific targets and fly in swarms, g) AI programmed weapons that can work autonomously, h) the sophistication and proliferation of non-state actors such as the Houthi and Hezbollah, and i) climate warming as huge swaths of the world, especially in the Middle East, race past the 1.5°C threshold set by the United Nations and become uninhabitable, and scarce resources such as water literally dry up.

The conduct of war in the twenty-first century has evolved significantly from that of the twentieth century, reflecting changes in technology, geopolitics, and the nature of conflict itself.[10] Among the main drivers transforming the ways in which warfare is carried out are the following. a) Asymmetrical warfare: in the twentieth century, conflicts often involved conventional warfare between nation-states with relatively similar military capabilities. The twenty-first century, however, has seen a rise in asymmetrical warfare between state and non-state actors, with vastly different military capabilities and strategies. This includes guerrilla warfare, terrorism, and cyberattacks. b) The digital revolution has introduced cyber warfare as a critical component of modern conflict. State and non-state actors engage in hacking, disinformation warfare, and cyberattacks to disrupt, degrade, or spy on each other's infrastructure and communications. c) Hybrid warfare combines conventional military tactics with irregular tactics. It blurs the lines between military and civilian targets, and between war and peace, making it more challenging to identify aggressors and respond effectively. d) The use of unmanned aerial vehicles (UAVs), commonly known as drones, and the development of autonomous weapons systems represent a significant shift. These technologies allow for remote or automated engagement in conflict, reducing the risk to human soldiers and changing the dynamics of surveillance, targeting, and strikes. e) The privatization of war: there has been an increase in the involvement of private military and security companies (PMSCs) in conflicts. These entities offer a range of military and security services, from logistical support to direct combat roles.

According to a February 2024 article in *Foreign Affairs*, "The Perilous Coming Age of AI Warfare," at least thirty countries use defense systems that have autonomous modes. Some analysts say that it is only a matter of time before "drones will be used to identify, select, and attack targets without help from humans."[11] Paul Scharre of the Center for a New American Security outlined a number of possible near-term futures, from autonomous drone swarms battling each another "as independently as high-frequency trading bots to the possibility that AI may be given authority over existing nuclear arsenals."[12] He calls for governments to agree to human supervision of military, ban AI weapons that target humans, and protocols that only humans have control over nuclear weapons. "Without limits, humanity risks barreling toward a future of dangerous, machine-driven warfare," Scharre writes, and the window to act is "closing fast." Other analysts disagree with his conclusion of a possible apocalyptic future, but most agree that in future wars, big data will play a pivotal role. "It [a military] will have to master digitized information flooding through the battle space," he writes. "Humans simply do not have the capacity to do this." AI most probably will.

In the Israel-Hamas conflict there are credible investigations showing that the Israeli Defense Force (IDF) uses two systems Habsora (the Gospel) and Lavender, AI algorithms to identify targets in Gaza, the former to identify where the army believes militants are operating from and the latter used to compile a "kill list" of suspected combatants. The IDF, as it does all matters related to its security, denies the report.[13]

The Ukraine-Russia War is the best example of how the near future in warfare between states might be conducted. Ukraine is fostering innovation through initiatives like the Brave1 Cluster, a technology incubator that supports collaboration between the defense sector and industry, enhancing its innovative bandwidth. Over 300 companies are involved.[14] This has led to the development and testing of numerous drones and unmanned ground vehicles (UGVs), many of which have already been deployed in combat scenarios.

The *Washington Post* calls Ukraine a "super laboratory of invention" regarding autonomous weapons innovations.[15] Some Ukrainian UGVs are equipped for direct combat and tactical missions. Its naval drones, "Sea Baby" and Toloka, the country's uncrewed underwater vehicles, have disabled one-third of the Russian fleet in the Black Sea and opened a passageway for exports of grain, the sustenance of the Ukrainian economy.[16]

Other drones are armed with machine guns and are used to attack enemy positions, conduct reconnaissance, and provide fire support. Despite these advancements, the deployment of UGVs also presents challenges, including vulnerability to enemy drones (dogfights in the air), but further technological refinement will enhance their effectiveness and survivability on the battlefield.[17]

Starlink, a satellite internet service provided by SpaceX, has become a critical component of Ukraine's military communications infrastructure. It enables Ukraine to maintain high-speed, reliable communication channels for various military and civilian applications, especially in the face of Russian attempts to disrupt its telecommunications. After a cyberattack by Russia that disabled a significant portion of Ukraine's satellite communications network, managed by Viasat, the Ukrainian government reached out to SpaceX. Elon Musk, the CEO, activated Starlink service over Ukraine and sent terminals to the country. This quick deployment allowed Ukraine to reestablish its communications capabilities, crucial for command and control of military operations. Starlink's low-orbit satellite network has provided Ukraine with several strategic advantages. It has enabled real-time communication and coordination across military units, which is vital for operational success in a dynamic battlefield environment. The service, which the Pentagon pays SpaceX for, has also supported the use of drones and other technology-dependent systems, enhancing Ukraine's surveillance and reconnaissance capabilities.[18] However, there is evidence that Russia has pierced the Starlink veil and has been purchasing Starlink terminals on the black market for its troops' use.[19]

Russia has responded to these developments with its own innovations.[20] The key developments include the following. a) Artillery shells: Russia is on track to produce nearly three times as many artillery shells in 2024—almost three million—as the United States and Europe combined (about 1.2 million). This includes receiving over one million rounds from North Korea. b) Russia has significantly increased the production of its Iskander-M ballistic missiles, and the Kh-101 cruise missile, from thirteen to thirty, and c) relied heavily on "kamikaze" drones. d) Russia has acquired Fareh-110 and Zolfaghar short-range ballistic missiles and Shahed drones from Iran, which it has deployed in large numbers to strike Ukrainian infrastructure and military targets.[21] e) Glide bombs: Russia has been using glide bombs, which are old Soviet dumb bombs equipped with guidance kits, as one of its most effective aerial weapons against Ukrainian troops, and f) supersonic missiles, specifically the Kinzhal (Dagger) air launched ballistic missile, which can travel at Mach 10 (over 7,600 mph) and is designed to evade Ukraine's air defense systems. The US-supplied Patriot missile has intercepted some of these, despite their speed of approach.

The articles in this volume address different facets of how war and peacemaking are undergoing structural changes in the first decades of the twenty-first century. Some wars are of the old-fashioned type, but with technological differences. In Ukraine the trench warfare is reminiscent of WWI, despite a variety of technological innovations. Russian and Ukrainian forces engage in the closest thing to face-to-face combat. Costly battles are fought over inches of ground, which can change hands on numerous occasions. But Ukrainian troops, even in their trenches rely on their laptops and phones to pinpoint Russian troop movement and as I have described, a wide variety of home manufactured drones, adapted for multipole uses.

In his wide-ranging essay "New Technologies in Wars, Old and New," Lord John Alderdice, guest editor of this special issue of the journal, The Changing Character of War and Peacemaking, and a member of the House of Lords Select Committee on International Relations and Defence, among his many distinguished affiliations, observes that the constant advancement of drone capabilities is merely part of a larger story. Drones are integrated into a hybrid approach that is continuously evolving and developing, following the principles described by Brian Arthur. He highlights that technologies not only adapt through changes to their individual elements, such as miniaturization and increased power, but they also combine with one another, giving rise to novel structures and capacities.

Just as the character of war is changing, he writes, so too is the nature of peacemaking. A survey of "experienced negotiators from the UN and other national and international agencies and NGOs" revealed "an almost universal sense that the old ways of peacemaking no longer worked but that it was not yet clear what might replace them."

Alderdice warns against a future described by the philosopher John Gray, where "instead of the belief that humankind, albeit in fits and starts, was moving inexorably toward a peaceful, rational, liberal, well-ordered, and prosperous future, he says that we are falling into a world dominated by authoritarianism, intolerant nationalisms, and unreason." Gray argues that the relatively short period when the liberal trajectory seemed to be in the ascendant was, in historical terms, a passing blip, an aberration that is already dissolving away.

As an alternative, Alderdice suggests three developments that may point toward the next evolutionary way station for humankind: the emergence of complexity science, an appreciation that our emotions are a positive evolutionary advantage rather than a flaw to be overcome, and a focus on relationships rather than solely on individuals.

Drawing on psychodynamics as a framework, Eugen Koh provides an analysis of the factors heightening the risk of armed conflict between the two superpowers in the "Psychological Risks of War Between the United States and China." The article delves into how the deteriorating US-China relationship—marked by a shift from collaboration to competition, mutual perceptions of enmity, and escalating threats exacerbated by historical traumas—can precipitate a collapse of rational thinking and unleash uncontrollable emotionality.

Koh underscores the perils of disregarding or exploiting these trauma-related sensitivities for domestic political expediency or strategic gains, as such actions risk escalating accidents into conflicts, and conflicts into outright war. Drawing upon the concept of Thucydides's Trap, which posits the inevitability of conflict when a rising power challenges an established one, Koh explores pathways to circumvent this dynamic.

Central to Koh's proposed psychodynamic approaches is the need to anticipate and counter regressive forces driven by fear, contain overwhelming emotionality, and restore the capacity for nuanced, complex thinking to find creative solutions to potential impasses. It accentuates the criticality of recognizing and managing the emotional and cognitive factors that can fuel conflict escalation between the two powers.

In "Employing Multi-Agent AI to Model Conflict and Cooperation in Northern Ireland," Katherine O' Lone, Michael Gantley, Justin E. Lane, and F. LeRon Shults develop a multi-agent artificial intelligence (MAAI) model to investigate the primary catalysts of conflict and cooperation in Northern Ireland's post-Agreement era. Insights from the model reveal that perceptions of fairness and emotions of sadness are leading drivers of cooperation. Conversely, anxiety and perceived moral authority stand out as prominent instigators of conflict.

The article contextualizes these findings within prior computational modeling efforts focused on Northern Ireland, the social psychological literature on intergroup conflict, and the prevailing geopolitical landscape. It outlines MAAI's potential for providing policymakers with powerful digital tools to model and predict conflict and cooperation dynamics and discusses previous modeling work on intergroup conflict and reconciliation in Northern Ireland, which laid the foundation for their research. The methodological approach, including sentiment analysis and creating a "digital twin" to simulate conditions for social stability (or instability) in Northern Ireland, is outlined, with a focus on the implications of removing "peace walls." Ultimately, the authors advocate for leveraging MAAI technology to inform policymaking while addressing ethical considerations surrounding its application in peacebuilding and reconciliation initiatives.

In "Brothers and Sisters from Another Mother—Promoting Inter-cultural Understanding, Conflict Reduction, and Solidarity Among Partner Forces in the Sahel," Alain Tschudin and James Smith, cognizant of the changing nature of warfare and of global extremist challenges, propose fresh innovations in the training of international and African partner forces tasked with collaborating to address security threats in the Sahel region.

This article advocates for a contemporary peacebuilding approach rooted in transformative, dialogical methodologies that promote greater intercultural understanding between local security forces and their external allies. They emphasize the complexities of cultural pluralism in combat, including the importance of shared language. Such an intervention is posited as cost-effective, sustainable, adaptable, and replicable, fostering unity, shared understanding, and reducing direct and indirect violence such as green-on-blue casualties and resentment toward diverse troops. It heightens motivation, strengthens solidarity in the field, aligns efforts toward shared goals, and enhances operational effectiveness, ultimately contributing to conflict reduction and a more enduring peace.

Kumar Ramakrishna argues in "Understanding the Indirect Strategy Moment in Global Affairs" that the ongoing conflict between Russia and Ukraine highlights the relevance of "indirect strategy" in modern geopolitical competition. While the prospect of an end to the fighting remains uncertain, the threat of escalation through nuclear weapons has emerged as a worrying possibility. However, this overt military conflict is an anomaly compared to the past decade, where he says low intensity "'hybrid conflict' has been the norm in the standoff between Moscow and Kyiv. Hybrid conflict broadly refers to the methods and tools used by individual state or non-state actors to pursue their objectives, spanning the conflict continuum from disinformation to cyber war, energy supply disruption, and traditional warfare. Moscow had in fact been engaging in hybrid conflict with Ukraine since the 2014 intervention" in eastern Ukraine by Russian troops in unmarked uniforms, the so-called "little green men."

"Russian President Vladimir Putin's decision to switch to an outright 'special military operation' in February 2022," Ramakrishna writes, "has not yielded the desired outcome of Ukrainian military and political capitulation." Instead, US intelligence assessed that Russia has suffered staggering losses, including eighty-seven percent of its active-duty ground troops and two-thirds of its pre-invasion tanks. He continues, "Against such a backdrop, it is not far-fetched to imagine that a ceasefire between Kyiv and Moscow might eventually ensue. Putin may then revert to his previous and relatively far more cost-effective hybrid warfare playbook as the main means to secure his geopolitical objectives vis-à-vis Kyiv."

Ramakrishna notes that a recurring theme in this "indirect strategy moment" is that the line between peace and war has become increasingly blurred. Adopting an "indirect strategy lens" is crucial to frame current and ongoing geostrategic developments across various issues and domains, "from economic and technological de-risking to the preservation on domestic socio-political cohesion in the face of foreign influence campaigns by hostile state actors."

The opening premise of Cedric de Coning's "Coping with the Complexity of the Changing Character of War: Toward a New Paradigm of Adaptive Peace" is that conflicts and related casualties continue to rise, underscoring the inadequacy of the mainstream approach to peace and security. It contends that a critical factor behind the international community's faltering peace and security efforts lies in the inherent shortcomings of the prevailing approach and methodology employed to foster, maintain, and build peace in conflict-ridden societies This article advocates for a paradigm shift:

an adaptive mindset that embraces the dynamism and unpredictability of conflict environments, and a context-specific methodology that can effectively address the underlying drivers of violent conflict and foster lasting peace. By doing so, it offers a new lens through which to navigate the evolving character of war and peace. By reframing our understanding of conflict's complexities and embracing adaptive methodologies, de Coning argues, we can transcend the limitations of predetermined strategies. This shift in perspective is pivotal to achieving lasting peace in volatile environments where linear models have consistently fallen short.

As the quest for a lasting solution to the Israeli-Palestinian conflict continues, Ciarán Ó Cuinn maintains in "Muscat, Madrid, Ulster, and the Holy Land: the MEDRC Model of Environmental Peacebuilding in a Revived Middle East Peace Process," that MEDRC stands out as a unique institution facilitating the Middle East peace process through environmental diplomacy. While other initiatives have faltered, MEDRC's distinct institutional and operational approach to conflict resolution has enabled its perseverance.

Examining MEDRC's methodology, he writes, holds significance not only for combating transboundary climate and environmental threats but also for leveraging these challenges as entry points into peace processes. This article presents, for the first time, the detailed elements of the MEDRC Model and its underlying Conflict Resolution Process Guidelines, exploring their broader implications for environmental peacebuilding and a revitalized Middle East peace process.

Through this exploration, the article sheds light on the potential of environmental diplomacy to transcend deeply rooted conflicts. It offers insights into the design and implementation of peace processes that harness the power of shared environmental challenges as catalysts for dialogue, cooperation, and ultimately, lasting peace. By examining the transferable elements of this approach, the article offers insights for practitioners and policymakers seeking innovative pathways to address complex, protracted conflicts through environmental cooperation and diplomacy.

In "The Middle East: From an Inflammable Region to A Resilient Land of Opportunities; A Case Study of EcoPeace Middle East's Unique Approach to Conflict and Environmental Action," Yana Abu Taleb and Thalsa-Thiziri Mekaouche observe that while the global community strives to limit temperature rise to 1.5°C, the Middle East is projected to experience a four-degree increase. Vast swaths of the region will become uninhabitable during the extended summer months. This climate vulnerability is further compounded by dependencies on food imports and reliance on fossil fuels. Additionally, the Middle East is the world's most water-scarce region, straining ecosystems, economies, and population well-being. Moreover, it is already grappling with high levels of conflict and violence. The ongoing Israel-Hamas war has caused over 36,000 deaths in the first seven months, and they point out that the region already had the world's highest number of battle-related deaths (26,270 in 2021), primarily due to the escalating conflict in Yemen.

Amid this convergence of crises, EcoPeace Middle East, a 2024 Nobel Peace Prize nominee, has developed a theory of change that seeks to simultaneously address climate change and conflict resolution in Jordan, Israel, and Palestine. This article focuses on their paradigm and offers "insights into the prospects of reversing the narrative attached to the Middle East: from a climate-vulnerable and conflict-prone region to a resilient and peaceful land of opportunities."

In "Pioneering the Digital Frontier: CMI"'s Approach to Forward-Looking Dialogues," Johanna Poutanen and Felix Kufus outline how the CMI – Martti Ahtisaari Peace Foundation (CMI) integrates technology-enhanced foresight methods into dialogue and mediation efforts. Digital tools, such as software dedicated to data analysis and visualization, play a pivotal role in their approach by allowing for broad-based data collection and participatory analysis. Interactive visual aids foster collective sense-making and aid in challenging the entrenched mindsets of conflict stakeholders. They explain how foresight approaches can be employed "to develop shared future visions and facilitate collaboration even in the context of stalled peace processes." The article provides an overview of CMI's work in integrating these methods into future-oriented dialogue processes across various countries, including Yemen, Libya, Palestine, and Armenia. The fundamental aspect of this approach is the utilization of software that aids in mapping and displaying diverse stakeholder perspectives, grounding discussions in factual realities, and facilitating participatory scenario-building. The article concludes by presenting two case studies that illustrate CMI's use of digitally augmented foresight in dialogue processes in Armenia and Libya, suggesting key benefits, limitations, and broader potential of foresight and accompanying digital approaches for peacemaking.

In "Scaling Expertise: A Note on Homophily in Online Discourse and Content Moderation," Dylan Weber examines how online discussions naturally tend to favor homophily, meaning users prefer interacting with content and people similar to themselves. This tendency, he shows, leads to a narrower range of information and a higher risk of spreading misinformation. He interrogates the widespread presence of homophily in online discourse and its negative impacts. Additionally, he evaluates the current moderation systems used by major social media platforms, noting their inadequacies in addressing these structural issues. Finally, Weber proposes a new moderation framework focused on "scaling expertise," which aims to handle the vast scale of online interactions while being sensitive to different contexts and cultures.

Finally, In "Personal Reflections from a Grassroots Peacebuilding Journey," Mark Clark shares his diverse experiences over thirty years, working at the intersection of leadership development, complexity, and conflict. It highlights the author's journey across various conflict regions, including Iraq, where he was Minister for Youth and Sports in the Paul Bremer era that followed the ousting of Saddam Hussein by a US-led coalition, violence reduction and post-conflict reconciliation initiatives in Papua New Guinea, humanitarian work in remote areas in the Democratic Republic of the Congo, and his thirteen years as CEO of Generations For Peace, the Jordan-based global international peacebuilding organization supporting grassroots peacebuilding efforts in fifty-two countries.

Peacekeeping and peacebuilding are two different areas of intervention and require separate, though on occasion overlapping, strategies. The sum of his experiences lead Clark to prescribe a number of variables as necessary to underpin successful peacemaking—courageous leadership, high-quality data, participatory engagement that engages diverse perspectives in generative dialogue, and accountability and incentive mechanisms. The sum of his experience leads him to conclude that peacemaking and peacebuilding should be essentially viewed as a change process—an adaptive leadership challenge within complex adaptive systems.

Recurring themes that emerge from these eleven articles are a) the geopolitical landscape is both unstable and dynamic, b) too many crisis situations have too many tipping points drawing not just countries but alliances into conflict, and c) the lines between war and peace are increasingly blurred, not auguring well for the near.

Notes

1   Francis Fukuyama, *The End of History and the Last Man* (New York: Free Press, 1992).

2   David E. Sanger, *New Cold Wars: China's Rise, Russia's Invasion, and America's Struggle to Defend the West* (New York: Crown, 2024).

3   Bryony Cottam, "Autocracies on the Rise, Democracies in Decline," *Geographical*, November 10, 2022, https://geographical.co.uk/geopolitics/autocracies-on-the-rise-democracy-in-decline; Vanessa A. Boese et al., "State of the World 2021: Autocratization Changing Its Nature?," *Democracy* 29, no. 6 (2022): 983–1013, https://www.tandfonline.com/doi/full/10.1080/13510347.2022.2069751; Mike Smeltzer and Noah Buyon, "From Democratic Decline to Authoritarian Aggression," Freedom House, 2022, https://freedomhouse.org/report/nations-transit/2022/from-democratic-decline-to-authoritarian-aggression; Rodrigo Menegat Schuinski, "When Democracies Falter, They Rarely Recover," Deutsche Welle, September 15, 2022, https://www.dw.com/en/as-autocrats-ascend-gloomy-data-on-democracies-decline/a-62674756; V-Dem Institute, "Democracy Report 2023: Defiance in the Face of Autocratization," 2023, https://www.v-dem.net/documents/29/V-dem_democracyreport2023_lowres.pdf.

4   Thomas B. Edsall, "The Seeds Had Been Planted. Trump Didn't Do It Himself," *New York Times*, May 15, 2024, https://www.nytimes.com/2024/05/15/opinion/trump-authoritarianism-democracy.html.

5   Roger Cohen, "A Would-be Assassin Stirs Europe's Violent Ghosts," *New York Times*, May 18, 2024, https://www.nytimes.com/2024/05/18/world/europe/fico-shooting-slovakia-europe-politics.html.

6   Joe Leahy, Kai Waluszewski, and Max Seddon, "China-Russia: An Economic 'Friendship' That Could Rattle the World," *Financial Times*, May 15, 2024, https://on.ft.com/3K9Qgzz; Alexander Gabuev, "The West Doesn't Understand How Much Russia Has Changed," *New York Times*, May 16, 2024, https://www.nytimes.com/2024/05/15/opinion/putin-china-xi-jinping.html.

7   Padraig O'Malley, Paul L. Atwood, and Patricia Peterson, eds., *Sticks and Stones: Living with Uncertain Wars* (Boston: University of Massachusetts Press, 2006).

8   "Russia Announces Nuclear Weapon Drills after 'Provocative' Western Threats," *Al Jazeera*, May 6, 2024, https://www.aljazeera.com/news/2024/5/6/russia-announces-nuclear-weapon-drills-after-provocative-western-threats

9   Anton Troianovski, "Russia to Hold Drills on Tactical Nuclear Weapons in New Tensions with West," *New York Times*, May 6, 2024, https://www.nytimes.com/2024/05/06/world/europe/russia-tactical-nuclear-weapons-drills.html; "Russia Warns Britain and Plans Nuclear Drills over the West's Possible Deepening Role in Ukraine," Associated Press, May 6, 2024, https://apnews.com/article/russia-ukraine-war-nuclear-drills-b007cffdc4fc57922042a35fbe47907f.

10 Piero Scaruffi, "Wars and Casualties of the 20th and 21st Centuries," 2009, https://www.scaruffi.com/politics/massacre.html; "What Is War Today?," The Changing Character of War Centre, https://www.ccw.ox.ac.uk/what-is-war-today; Bastian Herre et al., "War and Peace," Our World in Data, https://ourworldindata.org/war-and-peace; Herfried Münkler, "The Wars of the 21st Century," *IRRC* 85, no. 849 (March 2003): 7–22, https://www.icrc.org/en/doc/assets/files/other/irrc_849_munkler.pdf; "21st Century," Helion & Company, https://www.helion.co.uk/periods/21st-century.php; Rob Johnson, Martijn Kitzen, and Tim Sweijs, eds., *The Conduct of War in the 21st Century: Kinetic, Connected and Synthetic* (New York: Routledge, 2021); Shmuel Shmuel, "The American Way of War in the Twenty-First Century: Three Inherent Challenges," Modern

War Institute at West Point, June 30, 2020, https://mwi.westpoint.edu/american-way-war-twenty-first-century-three-inherent-challenges/; "Timeline of 20th And 21st Century Wars," Imperial War Museums, https://www.iwm.org.uk/history/timeline-of-20th-and-21st-century-wars; Michael Ray, "8 Deadliest Wars of the 21st Century," Britannica, https://www.britannica.com/list/8-deadliest-wars-of-the-21st-century; "List of Battles in the 21st Century," Wikipedia, https://en.wikipedia.org/wiki/List_of_battles_in_the_21st_century.

11 Paul Scharre, "The Perilous Coming Age of A.I. Warfare: How to Limit the Threat of Autonomous Weapons," *Foreign Affairs*, February 2024, https://www.foreignaffairs.com/ukraine/perilous-coming-age-ai-warfare.

12 Ibid.

13 David Wallace-Wells, "What War by AI May Actually Look Like," *New York Times*, April 10, 2024, https://www.nytimes.com/2024/04/10/opinion/war-ai-israel-gaza-ukraine.html.

14 Inna Chefranova, "Empowering Innovation: Brave1's Role in Ukraine's Military Technology Development," EU Today, May 11, 2024, https://eutoday.net/brave1-in-ukraines-military-technology-development/; John Hudson and Kostiantyn Khudov, "The War in Ukraine Is Spurring a Revolution in Drone Warfare Using AI," *Washington Post*, July 26, 2023, https://www.washingtonpost.com/world/2023/07/26/drones-ai-ukraine-war-innovation/.

15 Hudson and Khudov, "The War in Ukraine"; "War Turns Ukraine from Agrarian State to Super Lab of Inventions – WP," *Ukrainska Pravda*, July 26, 2023, https://www.pravda.com.ua/eng/news/2023/07/26/7412971/; David Ignatius, "How Ukraine's Tech Army Is Taking the Fight to Russia," *Washington Post*, April 5, 2024, https://www.washingtonpost.com/opinions/2024/04/05/ukraine-russia-tech-drone-warfighting/; "Ukrainian Defense Innovations," Brave1, https://brave1.gov.ua/en/.

16 Jake Epstein, "Ukraine Made the Naval Drones Sinking Russian Warships 'Deadlier' by Arming Them with Bigger Warheads, General Says," Business Insider, March 1, 2024, https://www.businessinsider.com/ukraine-made-naval-drones-deadlier-larger-warheads-general-says-2024-3.

17 "War Turns Ukraine"; David Hambling, "Ukraine Prepares to Roll Out an Army of Ground Robots," Forbes, March 14, 2024, https://www.forbes.com/sites/davidhambling/2024/03/14/ukraine-prepares-to-roll-out-an-army-of-ground-robots/; David Axe, "Robot War in Ukraine: Unmanned Systems Clash on the Front Lines," *The Telegraph*, April 7, 2024, https://www.telegraph.co.uk/news/2024/04/07/russia-war-ukraine-uav-ugv-drone-robot-unmanned-weapons/; Ellie Cook, "Ukraine Deploying Machine-Gun Mounted Robots to Attack Putin's Troops," *Newsweek*, January 29, 2024, https://www.newsweek.com/ukraine-ugvs-machine-gun-combat-robots-drones-1864843; Elisabeth Gosselin-Malo, "Ukrainian Officials See Ground Robots as 'Game Changer' in War," DefenseNews, March 14, 2024, https://www.defensenews.com/global/europe/2024/03/14/ukrainian-officials-see-ground-robots-as-game-changer-in-war/; Miriam McNabb, "FPV Drones vs. Ground Robots in Ukraine," DRONELIFE, April 1, 2024, https://dronelife.com/2024/04/01/fpv-drones-vs-ground-robots-in-ukraine/; Alistair MacDonald and Ievgeniia Sivorka, "Robots Are Entering the Ukraine Battlefield," *Wall Street Journal*, March 22, 2024, https://www.wsj.com/world/europe/robots-are-entering-the-ukraine-battlefield-fab195d2.

18 Alex Horton and Serhii Korolchuk, "Whatever the Fuss over Elon Musk, Starlink Is Utterly Essential in Ukraine," *Washington Post*, September 8, 2023, https://www.washingtonpost.com/world/2023/09/08/elon-musk-starlink-ukraine-war/.

[19] Nick Paton Walsh et al., "Ukraine Relies on Starlink for Its Drone War. Russia Appears to Be Bypassing Sanctions to Use the Devices Too," CNN, March 26, 2024, https://www.cnn.com/2024/03/25/europe/ukraine-starlink-drones-russia-intl-cmd/index.html; Thibault Spirlet, "Ukraine Goes After Elon Musk, Disputing His Claim That Russia Isn't Buying and Using Starlink," Business Insider, February 16, 2024, https://www.businessinsider.com/ukraine-goes-after-musk-disputes-claim-russia-not-using-starlink-2024-2.

[20] "Russia Ramps Up Arms Production as US Boosts Support for Ukraine," Reuters, May 1, 2024, https://www.reuters.com/world/europe/russias-defence-minister-orders-more-weapons-ukraine-operation-2024-05-01/.

[21] Alexander Hill, "Both Sides in the Russia-Ukraine War Are Using New and Old Technologies for Warfare," The Conversation, March 14, 2024, https://theconversation.com/both-sides-in-the-russia-ukraine-war-are-using-new-and-old-technologies-for-warfare-225451; David E. Sanger, Julian E. Barnes, and Kim Barker, "White House Worries Russia's Momentum Is Changing Trajectory of Ukraine War," New York Times, May 14, 2024, https://www.nytimes.com/2024/05/14/us/politics/russia-momentum-ukraine-war.html; Hanna Arhirova, "Ukraine Ramps Up Spending on Homemade Weapons to Help Repel Russia," Associated Press, March 27, 2024, https://apnews.com/article/ukraine-weapons-russia-drones-90b03d92f72f878c8c2ac04b0d12f804.

INTRODUCTION TO THE SPECIAL ISSUE

John, Lord Alderdice

Harris Manchester College, University of Oxford; Changing Character of War Centre, Pembroke College, University of Oxford; Global Humanity for Peace Institute, University of Wales Trinity Saint David; House of Lords Select Committee on International Relations and Defence; The Concord Foundation

After the two terrible global wars of the first half of the twentieth century, the last millennium seemed, to Western observers at least, to end well. There had not been a war in Western Europe for some decades and it was assumed that the collapse of the Soviet Union and the end of the Cold War would result in a world that was less deeply divided and with a much-reduced risk of catastrophic nuclear war. Despite its difficulties, the United Nations system had survived, and the prospect of a relatively peaceful world governed under a liberal, international, rules-based order appeared to be within reach. The development of the global internet and the resultant extraordinary expansion of communication worldwide as well as the establishment of the World Trade Organization to administer the growing body of multilateral trade agreements added to the conviction that globalization was rapid, irreversible, and bound to result in greater global cooperation and peaceful relations. It was widely and confidently believed that the liberalizing of trade, travel, and communication would lead to a more liberal and tolerant politics across the world.

John, Lord Alderdice is a Senior Research Fellow at Harris Manchester College, Oxford, Executive Chairman of the Changing Character of War Centre, and an Honorary Fellow at Pembroke College Oxford. He directs the Conference on the Resolution of Intractable Conflict, is a professor of practice in the Global Humanity for Peace Institute at the University of Wales Trinity Saint David, and since 1996 he has been an active Liberal Democrat member of the House of Lords where he is currently a member of the House of Lords Select Committee on International Relations and Defence. He is the Founding Chairman of The Concord Foundation and an honorary fellow of the Royal College of Psychiatrists.

While the devastating Al Qaeda attacks in the United States on September 11, 2001, challenged the view that we were moving inexorably toward a more tolerant and less violent world, the illusion was sustained by a view, shared by many world leaders from East and West, North and South, that the problem was now 'terrorism.' There was, it was reasoned, no prospect of wars between major states, and the 'new wars,' which seemed to consist of intrastate conflicts involving non-governmental terrorist actors, could surely be addressed by international collaboration on a 'war on terrorism,' though how one could mount a war against a tactic was never clear.

Unfortunately, it did not take long for old differences to reemerge. The World Federation of Scientists (WFS), which had previously been able to maintain a degree of unity in shared efforts at nuclear de-escalation, found after 9/11 that on the question of terrorism, Western scientists wanted to use their knowledge to mitigate the growing problem, while scientists from the East thought it more important to try to understand the motivations of people who engage in terrorism and jeopardize their own welfare as individuals and communities. Debates around these questions led to the establishment of two WFS Permanent Monitoring Panels—one on the Mitigation of Terrorism and the other on the Motivations for Terrorism. Out of this collaboration emerged the Centre for the Resolution of Intractable Conflict (CRIC), bringing together scholars from different countries and disciplines including psychology, anthropology, and political science to explore the causes of intractable violent political conflict and how it could be addressed. A detailed account of the genesis of CRIC was given in a previous issue of this journal.[1]

One of the most important initiatives taken by CRIC was the creation of an annual conference held each September in Harris Manchester College at the University of Oxford. The first conference was held in 2014 and ten years later it has become something of an institution. The attendees at the annual invitation-only events come from across the globe and many now collaborate throughout the year in research work, writing, and consulting in the field. As a result, the conference has taken on a life of its own. It is currently hosted by The Concord Foundation, a newly established independent not-for-profit company (theconcordfoundation.org).

The tenth anniversary Conference on the Resolution of Intractable Conflict was held in September 2023 in collaboration with the Changing Character of War Centre at Pembroke College, University of Oxford (www.ccw.ox.ac.uk) and the Global Humanity for Peace Institute at the University of Wales Trinity Saint David (ghfp.institute). It offered an excellent opportunity for colleagues to explore both the changing character of war and the changing character of peacebuilding. The *nature* of war, and of peacebuilding, do not change. War always involves one community attempting to force another community, by physical force, to bend to its will, and when this is resisted by physical means, war is the result. Building peace always involves communities that have different perspectives finding ways of conducting their differences without the use of physical force. However, while the nature of war and peacebuilding do not change, their character does change, and understanding and responding to the rapid and profound changes of recent years is a challenge.

At the time of our first conference in 2014 there was still a considerable degree of structure and stability in international relations. Notable progress had been made in resolving the long-standing conflicts in Northern Ireland and South Africa and these peace processes had benefited from the international collaboration facilitated by the end of the Cold War and the development of initiatives by the United Nations and the European Union. While the challenges were clear, there was optimism among CRIC participants that with creativity and commitment we could deepen our understanding of why some conflicts become intractable, and find ways to reframe them and make progress in resolving them. The annual conferences that followed facilitated this work and substantial progress was indeed made, but persuading governments to implement policies based on this knowledge was very difficult, especially when the policy proposals challenged power structures and traditional perspectives. Public and private warnings were made to Western governments about the dangers to global stability if there was not a change of course, but it soon became clear that the trajectory toward global conflict would be difficult to arrest.[2]

The work and the annual conferences continue, and our understanding of the nature, causes, and character of violent political conflict has widened and deepened. We also came to appreciate that some of the developments that had been expected to mitigate conflict—globalization, the internet, and rapid mobile communications—were actually exacerbating the division and advancement of technology was being used at least as much for war as for peace.

Now the post-war international political structures that had shown so much promise seem to be dissolving. The United Nations had provided a table around which states could negotiate about their differences and collaborate to address international social, economic, environmental, and political problems, and provide a system of international law. But states are increasingly signing up to conventions that they have no intention of observing and are disregarding the requirements of international law. Even the five permanent members of the UN Security Council cannot be depended upon to support the rule of law if it does not seem to be in their own selfish short-term interests. The internet was expected to provide a new way of communicating that would democratize knowledge and ensure that malign forces could not hide their activities behind physical borders. However, paradoxically, people are more likely to restrict their viewing to that which fits with their prejudices and false information has spread much more rapidly than the truth. In the meantime those engaged in organized crime, sexual exploitation, especially of women and children, terrorists, and other malign state and non-state actors, have been much more successful than expected in using the new opportunities of cyberspace, resulting in a massive growth in illegal activity online.

It would be easy to lose faith that a better world is possible, as some have done. Others seem to bolster their hopes with shallow and unrealistic optimism. In our CRIC collaboration we have seen the situation differently. We are fully conscious of the dangers of climate catastrophe and nuclear holocaust, but we have also concluded that it is in times of such existential crisis that the human family is motivated to find new ways of thinking. By continuing to investigate scientifically and reflect philosophically on the challenges, we have begun to see ways to turn conflict into cooperation through our investigations of the new paradigms of complexity science and a more relational psychology.[3]

This Special Issue makes available articles based on many of the presentations at CRIC 2023 and you can view the presentations on the CRIC YouTube channel at www.youtube.com/@cric-oxford. We hope that you will be encouraged in your own thinking and research on war and peace and we invite you to follow up with us, as individual researchers, or through CRIC or The Concord Foundation.

Notes

[1] John, Lord Alderdice, "Why We Have the Center for the Resolution of Intractable Conflict in Oxford," *New England Journal of Public Policy* 29, no. 1 (2017): Article 3, http://scholarworks.umb.edu/nejpp/vol29/iss1/3.

[2] John, Lord Alderdice, "…The Lamps Are Going Out Again…" August 15, 2016, https://lordalderdice.com/index.php/2016/08/15/the-lamps-are-going-out-again/.

[3] John, Lord Alderdice, "Conflict, Complexity, and Cooperation," *New England Journal of Public Policy* 33, no. 1 (2021): Article 9, https://scholarworks.umb.edu/nejpp/vol33/iss1/9.

NEW TECHNOLOGIES IN WARS, OLD AND NEW

John, Lord Alderdice

Harris Manchester College, University of Oxford; Changing Character of War Centre, Pembroke College, University of Oxford; Global Humanity for Peace Institute, University of Wales Trinity Saint David; House of Lords Select Committee on International Relations and Defence; The Concord Foundation

ABSTRACT

Wars are often marked by technological advances and while the front line in the confrontation in the Russia-Ukraine War is between the two countries concerned, many other countries are also involved in bringing a range of weapons to bear. Some, such as drones and satellite communications, are not entirely new, but are playing a greater role than before. They are also being combined with more definitively new technologies such as artificial intelligence. However, the older ways of warfare are still center stage. Not only has there been a return of war in Europe between major powers, but even the trench and tank warfare that some had thought were consigned to military history have returned with brutal consequences. The faltering of the post-war international structures that had given stability and a foundation for international law, has also undermined confidence in the peacebuilding processes based on them and so the author proposes a new set of foundational principles.

John, Lord Alderdice is a Senior Research Fellow at Harris Manchester College, Oxford, Executive Chairman of the Changing Character of War Centre, and an Honorary Fellow at Pembroke College Oxford. He directs the Conference on the Resolution of Intractable Conflict, is a professor of practice in the Global Humanity for Peace Institute at the University of Wales Trinity Saint David, and since 1996 he has been an active Liberal Democrat member of the House of Lords where he is currently a member of the House of Lords Select Committee on International Relations and Defence. He is the Founding Chairman of The Concord Foundation and an honorary fellow of the Royal College of Psychiatrists.

Few pressures concentrate the inventive mind of a community more than the threat of death or defeat, and so major wars often result in significant technological advances as those who are prosecuting the conflict seek to apply every possible improvement in scientific understanding to achieve military advantage.

The First World War produced important innovations in existing weapons such as grenades, machine guns, and artillery, along with new weapons in the familiar war spaces on land and at sea, including tanks and poison gas on land and submarines at sea, but also extending into the air with the use of zeppelin airships and warplanes.

The Second World War saw the use of medical advances, with vaccines, penicillin, and blood plasma transfusions playing a part in the war; low level technology that had important contributions, including synthetic rubber, superglue, and duct tape; but more obviously and directly the creation of the jeep, the invention of radar, and the building of electronic computers, especially for code-breaking; and further major advances in tanks, naval vessels, and airplanes. Most dramatic and earth-shattering was the creation and detonation by the US of two atomic bombs at Hiroshima and Nagasaki in Japan.

Throughout the Cold War, the development of traditional weapons, war vehicles, and communications technology continued, and the USSR responded to each advance in nuclear weapons by the US with a development of their own, and vice versa. While the Soviets tended to concentrate on more powerful weapons, the Americans also improved the sophistication and accuracy of their systems. Both sides massively expanded their numbers so that, while some military strategists maintained that limited or theater nuclear warfare was possible, the stockpiles were such that by the 1980s there was the capacity for, and risk of, global 'mutually assured destruction' many times over.[1]

With the end of the Cold War there seemed to be a thawing of relationships and the negotiations on Strategic Arms Reduction Treaties (START) began to have an effect on both the numbers and types of nuclear weapons. The two major powers also avoided direct confrontation by operating with or through proxies who were often using terrorism as their tactic. The anxiety levels in civil society diminished and the issue became less of a preoccupation. By the late 1980s Mueller, Mandelbaum, and others were arguing that major war was now obsolete, and some even said that inter-state war was no longer possible.[2] Through the 1990s authors such as John Keegan and Mary Kaldor wrote that Clausewitz-type wars were a thing of the past and in the future war would be waged by non-state actors, guerrillas, and terrorists instead of states.[3] The attacks on the United States on September 11, 2001 might have seemed to confirm this analysis but, as we shall see, the reality was much more complex and less reassuring.

In the meantime, and since then, the pace of technological change has been so rapid as to be unsteadying. The military-industrial-complexes in major countries were working energetically on a range of scientific advances and their technological applications in a wide range of domains—computer power, communications technology, satellite exploitation, artificial intelligence (AI), and biological genetic modifications. In addition to operating on land, sea, and air, space and the whole new cyber world were added to the contexts where war can be conducted. There was a great deal of excitement as well as anxiety about how these new capacities might be exploited in warfare, but it is only in the context of a 'hot war' that we can be clear about which of these technological developments has the most impact.

Inter-state War Returns

Despite the new capacities for surveillance that were making ever more global information available to both intelligence agencies and private individuals, in the months prior to the Russian attempt to extend its invasion and occupation of Ukraine in February 2022, many leading politicians found it difficult to contemplate the possibility of a return to a major war in Europe. Though there was substantial data about the assemblage of military forces around the borders of Ukraine, and clear, detailed, threatening statements were being issued, sometimes at great length, by President Putin and his entourage, with few exceptions beyond the US, Poland, and the UK, most NATO members were not really expecting that the Russian president, Mr. Putin, would actually embark on what he still insists on describing as a 'special military operation.' The failure was not of information gathering, but of the mature capacity to use the available intelligence and face the reality of humanity's aggressive and destructive tendencies.

The Russian president clearly expected that Ukraine would fall into his hands relatively easily and the reasons why it did not will be a matter of study for many years, but he is absolutely committed to proceeding with his invasion and war because it is part of a wider and deeper determination to avenge what he sees as the disastrous humiliation of the collapse of the Soviet Union. That is why we must assume that if the result of the Russia-Ukraine War is that he is seen to be successful, at least in his own terms, he will be emboldened either by that victory over Ukraine, or through the war spreading elsewhere, and he will not stop there. While he has put the Russian economy on a permanent war footing, the West remains unprepared both psychologically and militarily for full-scale war. This could be catastrophic not only for some of the countries concerned, but for liberal democracy globally.

Ukraine is not the only front in this war. The Middle East has its own internal and regional dynamics, but the meeting that President Putin hosted with Hamas and Iranian leaders in Moscow in October 2023, which he described as representing the Axis of Resistance, followed up with further meetings, including with Houthi rebel leaders in January 2024, shows how his ambitions go well beyond re-establishing the old borders of the USSR, though not of course beyond the boundaries of its influence and involvement, which were global. However, this emerging geo-political re-alignment goes further than merely a return to the status quo ante. The appearance of an increasingly powerful and assertive China under President Xi Jinping, who intends to bring Taiwan back into the arms of the Chinese state and of the Chinese Communist Party and has been extending his country's influence well beyond any past extent, also raises profound anxieties.

These political developments are further reflected in the sharing of military technology. For example, Iran has been providing Shahed drones to Russia for use in Ukraine as well as drones and missiles to the Houthis in Yemen, and China and North Korea have not only been providing military hardware, but along with many other countries in the region, in cooperation with most of the Global South, have been frustrating Western efforts to maintain economic sanctions on Russia. The profoundly serious conflicts in Africa, whether in Libya, the even more destructive war in Sudan, or elsewhere, are also being caught up into this new global division.

The New Adds to, but Does Not Replace, the Old

Prior to this spiral into chaos, it had been expected that if new wars did arise involving sophisticated and developed countries, they would be very different from the wars of the past. It was thought, for example, that much of their impact would be through cyber operations. There have certainly been significant cyber operations, not least using social media to create disinformation, fracturing, and confusion, but to date they seem to have been less successful in striking key elements of critical infrastructure. This is not so much because there have been no attacks on critical infrastructure but is a result of the better preparedness that has frustrated the attacks that have taken place and protected against them. However, much of the military engagement in Ukraine has been anything but modern. Indeed it is horribly reminiscent of the trench warfare and attritional artillery bombardment of 1914–1918 or the major tank maneuvers of 1939–1945. The operations of Israel in its latest war in Gaza have produced a similar outcome to the carpet-bombing of the 1930s and 1940s, and this despite such bombing of cities, towns, villages, or other areas containing a concentration of protected civilians having been considered a war crime since 1977 through Article 51 of Protocol I of the Geneva Conventions.

We have not moved to wholly new wars, in the sense of abandoning the old ways. The control of territory, whether protecting one's own territory or seeking to seize control of the territory of the enemy, and destruction of the enemy, both people and power structures, remain central to the struggles at the heart of today's wars. The major vulnerability of the Ukrainians is a shortage of weapons and ammunition, exacerbated by the relatively low stocks and remarkably feeble replacement capacity of their European allies. All of this is not redolent of 'new wars' but of very traditional military logistical challenges.

Drones

That being said, there are new technologies, and they are playing a major role. Perhaps the prominence of drones, or so-called 'uncrewed systems,' is one of the most dramatic developments. The use of 'uncrewed systems' is not itself new. Aerial target drones and boats controlled at a distance were used during World War I to deliver explosives, but the recent rapid advance of cheap, effective technology has completely changed their use.[4] While the governments of the US, UK, France, and others worked on developing uncrewed and autonomous systems conceived of as unmanned airplanes which, like their crewed versions, are large, sophisticated, and thus very expensive, to date the most effective use of drones has been through the technical and tactical modification of small, inexpensive civil drones. The Ukrainians have been particularly creative in the development and use of this technology.

Drones had previously made a significant impact in the conflict in Libya. While initially the arrival of Chinese-made Wing Loong drones in 2016 improved the capabilities of General Haftar's self-styled Libyan National Army (LNA), when Türkiye intervened in 2019 with a supply of Bayraktar TB2 drones in support of the UN-recognized Government of National Accord (GNA), it had a dramatic effect and the UN special representative to Libya, Ghassan Salamé, described it, at that time (May 2020) as "the largest drone war theatre in the world."[5]

However, it is in the war in Ukraine that the use of drones has expanded exponentially. James Cartlidge MP, the UK Minister for Defence Procurement, described it as "a very visible representation of a 'new way of war,' one characterized by innovation, the proliferation of technology, digitization of the battlefield and the need to rapidly develop capability for the tempo of operations."[6]

There are different types of drones with various capabilities that are being used. Small inexpensive drones have been used by Ukraine for reconnaissance missions, providing both intelligence and propaganda material, but at least as importantly they can be used in combination with artillery to produce much faster and more accurate targeting on the front line. So, while both traditional and modern artillery have been used in the war, these cheap drones have massively increased the speed and accuracy with which their operators can target and take out enemy ground forces. Of course, what is true for one side is quickly true for the other side too and so it is now more difficult for soldiers from either side to find hiding places on the battlefield. The only way either military can function and survive is to operate as small, highly mobile units that are constantly aware that when they fire their weapons they must immediately relocate and conceal themselves to avoid being targets.

Ukraine has also used low-cost first-person view (FPV) drones, which are constructed from cheap commercial products that are modified to carry small explosive devices, and these have proved to be effective anti-tank weapons. Tanks are traditionally best reinforced with hard skins around the outside but are vulnerable 'up top' where there is less reinforcement, in order to keep the weight of the vehicle to a manageable level. If a drone with an explosive payload can fly overhead and drop a device on top of the vehicle it can be devastating.

As I have already noted, Iran has been providing Russia with long-range kamikaze Shahed drones that are relatively inexpensive, can fly long distances, and deliver a substantial payload. These drones can be manufactured and used in large quantities and NATO has no 'cheap' equivalent weapon. Not only is this inequality in drone costs proving to be significant in Ukraine, it is even more dramatically for the Yemeni Houthis in their attacks on Western shipping in the Red Sea. They are using two-thousand-dollar drones and the US is trying to take out the Houthi drones with two-million-dollar missiles. This is not an economically viable strategy.

One of the most dramatically successful of Ukraine's drone tactics has come with the use of maritime drones, which include both surface and underwater uncrewed weapons. They have been able to target Russian ships and make much of the Black Sea a 'no-go' zone for Russia and a protected space for exporting Ukrainian products. The Houthis are also now using maritime drones, with limited success to date, but that may simply be a matter of time and development.

As the Russia-Ukraine War continues, and replacement ammunition has become a problem, the Ukrainians are being very inventive in their attacks. One method has been the use of a range of old Soviet-era Tupolev Tu-141/143 drones that were initially retired four decades ago by the Russians. They are around seven tons in weight and forty-seven feet long and they can carry a significant and very destructive explosive payload. They have been effective in deep strikes by Ukraine into Russian territory, inflicting significant damage on oil facilities. Even more ingeniously they have found ways of converting light civil aircraft such as the Cessna into exploding drones. These can be packed with explosives and with their low radar signature they can be flown slowly, at low altitude and erratically, under robotic control, hundreds of miles into Russia and detonated upon reaching the target. Perhaps surprisingly, these have proved quite effective. Because in the past the Soviet Union was surrounded by 'friendly' buffer states, the Russian air defenses were designed to deal with the more sophisticated, long-range, high-tech US missile systems. They have found it more difficult to adapt to creative Ukrainian low-tech inventions.

It would however be superficial and misleading to characterize these less expensive drones as an answer to the conduct of war, even during the current conflict. Every significant innovation by one side is quickly examined and responded to with a technical advance by the other side. Ukrainian allies are working on newer technologies, for example Estonia and the UK recently announced collaboration on a long-range drone system designed for the Russia/Ukraine theater, but Russia and its allies are similarly seeking out advances.

Hybrid War

This constant ratcheting up of drone capacities is still only part of the story for they are part of a hybrid approach that is itself in a constant process of revision and development, the principles of which are well-described by Brian Arthur. As he points out, not only do technologies adapt by changes to their own individual elements—for example, being miniaturized and becoming more powerful—but they also combine with each other and bring about novel structures and capacities. Combining existing technologies can result in new technologies that yield new and sometimes unexpected effects.[7]

So, it is possible to use drones for surveillance and intelligence gathering, which is then fed back to the gunners manning the artillery and missile launchers through the use of rapid communications, especially the Starlink satellite system provided by Elon Musk and SpaceX. Starlink brought high-speed internet access to almost anywhere on the globe. It is then a relatively short step, at least in principle, to connect the intelligence-gathering function of the small drones to the attack weapons without the time delay required by a human operator. The next generation of drones will undoubtedly be enabled by artificial intelligence to operate increasingly autonomously and collaboratively. There have been reports that Israel has been using a previously undisclosed AI-powered database system called Lavender that is said to have identified 37,000 potential targets for attack based on their apparent links to Hamas.[8] Such AI programming takes out human judgment and speeds up the process of attack, but it was often this human element that saved us from accidental nuclear conflict during the Cold War when the technology misinterpreted what was happening and human hesitation in decision-making prevented catastrophic escalation.[9]

Not only does AI enormously increase the speed and targeting capacity of the military, but, because the cost of smaller drones is so low, various militaries are contemplating the production of huge numbers of them. In the UK, Chief of Defense Staff Admiral Sir Tony Radakin stated in February 2024 that the Army, Navy, and Royal Air Forces intend to procure 'hundreds of thousands more drones' and Ukraine announced that it intended to produce a million drones in 2024. AI will soon enable them to be operated in 'swarms' and defense against huge swarms of autonomous drone weapons will be much more difficult. These drones will not be obtained through the usual laborious, specific military planning and procurement processes that have bedeviled efficient provision of arms and machines. Instead, many of them will be obtained 'off the shelf' from civil supplies, which can then be adapted as required. The expensive and inefficient bureaucracy in which military procurement has become entrenched may be one of the many reasons why some of the most powerful states are no longer able to be successful in their military ventures.

In recent decades, supposedly weaker conflict actors are regularly outpowering stronger actors. This is also because they are 'devoted actors' driven by faith in defending or advancing their nonnegotiable 'sacred values,' whether religious or secular.[10] As I have pointed out elsewhere, bringing together insights from large group psychology, neuroscience, epigenetics, and political science gives us some of the human answers to the success of these 'weaker actors' in terms of individual and large group functioning, but the inefficiencies of large democratic societies also plays a part.[11] It is striking how in Afghanistan and Iraq, but also in Gaza with Hamas and with the Houthi rebels in Yemen, much wealthier and more apparently powerful states—the US and its allies, Israel, and the Kingdom of Saudi Arabia—have been denied military victories, and an important element of these outcomes has been the creative adaptation of unsophisticated technologies. A striking example is the use of drones by the Houthis to close down critical global shipping lanes, send the price of oil soaring, and contribute to inflation in the West. The impact on the US presidential election on the other side of the world is significant because despite being so far away and so much less well resourced, they are making the reelection of the incumbent, President Biden, more problematic.

Globalization and the Changing Character of War

The role of globalization in minimizing the significance of geographical distance has been much more complex than its early supporters imagined. The technological advances that resulted in such remarkable increases in the speed of communication and travel were seen by developed Western countries as opening up new markets, expanding liberal democracy, and making the world a more collaborative and safer place. They assumed that a more connected and more prosperous world would welcome Western culture and liberal politics. The actual result has been an empowerment of the Global South, which for years resented the colonial history and political hypocrisy of countries that proclaimed a commitment to democracy but only accepted election results that were in their favor. While Western countries trumpeted their commitment to human rights they often allied themselves with authoritarian and oppressive rulers if it was in their perceived interests. Free markets increased the wealth of developing countries, which could then afford to purchase and adopt the improved technology of warfare, but without adopting Western liberal values or political norms.

This disenchantment was exacerbated when the global pandemic struck and developed countries made remarkably little effort to share the benefits of COVID-19 vaccinations. Meantime, while China may have contributed to the spread of the pandemic in the first place, it made more effort to share its vaccines, even if they were not always of the highest quality. China also cooperates in development projects and provides loans to risky ventures, asking no awkward questions about human rights or environmental protections. It is true that when it comes to paying back loans, the glitter may fade, but nevertheless, what we are increasingly calling the 'Global South' identifies more with China, and even Russia, than with what we call 'the West.' The attractions of liberal democracy and freedom to trade have proved to be more modest than expected and the freedom to travel has vanished with increasing Western restrictions on immigration and asylum.

The democratizing of economic, political, and military power has also resulted in the spread of violent conflict and war, and a growing number of failed states, often a consequence of Western interventions. Writers such as Steven Pinker, who insisted that the world was becoming more peaceful, and Francis Fukuyama, who claimed that humanity had reached "the end-point of mankind's ideological evolution and the universalization of Western liberal democracy as the final form of human government," have been shown to have made shallow judgments not based on the reality of human nature.[12] The threat of war fought with nuclear weapons is back on the agenda in a profoundly threatening way, not just in the traditional theaters of conflict in Europe and the Middle East, but, in the longer term, between China and the West.[13]

New Challenges for Peacebuilding

A generation ago there was reason to believe that what was called 'the developing world' looked to the social, economic, political, and cultural life of Europe and North America as an ambition and even a source of envy, however things have changed. It is clear that not everyone in the West benefits from its wealth, and its systems of welfare and healthcare are faltering. The rule of law, which previously gave confidence about fairness and integrity, now appears to many people to make unreasonable demands for acute sensitivity to the wishes of minority religious and other groups, while dismissing and even delegitimizing the views of substantial elements of the community, and too many leading figures in countries that claimed to promote fairness and integrity have demonstrably lacked either of them. Military might has resulted in almost constant interventions based on the selfish strategic and economic interests of Western powers, resulting in death, destruction, and failed states, rather than prosperous societies based on the values of liberal democracy. Almost everyone still wants the science, technology, and medicine that resulted from the Enlightenment, but people are much less sure about the rest of the package. Those who live in North America and Western Europe seem to lack confidence in their own systems and question whether the military interventions embarked on by their governments are worth the cost in blood and treasure, or that they bring positive results for anyone. Even development aid is being questioned, and in some cases radically reduced or re-directed.

This wish to withdraw from military engagement and the funding of development aid accompanied by a loss of confidence in liberal democracy, is mirrored by uncertainty and lack of direction among those who have previously been active in, and committed to, peacebuilding. When the journalist Matt Waldman, who is a senior advisor at both the European Institute of Peace and the United States Institute of Peace and a former special advisor to UN envoys, used the period of the global pandemic lockdown to conduct online interviews with some eighty-six experienced negotiators from the UN and other national and international agencies and NGOs, and asked them about their work, he found an almost universal sense that the old ways of peacemaking no longer worked but that it was not yet clear what might replace them.[14] The Conflict Management Initiative, now known as CMI – Martti Ahtisaari Peace Foundation, established by the former president of Finland and Nobel Peace Laureate, is one of the world's leading organizations in the field. In recent years they have found themselves running into new hurdles in their peacemaking work and began to realize that something had changed about the context. If the technology of making war had changed, it seemed the technology of making peace also needed to adapt to the new circumstances.[15]

The events on September 11, 2001 and the responses re-shaped the fields of conflict and peacebuilding and it was thought for a time that the twentieth century problems of conflicts between states were being replaced by a new security landscape where non-state actors and terrorism would be the main threats, and states with competing interests would collaborate within post-war international institutions on counterterrorism and stabilization efforts. But twenty years on, the deepening of the invasion of Ukraine in 2022 suggests that the conflict paradigm was returning to inter-state conflicts, leaving the key multilateral organizations, both intergovernmental and non-governmental, in a state of profound uncertainty.

Must We Fall Back or Can We Move Forward?

In his 2023 book, "The New Leviathans: Thoughts after Liberalism," the iconoclastic English philosopher, John Gray, sets out a challenging perspective that returns to a Hobbesian analysis of international relations. Instead of the belief that humankind, albeit in fits and starts, was moving inexorably toward a peaceful, rational, liberal, well-ordered, and prosperous future, he says that we are falling into a world dominated by authoritarianism, intolerant nationalisms, and unreason. He proposes that the relatively short period when the liberal trajectory seemed to be in the ascendent, should be regarded as, in historical terms, a passing blip, an aberration that is already dissolving away.[16]

He may be right, but in a previous article I have described an alternative perspective in which I agree that the old forms based on the Enlightenment are dissolving, but that this is the inevitable course of progress.[17] All forms of governance and culture have their day, and if there is to be progress and new ways are to emerge, the old ways must be seen to have run their course and begin to fragment and dissolve so that a new paradigm can emerge. I have proposed that three developments may point toward the next evolutionary way station for humankind:

- the emergence of complexity science,
- an appreciation that our emotions are a positive evolutionary advantage rather than a flaw to be overcome, and
- a focus on relationships rather than simply on individuals.[18]

Such a 'new Enlightenment' will not come easily because it will be opposed by both those who remain attached to the thinking based on the European Enlightenment of the seventeenth and eighteenth centuries and those who gain from a return to the Hobbesian world that Gray describes. But, if we do not destroy ourselves through climate catastrophe or nuclear holocaust, we have the possibility of moving through the painful transition of the present times into a new way of engaging with each other and our wider global environment. Our survival and that of many other species on our planet depends on whether we can produce such an outcome from our present travails.

Notes

1. Paul Rogers, *Losing Control: Global Security in the Twenty-First Century*, 4th ed. (London: Pluto Press, 2012).

2. John Mueller, *Retreat from Doomsday: The Obsolescence of Major War* (New York: Basic Books, 1989); Michael Mandelbaum, "Is Major War Obsolete?," *Survival* 40, no. 4 (1998): 20–38.

3. John Keegan, "The End of War?," *Daily Telegraph* August 4, 1997; Mary Kaldor, *New and Old Wars: Organized Violence in a Global Era* (Cambridge: Polity Press, 1999), 138.

4. UK Ministry of Defence, *Defence Drone Strategy: The UK's Approach to Defence Uncrewed Systems*, 2024, https://assets.publishing.service.gov.uk/media/65d724022197b201e57fa708/Defence_Drone_Strategy_-_the_UK_s_approach_to_Defence_Uncrewed_Systems.pdf.

5. Alex Gatopoulos, "'Largest Drone War in the World': How Airpower Saved Tripoli," *Al Jazeera*, May 28, 2020, https://www.aljazeera.com/news/2020/5/28/largest-drone-war-in-the-world-how-airpower-saved-tripoli.

6. UK Ministry of Defence, *Defence Drone Strategy*.

7. W. Brian Arthur, *The Nature of Technology: What It Is and How It Evolves* (New York: Free Press, 2009).

8. Bethan McKernan and Harry Davies, "'The Machine Did It Coldly': Israel Used AI to Identify 37,000 Hamas Targets," *The Guardian*, April 3, 2024.

9. Rogers, *Losing Control*.

10. John Thomas Alderdice, "Sacred Values: Psychological and Anthropological Perspectives on Fairness, Fundamentalism, and Terrorism," *Annals of the New York Academy of Sciences* 1167, no. 1 (June 2009): 158–73, https://doi.org/10.1111/j.1749-6632.2009.04510.x.

11. John, Lord Alderdice, "New Insights into the Psychology of Individuals and Large Groups in a World of Changing Conflicts," *International Political Science Review* 45, no. 1 (2024): 94–105, https://doi.org/10.1177/01925121231177444.

12. Steven Pinker, *The Better Angels of Our Nature: A History of Violence and Humanity* (London: Penguin, 2012); Francis Fukuyama, *The End of History and the Last Man* (New York: Penguin, 1992).

13. Kevin Rudd, *The Avoidable War: The Dangers of a Catastrophic Conflict between the US and Xi Jinping's China* (New York: Public Affairs, 2022).

14. Matt Waldman, "Peace-Making in Trouble: Expert Perspectives on Flaws, Deficiencies, and Potential in the Field of Mediation," unpublished presentation, CRIC 2023.

15. Itonde Kakoma and Edward Marques, *The Future of Mediation in the Post-COVID World*, Geneva Centre for Security Policy, August 2020, Issue 12, https://dam.gcsp.ch/files/images/the-future-of-mediation-in-the-post-covid-world.

16. John Gray, *The New Leviathans: Thoughts After Liberalism* (London: Allen Lane, 2023).

17. John, Lord Alderdice, "Conflict, Complexity, and Cooperation," *New England Journal of Public Policy* 33, no. 1 (2021): Article 9, https://scholarworks.umb.edu/nejpp/vol33/iss1/9.

18. Alderdice, "Conflict, Complexity, and Cooperation."

THE PSYCHOLOGICAL RISKS OF WAR BETWEEN THE UNITED STATES AND CHINA

Eugen Koh

Melbourne School of Population and Global Health, University of Melbourne

ABSTRACT

The relationship between the United States and China has deteriorated over the past two decades and fears of escalating risks of war are regularly reported in global media. This article explores the psychological factors that contribute to the two superpowers shifting from a collaborative relationship to a competitive relationship, seeing each other as enemies, feeling increasingly threatened by each other, failing to consider the heightened sensitivities that arise from their respective traumatic pasts, triggering the collapse of thinking and unleashing of uncontainable emotionality, escalating accidents to conflict, and escalating conflict to war. It highlights the dangers of ignoring heightened trauma-related sensitivities, or worse, the humiliation of the Other for domestic political gain or strategic advantage. This psychodynamic analysis of the psychological risks of war between the two superpowers considers the dynamics of Thucydides's Trap and ways to avoid succumbing to the dynamics of inevitability. The essence of the psychodynamic approaches to managing these risks is to anticipate the seemingly irrational and inevitable by preparing to counter the regressive forces driven by fear, contain the overwhelming emotionality, and restore the capacity for complex thinking in order to fully understand the nuances of the situation and find creative solutions to a potential impasse.

Eugen Koh is a psychiatrist and psychoanalytic psychotherapist, a consultant in art, culture, trauma, and peacebuilding, and a senior fellow at the Melbourne School of Population and Global Health, University of Melbourne, Australia.

This article is based on lectures of the same title delivered at The Center for Peace, Hiroshima University, in 2023; the Changing Character of War Centre, University of Oxford, in 2023; and S. Rajaratnam School of International Studies, Nanyang Technological University, Singapore, in 2024.

After five years of research into the cause of the global financial crisis of 2007–2009, Alan Greenspan, the former chairman of the US Federal Reserve bank, concluded that it was a result of what John Maynard Keynes famously referred to as "animal spirits"—the market was simply driven by fear and greed.[1] The historian Christopher Clark's highly regarded, detailed analysis of the events and factors that led to the First World War, *The Sleepwalkers: How Europe Went to War in 1914*, highlighted how personalities and relationships play a major part in the formation of alliances and decisions that ultimately lead to war.[2] Sleepwalking is, physiologically, a state when our rational mind is asleep but the body operates automatically and is driven by 'inapparent' impulses. From a psychodynamic perspective, while some impulses might not be immediately apparent, they are not necessarily unknown and could be known. The role of psychology in propaganda and warfare is well known to those working in the field of national security and international relations. The useful application of psychodynamic thinking in diplomacy, negotiation, the prevention of conflict, and peacebuilding is regrettably much less appreciated.

This article aims to highlight the psychological factors that influence the relationship between the United States and China from a psychodynamic perspective. It will discuss how understanding some of these factors could be useful in dialogue and diplomacy to de-escalate the risk of war and manage critical events to prevent accidents from turning into conflict, and conflict from turning into war.

Psychodynamic Approaches

Psychodynamic thinking considers both the conscious (apparent) and unconscious (not apparent) of individuals, collectives, and systems. Traditionally, the study of thinking and behavior in the conscious realm is the focus of psychology, while attempts to understand the territory that is beyond our awareness, that is the unconscious, is the domain of psychoanalysis. Psychodynamic approaches usually incorporate knowledge from both psychology and psychoanalysis.

In its application to international relations, psychodynamic thinking treats countries as singular entities, each with its unique national psyche, in the way that everyone has a mind of their own. It is, however, not as simple as making inferences extrapolated from our understanding of an individual's mind. It might be argued that the psychodynamics of collectives, such as nations, are far more complex because countries might not consist of sufficiently homogenous populations to be considered unified entities. Most countries will, however, overcome these differences through the collective agency of their government, which will ultimately determine foreign policies. This article will briefly highlight how a government's approach to its international relations is influenced by its domestic politics, that is, the dynamics between distinguishable groups and political factions in the country. However, the main focus of this article is the psychodynamics between two countries.

Vamik Volkan, the pioneer of the systematic application of psychodynamic thinking to diplomacy and conflict resolution, preferred to conceptualize the consciousness of countries and factions within them in terms of large group psychology. The psychodynamic approach adopted in this article is influenced by Volkan's work and I recommend his book *Psychoanalysis, International Relations and Diplomacy* for those who wish to understand such an approach more thoroughly.[3]

Some argue that conceptualization of a country as a single mind or psyche imposes a reductionistic categorization that fails to account for the rich and complex culture, history, and varied experiences and views of the people. They consider it offensive to speak of the American mind or the Chinese psyche. Yet the notion of a single consciousness is central to the psychology of nationalism, as Americans consider themselves 'patriots under one flag,' and the Chinese government recently proposed laws against 'hurting the nation's feelings.'[4] This article is mindful of nationalism's complexities and much more can be elaborated through political science and other disciplines. With acceptance of these caveats and other limitations, and without any intention to oversimplify or offend, the psychodynamic approach is proposed here as a contribution that could usefully add to the more traditional approaches that help in understanding international relations and negotiating the complex tensions between two superpowers to avoid the possibility of a catastrophic war.

From Collaboration to Competition, to Creation of the Enemy

The United States and China established a full diplomatic relationship in 1979, seven years after President Richard Nixon and Secretary of State, Henry Kissinger, met with Chairman Mao Zedong. China soon embarked on economic reforms under the collective leadership of Deng Xiaoping. The Clinton administration tentatively gave China 'most favored nation' status in 1993, with its low tariff and trade privileges. This was reviewed and renewed annually, before it was made permanent in 2001 by the Bush administration; both administrations supported its membership to the World Trade Organization, formalized that same year.[5]

How did such a collaborative relationship turn into strategic competitiveness and escalate to both countries treating the other as the enemy? After a decade of collaboration in the 1990s, driven by what was simply bilateral economic opportunism, the relationship began to sour over the next two decades, as American manufacturing continued to decline while China's economic growth accelerated through the unprecedented growth of its manufacturing sector, and the balance of trade gradually slid toward China's favor. The global financial crisis toward the end of that decade wreaked havoc on Western economies (while China was relatively spared), precipitating an even greater trade imbalance, with an accompanying deterioration of the relationship between the two countries.

The gradual shift in economic power in the final two decades of the twentieth century accelerated over the first two decades of the twenty-first century. This economic shift saw more decline of manufacturing in the US while China became the factory of the world. The US had been militarily drained by wars in Iraq and Afghanistan, while China expanded its military significantly and built what is now one of the world's largest naval fleets. This period was accompanied by the emergence of renewed Chinese nationalism, which had begun under President Jiang Zemin at the time of the Clinton administration, with his concerted, nationwide 'patriotic education campaign.' Against this backdrop of shifting economic and military power, a sense of alarm has grown over the past decade with the rise of President Xi Jinping, who consolidated power within the Chinese Communist Party (CCP) and has been strident in his proclamation of this new Chinese confidence.

There are several more threads to be woven into this narrative from a psychodynamic perspective, especially to explain the more recent escalation from competing to becoming enemies.

One of the fundamental psychoanalytic ideas is that the mind, either individual or collective, will rid itself of unbearable aspects of itself (bad parts) by projecting (externalizing) it onto Others, which then leads to it perceiving them as 'bad.' As such projections grow, the perception of 'badness' in the Other and the accompanying sense of threat becomes so great that the mind regresses and its ability to distinguish between what is real from that which is imagined begins to diminish.[6] I will elaborate on regression and the loss of capacity to think later in this article. This is the essence of how enemies are created, as understood from a psychodynamic perspective.

According to this theory, the increase in America's perceiving China as a threat is partly due to the emergence of some negative aspects within themselves that are unbearable and are consequently projected onto Others. Moreover, such projection occurs most easily to external entities that were historically viewed negatively. The US had seen China as inferior a long way back, since the early nineteenth century when it joined the British in selling opium to the Chinese.[7]

In the last two decades, the US has experienced several unbearable collective experiences that 'needed' to be discarded by projection. One of the most unbearable human experiences is humiliation. It is, perhaps, not a coincidence that the relationship began to deteriorate in the years after the terrorist attacks in September 11, 2001, followed by a failed disaster response to Hurricane Katrina in 2005 and the collapse of its proud financial sector during the global financial crisis from 2007 to 2009. It is significant that these three catastrophic events occurred in the context of an earlier and ongoing, but more insidious humiliation, exemplified by the Midwestern American experience of losing their proud and powerful manufacturing industries to China, an intolerable pain fueling movements like Make America Great Again.[8]

Although China has enjoyed unprecedented economic growth that has lifted more than half its population out of poverty over the past four decades, it too had its share of internal problems over that period.[9] The social upheavals from the Communist Revolution did not end with the Chinese Communist Party taking control in 1949.[10] The enforced change from an agrarian economy to an industrialized one (the Great Leap Forward, 1958 to 1962), with its reduced focus on food production compromised by bad weather, led to one of the worst famines in human history, with an estimated fifteen to fifty-five million people dying of starvation.[11] This catastrophic event was followed by the social turmoil of the Cultural Revolution (1966 to 1976) with its stated aim to reduce what was termed "the three major differences"—those separating intellectual from manual labor, worker from peasant, and urban from rural.[12] The personal and collective traumatic impact of the Cultural Revolution continues to this day.

From a psychodynamic perspective, the socio-emotional consequences of these massive collective trauma events do not just disappear. Even as the country went through a relentless period of economic boom over the next four decades, a concerted effort has been taken either collectively, or enforced politically, to deny or forget the painful past. The suppressed collective pain will inevitably erupt from time to time; perhaps the Tiananmen Square incident of 1989 was unconsciously driven by such an eruption.[13]

The projection of 'badness' will grow to such an extent that any realistic perception of the Other is completely lost. The psychological risk of war is greatest in the early phases of a domestic crisis when projection is the main mechanism for managing unbearable internal stress. As the crisis grows, projection is no longer adequate. In ordinary language, blaming others can only work for so long. The attempt by a government and other social institutions to solve their internal problems by projection is accompanied by an escalation of its sense of threat, as the 'badness' is externalized.[14] If these psychodynamic postulations are correct, the sense of threat between the US and China will be the greatest when one or both countries are experiencing recession or the beginning of an economic collapse and/or the emergence of social unrest.

Collective Trauma Heightens Sensitivity to Future Humiliation

Officially, the domestic events in China mentioned in the previous section, and its civil war between the Kuomintang (KMT) and the Chinese Communist Party (1927–1949), are not considered to be part of the traumatic events that have been condensed into what has been popularly referred to as *the century of humiliation*.[15] That historical period began with the Opium Wars (the first from 1839 to 1842, the second from 1856 to 1860) and the ceding of Hong Kong to the British, promptly followed by an escalation of demand for trade and territorial concessions by ten Western countries and Japan after the brutal suppression of the Boxer Rebellion (in 1899–1901), where more than 100,000 Chinese people were killed.[16] A few years earlier in 1895, China was forced to cede Taiwan to Japan after it lost a war over their contest for influence over Korea. More than twenty million Chinese people, mostly civilians, died from mass atrocities and famine when Japan later invaded China in 1937.[17] This century of national humiliation at the hands of foreigners finally ended with the Japanese surrendering upon their defeat in the Second World War in 1945.

The humiliation experienced by China over a century of foreign domination was utilized in Jiang Zemin's nationwide patriotic education campaign to foster nationalism and certainly influenced the CCP in its foreign policy. From a psychodynamic perspective, while such fostering of collective traumatic pain to fuel nationalism is common, it dangerously heightens a country's sensitivity to future humiliation.[18] Not surprisingly, China reacts very strongly to criticism, especially when it comes from countries that have contributed to its century of humiliation.[19] Such strong reactions are understandable when one considers how painful these criticisms might be when a traumatic wound is prodded, especially by those who inflicted it in the first place.

The internal stoking of historical wounds by a government for whatever aim, dangerously risks a buildup of collective emotional pain that could easily erupt in crises from domestic situations and foreign relations. The suppression of the pain from these wounds is not helpful either, because the pressure from cumulative trauma will only build. Until such historical traumatic wounds can be healed, the pain needs to be managed by a quiet and sensitive acknowledgment of its existence without either stoking or suppressing it.[20] This approach is necessary in the management of the psychological risk from such heightened sensitivity to humiliation, not only in a government's consideration of its people but also its relationships with other countries. Attention to these trauma-related sensitivities is a vital component of dialogue and peace processes.[21]

It is standard practice for diplomacy to manage anticipated sensitivities carefully. In the context of the US-China relationship, diplomats have been careful not to highlight the domestic problems of the Other. The media of the two countries have, however, been less restrained and there is virtually no such sensible reservation in the territory of social media. The extent to which widespread circulation of misinformation and conspiracy theories is the work of proxies of their respective governments is up for conjecture. The humiliation of a country's ordinary people will ultimately have a collective impact and as the Chinese government would say, 'hurt the nation's feelings.'[22]

There are those who revel in the humiliation of the Other, as the schoolyard bully does, and the psychopath. They create a potentially very dangerous situation. My colleague, the late Stuart Twemlow, a psychiatrist and psychoanalyst who studied the psychodynamic causes of school shootings in the US for the Federal Bureau of Investigation (FBI), found the shooter to be invariably a victim of extended bullying and humiliation, and shootings were usually acts of revenge.[23]

The media of both the US and China have used humiliation to gain a sense of moral superiority and triumph. The Chinese media and social media highlighted the social and political upheavals in the US; for instance, the civil unrest during the Black Lives

Matter protests across the country.[24] They may not have appreciated the depth of the emotional significance of those events to the American national psyche, nor its reach into the country's unhealed fractures that stem from its civil war (1861–1865) fought over the issue of slavery.[25] If Chinese media continues to purposely exploit the situation to cause further humiliation for Americans, it would be treading a very dangerous path as it could awaken a series of past traumatic events and unleash an emotional storm.

While the US might not have had a comparable century of humiliation, it has had several collective traumatic events since its civil war that would render heightened sensitivity. For a country that prides itself on capitalistic enterprise, the Great Depression (1929–1939) and the global financial crisis (2007–2009) would have injured its collective ego. Its pride in military strength was severely dented by the surprise attack on Pearl Harbor by the Japanese in December 1941 and the loss of the Vietnam War (1955–1975) remains a deep, traumatic wound in the American psyche.

The US has not explicitly formulated these major events as traumatic. Neither has it explicitly framed its loss of manufacturing in the Midwest and other parts of the country, its social divides, especially along economic and racial lines, its epidemic of opioid addiction, or the rolling turmoil of its financial sectors, as humiliating. It is, however, implied through social-political movements, such as Make America Great Again. The absence of explicitly acknowledging trauma and other humiliation, of course, does not mean that such heightened sensitivities do not exist. While the country debates the extent to which such pain and vulnerability is driving American lives collectively, and its domestic and foreign policies, it is prudent to take such sensitivity into account in diplomatic dealings with the US, especially when it is entering into domestic crises. It is in these early phases of a domestic crisis that projection and its accompanying distortion of perception are at their worst.

Regression and Collapse of Thinking

A failure to consider trauma-related sensitivities will lead one country to carelessly provoke the other country. If such provocation persists or takes place at a time of internal weakness and domestic crises, it could trigger a collapse of its collective psyche.

The collective mind, however, tries to regroup by activating a process of regression. Regression is a psychological concept akin to the notion of a military retreat to regroup at the next level of strength. The mind regresses to a simpler or more basic level of functioning. A collective mind, group, or system can regress in four ways: a collapse of thinking, increased preoccupation and sensitivity about boundary and identity, splitting and fragmentation, and implosion with internal conflict and violence.

The regression of thinking, which might lead to its complete collapse, begins with the loss of complex thinking, that is, an inability to consider the nuances of a situation and negotiate its complexities. When this happens, binary thinking takes over with its simplistic black and white, good and bad, dichotomy. It was in this state that President George W. Bush addressed Congress in the aftermath of the September 11 terrorist attacks, when he famously declared, "Either you are with us, or you are with the terrorists."[26] In that situation, there was only "us" or the enemies; there was no possibility of neutrality. At a societal level, the predominance of binary thinking manifests as polarized opinions and positions; along with its extremes at both poles, there is no possibility of a middle ground. In this situation, Chinese Americans are asked to abandon the complexity of ethnicity and national identity and are forced to take sides.

In binary thinking, there is at least room for two distinct, opposite positions and parties might agree to disagree. If the regression in thinking deteriorates further, the mind operates in an even simpler mode. I call this *unitary thinking*, where only one view is valid and allowed to exist, and all other views are wrong. This is the position of the fundamentalist mindset. Dialogue and negotiations become impossible when such thinking predominates. The insistence of other parties that their view is valid, even if it is not imposed on others, might be perceived as a threat that needs to be countered or eliminated. This was arguably the fundamentalist mindset of ISIS, where it was impossible for any country to negotiate with it.[27]

I am not suggesting that such a mode of thinking is currently operating in US-China diplomacy. However, binary thinking is common in the US at almost every strata of its society, most prominently among its political elite. Some might suggest that the thinking of authoritarian and totalitarian regimes, such as the CCP, approaches unitary thinking because there appears to be no room for debate or dissent and only the party's thinking is permitted. However, does China's more nuanced diplomatic stance in recent times and emphasis on bilaterality and multi-laterality in international relations suggest a renewed capacity for complex thinking?

Psychodynamic approaches predictably consider a mind's mode of functioning as ever changing (dynamic), as it negotiates stress and regresses to regroup to face challenges ahead. Volkan proposes that a large group, which may consist of thousands or millions of people, becomes preoccupied with identity and boundaries when they are under stress and regressing. This increased preoccupation takes the form of nationalism, a heightened focus on 'Othering' and increased concern about territoriality and borders. When there is greater economic stability and relative peace, they return to a more progressive level of functioning and become less concerned about their identity and boundary.

Applying these observations to the US-China relationship, we can expect heightened geopolitical tensions when there is global stress or domestic challenges within their respective countries. It is perhaps not surprising that the relationship between the two countries deteriorated to an alarming level early in the COVID-19 pandemic. While the relationship has regained some stability, we could expect China to become more preoccupied and sensitive about Taiwan and other territorial issues if the level of global stress increases again. Indeed, some would suggest that global stress might have already increased again since the pandemic with the war between Russia and Ukraine and the conflict between Israel and Hamas.[28] This stress could escalate dramatically if the Russia-Ukraine War draws in the rest of Europe and NATO or the Middle East situation spreads into a regional war.

If the Russia-Ukraine and Israel-Hamas wars were to draw the US and China into conflict, the devastating global economic impact would precipitate a worldwide regression that would tip the two countries into a full-scale war. I have already discussed how regression causes a collapse of thinking and heightens preoccupation about identity and boundary. The sociologist psychoanalyst Earl Hopper has described how a regressed, traumatized system splits and aggregates.[29] From an international relations perspective, this means diminishing multilateralism and increasing alliances. However, I have also consistently observed an overall fragmentation of relationships, with diminished trust and heightened sensitivity to humiliation within a deteriorating, regressed traumatized system. Such a situation predisposes itself to internal conflict and anarchic eruptions of violence within a country.

Studies of group dynamics have highlighted the rise of authoritarian leadership to avoid and manage such anxious situations; strongman leaders offer to rescue their country from the risk of descending into anarchy and paralysis. Some analysts might suggest that we are already facing such a situation in the US with the rise of Donald Trump, and in China, the rise of Xi Jinping.

The psychological risk of war increases significantly when the fate of the superpowers' relationship lies in the hands of two powerful leaders. When the checks and balances that are usually in place are swept aside by the strongmen, the system becomes dysfunctional, as fragmentation and internal conflict grow within their respective governments. With the collapse of thinking, decisions are driven only by unbridled emotionality. Any wish by one country to intentionally provoke another country to cause a collapse of thinking in the Other, is very dangerous indeed because it will unleash an emotional storm that engulfs all, and a catastrophic world war becomes inevitable.

Unleashing of Uncontainable Emotionality

The mind, both individual and collective, seeks to protect itself by wrapping up or encapsulating the traumatic experience and suppressing it to forget what happened. It also detaches the emotions associated with that experience by compartmentalizing and suppressing them separately from any memory of what happened. When the mind is triggered to remember the traumatic event, there is a strong risk that the associated suppressed and compartmentalized emotion is released. If the mind could reconnect reactivated emotions to the original traumatic experience in a measured way and make sense of why it is feeling that way, the emotionality is contained and the situation is manageable. If the mind cannot, the individual will be left anxious, overwhelmed, and bewildered. The collective mind is less able to reconnect this reactivated emotionality to what happened and is even less capable of making sense of it as one. Often, the emotions accumulated from a long history of trauma are unleashed in an uncontainable form, leading to riots and even revolutions.

The potency of pent-up collective psychic pain, most evident in the violence of riots driven by explosive eruptions of emotions and mob mentality, has been well documented since Gustave Le Bon published his book, *Psychologie des foules (Psychology of crowds)* in 1895.[30] I am unaware, however, if there have been any studies of how such emotionality manifests in the closed corridors of power and affects their decision-making. One might glean, from the US Congress's *Final Report of the Select Committee to Investigate the January 6th Attack on the United States Capitol*, the sense of chaos and turmoil in the Trump administration during the storming of the United States Capitol buildings.[31] We would prefer to believe that those in charge of the fate of countries, if not the whole world, will handle crisis in the consultative, thoughtful, and emotionally contained manner in which the Kennedy administration's handling of the Cuban Missile Crisis in 1962 is dramatically depicted in the film *Thirteen Days*.[32] Such a scenario would not have been possible if the administration had been embroiled by overwhelming emotionality.

I would be surprised if there is documentation, or dramatization, of the government of the People's Republic of China in chaos; the public display of disharmony is rarely visible in a regime whose ordinary operation is distinctively opaque. It is also characteristic of Chinese culture that emotional matters and potentially shameful situations are kept strictly private.

In assessing the degree of emotionality, it is important to take into account differences between emotional expressions of Eastern and Western cultures. In East Asian cultures, strong emotions are usually found in silence. Failure to take this into consideration might have caused the West to underestimate the profound humiliation and anger felt by China when China was blamed for the COVID-19 pandemic. China's relatively mild public, angry response underplayed how profoundly outraged and hurt they were. In general terms, the Chinese tendency to withdraw into silence when humiliated may have added to the thinking that China had something to hide and must therefore be guilty. There is a very great risk of miscalculation if the West expects China to respond in ways that they would. Indeed, the Chinese would only respond with the strong display of emotionality expected in the West when they are in the grip of uncontainable rage, by which time, it might be too late for diplomacy.

How Things Get out of Control Very Quickly

Emotions unleashed by the reactivation of dormant trauma associated with one event, can very quickly get out of control as the memory of one incident triggers another, like the explosion of one barrel of gunpowder igniting another, and another. The stress and strain of an escalating emotional outburst causes a collective mind or a system to regress further, with further loss of the capacity to think clearly and to manage a nuanced diplomatic response to a worsening crisis.

The speed of such escalation, from an incident to conflict and full-scale war that rapidly draws in allies, can be frighteningly fast as illustrated by the First World War. The match was lit with the Sarajevo assassination of Archduke Ferdinand of Austria on June 28, 1914, and by August 4, 1914, Britain, France, and Russia were at war with the Austro-Hungarian Empire and Germany. The Ottoman Empire joined in two months later in November, and a few months later Bulgaria, Italy, and Greece became involved in what was recognized by early 1915 as a world war. In less than a year, the war had engulfed the world with battles throughout Europe, the Middle East, the Pacific, and Asia.

A potential example of how such an escalating crisis, driven by rapidly growing emotionality triggered by a series of related traumatic events, might lead to a war between the US and China, is the seemingly 'minor' conflict between China and Japan over an ostensibly insignificant group of inhabitable rocky islands.

While these contested islands, called the Senkaku Islands according to Japan, or the Diaoyu Islands according to China, possess limited worth in themselves, they represent the unresolved aspects of the First (1894–1895) and Second (1937–1945) Sino-Japanese Wars. A seemingly minor conflict over these islands could trigger a disproportionate response from China, driven by the emotionality of their traumatic experience from these wars. As previously discussed, China not only suffered millions of civilian deaths during the Japanese occupation over those eight years (1937–1945), but many died in circumstances that constituted war crimes, such the extensive use of biological warfare and massacres of civilians by the tens of thousands, including the infamous incident known as the Rape of Nanking.[33] It began on December 13, 1937 and continued for six weeks, with the rape and slaughter of women and children, killing as many as 300,000 in some estimates.[34] The painful emotions from this incident alone are still palpable in China today with not infrequent reference to what happened in the media.[35] Such unresolved tension predisposes a minor conflict with Japan to quickly escalate into a war. The US has a treaty with Japan that promises to come to Japan's aid if it is attacked.

A conflict with Japan will also trigger another set of traumatic experiences for China. The loss of the First Sino-Japanese War forced China to cede Taiwan to Japan. Reminders of the ceding of Taiwan could also trigger another set of humiliating traumatic experiences related to the Opium Wars, which resulted in China being forced to cede Hong Kong. The painful reactivation of memory about this period, the beginning of the century of humiliation, would bring to life the deep resentment and grievance, if not hatred, of the West that has been fermenting over many years.

The Symbolic and Emotional Significance of Taiwan to China

The significance of an event or a territory to a country is what it means to its people and is usually tied to a particular shared historical emotional experience. If that shared experience can be symbolized, or put into words or a narrative, it is said to be embedded in its culture and history. Often the symbol formed means much more than the immediate event or a thing itself. Taiwan, therefore, could mean a lot more to the Chinese people than its geostrategic position in the South China Sea and the critical importance of its semiconductor industries. While the search for the symbolic meaning of Taiwan to China might need to go back several hundred years in both of their histories, it might be argued that emotionality related to the most recent events is closest to the surface, and this is where we should begin.

The present-day Taiwan as a self-governing territory separate from mainland China was established by Chiang Kai-shek, the leader of the Kuomintang government of the Republic of China, who fled to the island upon defeat by the Chinese Communist Party in 1949. The civil war had begun in 1927 and hostilities paused when both the KMT and CCP fought against the occupying Japanese from 1937 to 1945. The emotional pain associated with the civil war appears to have been covered over by the trauma of Japanese occupation and the subsequent devastating suffering during the Great Famine and Cultural Revolution.

There is no agreement on the approximate number that were killed during the civil war, with estimates ranging from 1.8 to 3.5 million, with many atrocities carried out by both sides.[36] The greater part of the suffering of the Chinese people from this period has been buried. Modern day, democratic Taiwan was created out of this civil war and remains the most visible reminder of that fratricide that most Chinese would prefer to forget. They do not wish to remember a time when their families, communities, and country were torn apart as people took sides and betrayal cost lives. For the CCP, Taiwan could be a reminder of unfinished business from their conflict with the KMT; perhaps in the mind of some, the civil war has not yet ended.

Sometimes the significance of an event or a thing cannot be put into words, or in psychodynamic terms, is not symbolizable. We might speak of such a phenomenon, not as having symbolic significance, but having a more general and undifferentiated, emotional significance. Often an individual or a collective might not know the full emotional significance of an event or experience to themselves. For instance, I have been struck by the response from several Chinese scholars and observers to a hypothetical scenario: if Taiwan declares independence, crossing the red line that the CCP has repeatedly asserted they will not tolerate and the US comes to its aid, but the CCP does not respond as it said it would, what will happen? The common response to this scenario was, "the people will be very angry." This suggests a belief among Chinese people, and not only the CCP, that the Celestial Kingdom will once again be complete and harmonized when Taiwan is reunited with the motherland. Such a belief in the profound importance of reunification may also be somehow tied to a deep but unacknowledged wish and need to heal from the unresolved pain and fractures of the civil war and more.

The loss of Taiwan, through its declaration of independence from China with support from the West, would therefore be intolerable. Perhaps, even more significantly, such a loss would trigger an unleashing of the suppressed pain and rage from the century of humiliation. A cascading series of past trauma, with its associated emotionality, would be reactivated, starting with the unresolved aspects of the First Sino-Japanese War, when China was forced to cede Taiwan to Japan, which reminds China of an earlier humiliation when it had to cede Hong Kong to the British following its loss in the Opium Wars. Memories of the Second Sino-Japanese War, which became part of the Second World War in the Pacific, is not far from the forefront of many Chinese minds. Painful traumatic memories will quickly become reactivated and the Rape of Nanking, which has become symbolic of the many atrocities carried out by the Japanese, will once again arouse hatred.

Instead of these convoluted associations, it could be suggested that a US intervention in Taiwan could simply bring to life the long list of China's grievances toward that country alone.[37]

The emotional significance of Taiwan might extend farther back in history.[38] For the Han Chinese, who make up most of the population of China, the century of humiliation was not only a result of bullying by Western powers, but they were also sold out by the abject failure of the foreign Qing-Manchu dynasty. When the Manchurians (Manchus) defeated the last Han Chinese dynasty in 1662, the surviving remnant of the Ming dynasty, led by General Zheng Chenggong, retreated to Taiwan.

Taiwan has been a part of China's realm of influence since much earlier times. Delegations from the Chinese imperial courts have regularly visited the indigenous-inhabited island from the time of the Three Kingdoms (AD 230). It was, however, the steady migration of Han Chinese that followed the settlement by General Zheng that led to the formation of what is known as modern Taiwan today.[39]

The fact that the formation of what Taiwan is today was twice ushered in by retreating Chinese generals, might not be as significant as the fact that those events were associated with two catastrophic eras of China's history: the end of the last Han Chinese dynasty and the Chinese Civil War. From a psychodynamic perspective, Taiwan is not simply a place, but a symbol of the great fractures from those events. Perhaps more important is Taiwan's emotional association with the great suffering of China. It has also become, in the imagination of the Chinese people, a panacea for pain and humiliation from the past 350 years—a belief that all will be well when Taiwan returns to the motherland. It would be a terrible mistake to dismiss the emotional significance of Taiwan to China, even if it largely rested on a phantasy.[40] In psychodynamic thinking, what is imagined is often a much more powerful driver of human behavior than what is real. Perhaps, that is why China has repeatedly stated that 'Taiwan is not negotiable.'

The Problem of Distrust

In his book *The Avoidable War – The Dangers of a Catastrophic Conflict between the US and Xi Jinping's China*, Kevin Rudd, previously the prime minister of Australia and currently the country's ambassador to the United States, devoted a whole chapter to "The Problem of Distrust." It offers a frank analysis of the historical origins of this problem between the two countries and its continuing impact:

> The View from Beijing – Americans typically believe that their country's approach to China has been driven by high ideals in defense of democracy, free trade, and the integrity of the global rules-based order but the Chinese view is that American strategy is nothing more than the prosecution of its core national interests. To pretend otherwise, in China's view is political hypocrisy. Moreover, as seen from Beijing, American strategy is rarely if ever cognizant – let alone respectful – of China's national aspirations. In China's perspective, this is reflected in 150 years of US commercial efforts to penetrate China's vast domestic market – from the age of opium to the age of Apple. It sees it in the history of American national security strategy. First, handing over Chinese territory to appease Japan after World War I, then, using the protracted Japanese occupation of China during World War II to keep the bulk of Japanese Imperial forces bogged down for the duration of the Pacific War instead of prioritizing a liberation of the Chinese mainland. And finally, leveraging Beijing against Moscow as part of an ultimately successful strategy to contain the Soviet Union during the Cold War.[41]

From the perspective of the Chinese people, "No young person could ever graduate from the Chinese school system without being exposed to the sign said to have been erected in the international concession in Shanghai in the 1920s proclaiming, 'No dogs or Chinese allowed.' Few in China grew up without at least a passing familiarity with America's history of anti-Chinese sentiments."[42]

According to Jon Bateman, "American economic sanctions against China, such as the current restrictions of export of technology, especially semiconductors, feeds these sentiments."[43] Rudd continues,

> The View from Washington – As of June 2021, 76 percent of Americans had an unfavorable opinion of China, according to polling by Pew Research. However, most of this ire is directed at the Chinese state, with only 15 percent expressing confidence in Xi Jinping to "do the right thing regarding world affairs." […] Most Americans have a positive view of Chinese civilization, including the depth of history and culture […] It is much harder, however, for Americans to understand what the Chinese Communist Party actually wants as opposed to the common, understandable desires of the Chinese people.

Rudd suggests that the absolute secrecy of the CCP fosters the tendency among American officials "to assume the worst and prepare accordingly."[44]

There is no shortage of conspiracy theories about China's hostile intentions. In psychodynamic thinking, those theories that flourish, from Huawei to TikTok, only needed a small element of truth and thick opacity to feed the wild imaginations of those who are already fearful. The state of turmoil and insecurity of the post-pandemic world has prepared a fertile ground for paranoia and distrust to grow, and so too will the psychological risks of war. China's assertive claim of the whole South China Sea, of course, provides realistic material that fuels any prevailing paranoia.[45] Its regular incursion into Taiwan's airspace and frequently reported contest with the Philippines over the disputed Spratly Islands confirms a negative perception of China in the mind of many Americans.

Distrust is also one of the core effects of traumatization, when one's fundamental trust that the world is safe and the Other can be trusted, is shaken. Even one's trust in oneself is questioned. The prevailing distrust between the two countries will escalate in a crisis that relates to a past trauma, such as a crisis over Taiwan that triggers China's traumatic experience of the Sino-Japanese Wars and the humiliation of the Opium Wars.

Psychology of Inevitability

When situations become too frightening, we resort to denial as a mechanism of defense, which might manifest as 'there isn't a problem' or 'it will sort itself out.' Those who do not deny there is a problem, but are too overwhelmed by it to act, could convince themselves of something along the lines of, 'there is nothing that can be done and therefore, nothing to do, and therefore, do nothing.' Simply put, it is inevitable and therefore there is no need to do anything, absolving one of any guilt and shame from doing nothing. In Eastern culture, this way of thinking is 'fate' and passive acceptance is the only way forward.

The fatalistic acceptance that war between the two great superpowers is inevitable is widespread among those who subscribe to the idea of Thucydides's Trap. Graham Allison, Professor of Government at Harvard University and previously the assistant secretary of defense in the Clinton administration, highlighted what the ancient Greek historian Thucydides observed in his treatise, *History of the Peloponnesian War*. He concluded that it was the rise of Athens and the fear that this instilled in Sparta that made the war inevitable. Allison came to the same conclusion after finding that war occurred in twelve out of the sixteen situations over the past five hundred years when a rising power threatened to displace a ruling power.[46]

Writing in 2022, Rudd, however, suggested that war between the two superpowers is not inevitable but more 'probable,' even as he noted, "many of the elements of Thucydides's Trap are already present in the US-China relationship today."[47] Refusing to accept the psychology of inevitability, he instead highlighted, "Allison's analysis of sixteen historical engagements between rising and established powers over the last five hundred years concluded that *one-quarter of them did not result in war.*" [48] He urged, "We can either allow the primordial dimensions of Thucydidean logic to simply take their natural course, culminating in crisis, conflict, or even war. Or we can identify potential strategic off-ramps, or at least guardrails, which may help preserve the peace."[49]

Some of the drivers of the Thucydidean Trap can be understood in terms of how normal competitiveness is overtaken by a growing sense of threat, with a diminishing ability to distinguish what is real from what is imagined, as unbearable internal problems are projected onto the Other. The failure to address the internal domestic problems will create dangerous destructive forces within each respective country. If these internal forces are accentuated by external regressive forces generated by traumatic world events, such as the global financial crisis or pandemic, a perfect storm starts to form, greatly escalating the risk of war. To add to this highly fragile situation, a poorly considered response to an accidental crisis by one country, puncturing a historical traumatic abscess, will unleash resentment, grievances, and hatred that has built up over generations.

The stress from an escalating perception of threat will precipitate regression in the officials and leaders, as well as in ways governments operate, with a rapidly diminishing capacity to think and manage a crisis. Further missteps, especially those that humiliate the Other, would trigger memory of previous traumatic humiliations, putting into motion cascading explosions, and blowing off the lids of barrels of pent-up emotions that have been brewing for generations. The release of such overwhelming and uncontained emotions collapses any remaining diminished capacity to think and contain an emerging conflict. It is hoped that such a dire situation could be saved by whatever goodwill is left between the two countries. Failing that, only their goodwill with a mediating third Other could save us all.

Managing the Psychological Risks of War

There are, however, several steps where psychodynamic-informed and assisted interventions could manage the situation described above, counter the dynamics of the Thucydidean Trap, and prevent the world from sleepwalking into a catastrophic war. First we need to wake up to psychological factors that could lead to the two countries to war. I will briefly outline some of these interventions.

Understanding the Situation

Psychodynamic approaches to any situation begin with an appreciation that a great deal more is going on, in individuals and collectives, than it appears. While this might be stating the obvious, often we are forced to face the obvious challenges happening in front of us, when we do not have the time or space to understand the more powerful drivers of the situation operating in the unconscious.

Even though this article has discussed the psychodynamics driving some of the psychological risks of conflict between the US and China, including those that might drive a Thucydidean entrapment, there is much more that needs to be understood.

This article has not addressed the psychological risks associated with alliances and protective treaties, and the tendencies for governments to operate within these relationships under the influence of 'groupthink' and the rapid spread of a contagion in the realms of the unconscious.[50] It has not discussed the risks of collapsing executive decision-making and chains of command in the face of overwhelming, collective emotionality. One must consider the risks that emerge from a situation where the hatred of the Other (either anti-American or anti-Chinese) among the people becomes so great that either the government is forced to act accordingly, or the possibility of rogue operatives within governments act out the wishes of the people. A better understanding of these psychodynamics will enable us to anticipate and manage these situations.

De-escalating the Present Tension

If both superpowers agree they do not want war, then there is an urgent need for their governments, politicians, media and other security related institutions, including think tanks of each respective country, to refrain from blaming the other for their internal problems. The dangers of purposely exploiting trauma-related sensitivities to humiliate the Other and claim a moral high ground and sense of triumph, cannot be overstated. The humiliation of the Other for strategic gain could backfire spectacularly, if the reaction of the Other activates an emotional storm that spins out of control. Politicians that peddle fear for personal gain should be reminded that there comes a point where fear is overtaken by denial.

While it is understandable how profit-making media benefit from focusing on fear, as its readership predictably increases when there is a sense of danger, it is necessary to remember that too much fear drives down consumer confidence, economic activities, and advertising. The suggestion that the media is one of the main drivers of conflict and war should not be surprising given how responsive leading politicians are to the 24/7 news cycle. While the dynamics between the media and leadership might be too obvious to require elaboration, some further work on how to address this problem from a psychodynamic perspective would be useful to expose the dangers of this relationship with respect to the psychological risk of war.

Meanwhile, any effort at all levels of society and governments that can promote a sensitive appreciation of each country's respective traumatic history, will help to counter the prevailing fear and encourage a more realistic, if not sympathetic, understanding of the Other.

Overcoming Impasse

There are many possible reasons why dialogue and negotiation might stall. Psychodynamic insights into why an impasse might be occurring could help both parties to address it to enable dialogue and negotiation to proceed again. One of the more common reasons for impasse is that both parties are stuck in entrenched regression with compromised capacities for complex thinking, excessive preoccupation with identity and boundary, and splitting and fragmentation occurring within their respective group.

Impasse is also likely when the sense of distrust reaches the point where fear is the overwhelming emotion. At this point, the capacity for realistic evaluation of a situation is usually severely affected. Hubris, a common reaction to humiliation, past, present, or anticipated, would not permit any compromise. There is often, instead, a wish to triumph in the game of upmanship. Perhaps, more commonly, both sides are stuck in their defensive positions.

A recognition of the prevailing dynamic at the time of an impasse might enable those mediating the process to disentangle the situation. Sometimes, a deeper psychodynamic analysis of the possible unconscious drivers of the situation is necessary.

Avoiding a Crisis

Crisis does not happen in a vacuum. It usually occurs as the end point of cumulative misunderstanding and missteps. It is often pointed out in psychoanalytic discourse that there is no such thing as an accident. A forensic retrospective analysis could usually identify a series of human errors occurring under the influence of forces that are not easily apparent, but powerful, nonetheless.

Dialogue between the two countries during peacetime that seeks to establish a mutual, deeper appreciation of each other's motivations and differences in cultural and communication styles, will help to avoid the accumulation of misunderstandings and missteps that set the scene for crisis to occur. Such a dialogue will not only help to reduce the risk of a crisis occurring, but also aid its de-escalation should it happen.

Psychodynamic observations and analysis of the interactions between two countries, such as those discussed in this article thus far, could identify some of the subtle misunderstandings and missteps that might not be apparent to those involved.

Managing a Crisis

The stress and strain of a situation, such as the Cuban Missile Crisis of 1962, could lead to a rapid collective loss of capacity to think clearly and contain emotions. If that crisis had occurred in the context of an even more unstable time domestically, such as an insurrection or recession, or globally, such as a pandemic or global financial crisis, the stress and strain on the leaders as individuals, and governments as a collective, would be so great that it would cause a collapse in thinking, heighten a sense of threat to its boundary or border, and cause overwhelming emotionality, fragmentation, and fear of annihilation.

In this dire situation, both countries need to rely on whatever goodwill they can muster in their relationship, or through their respective proxies, or mediation through a mutually agreed upon third party. Anticipatory conflict resolution mechanisms, including reliable channels of communication that could withstand such a potential collapse of thinking and manage the emotional storms, need to be set up well before a crisis erupts. These channels between the two countries would ideally include psychodynamic-informed officials working with the support of psychodynamic trained professionals familiar with conflict negotiations and international relations.

Conclusion

This article has provided a psychodynamic analysis of the psychological risks of war between the US and China. The essence of the psychodynamic approaches to managing these risks is to anticipate the seemingly irrational and inevitable by preparing to do the following: counter the regressive forces driven by fear, contain the overwhelming emotionality, and restore the capacity for complex thinking in order to fully understand the nuances of the situation and find creative solutions to potential impasse.

Acknowledgments

I gratefully acknowledge suggestions from members of the International Psychodynamic Study Group on the Prevention of War between the United States and China (IPSG) and assistance from Siena Koh in the preparation of this article.

Notes

1   Alan Greenspan, *The Map and the Territory: Risk, Human Nature, and the Future of Forecasting* (New York: Penguin Press, 2013).

2   Christopher Clark, *The Sleepwalkers: How Europe Went to War in 1914* (London: Harper Perennial, 2014).

3   Vamik D. Volkan, *Psychoanalysis, International Relations, and Diplomacy: A Sourcebook on Large-Group Psychology* (London: Karnac Books, 2014).

4   Benedict Anderson, *Imagined Communities* (London: Verso, 1983); "China's Draft Law Banning Speech and Behaviours That 'Harm the Feelings' of the Country Sparks Backlash," Australian Broadcasting Corporation, September 8, 2023, https://www.abc.net.au/news/2023-09-08/china-bans-items-that-harm-national-spirit/102829672.

5   Bill Clinton's statement announcing China's most-favored nation status in 1993 showed that this move was not without reservation. "Statement by the President on Most Favored Nation Status for China," May 28, 1993, https://china.usc.edu/statement-president-clinton-most-favored-nation-status-china-1993. Its annual renewal and it being made permanent by the Bush administration in 2001 were driven by economic opportunism.

6   An example of such failure to distinguish real from imagined threat was the decision by a US-led coalition to invade Iraq in 2003 due to the perceived threat that Saddam Hussein had weapons of mass destruction, although none were found. Robert Kelly, "Twenty Years Ago in Iraq, Ignoring the Expert Weapons Inspectors Proved to Be a Fatal Mistake," Stockholm International Peace Research Institute, March 9, 2023, https://www.sipri.org/commentary/essay/2023/twenty-years-ago-iraq-ignoring-expert-weapons-inspectors-proved-be-fatal-mistake.

7   The refusal of China to accept the terms of trade imposed by Britain (with indirect American involvement), including the sale of opium to the local Chinese, led to two wars, the first Opium War (1839–42) and the second Opium War (1856–60). Upon defeat, China was forced to accept unequal treaties, which included the ceding of Hong Kong to Britain.

8   Encyclopaedia Britannica, s.v. "MAGA movement (United States political movement)," updated March 1, 2024, https://www.britannica.com/topic/MAGA-movement; Karen Tumulty, "How Donald Trump Came Up with 'Make America Great Again,'" *Washington Post*, January 18, 2017, https://www.washingtonpost.com/politics/how-donald-trump-came-up-with-make-america-great-again/2017/01/17/fb6acf5e-dbf7-11e6-ad42-f3375f271c9c_story.html.

9   China has a sustained an average growth rate of nine percent of its gross domestic product (GDP) since the 1980s and lifted more than 800 million of its population out of poverty. Jikun Huang, Qi Zhang, and Scott Rozelle, "Economic Growth, the Nature of Growth and Poverty Reduction in Rural China," *China Economic Journal* 1, no. 1 (February 2008): 107–22.

10 Yu Xie and Chunni Zhang, "The Long-Term Impact of the Communist Revolution on Social Stratification in Contemporary China," *PNAS* 116, no. 39 (2019): 19392–97, http://doi.org/10.1073/pnas.1904283116.

11 Vaclav Smil, "China's Great Famine: 40 Years Later," *BMJ* 319, no. 7225 (December 1999): 1619–21.

12 Encyclopaedia Britannica, s.v. "China," "Social Changes," updated May 2, 2024, https://www.britannica.com/place/China/Social-changes.

[13] Tiananmen Square is the central square of Beijing in the foreground of the Forbidden City, the symbolic heart of imperial power of China, and has been the site of protests against governments. In the spring of 1989, for almost three months, thousands of students gathered demanding greater democratic freedom. The CCP accused Western countries of fomenting the protest and finally sent in the military to squash it on June 4, 1989, causing deaths, at the very least in the hundreds

[14] When attempts to solve internal problems by projection fail, a country will usually be stuck in the quagmire of a domestic crisis and concerns about the Other become insignificant, at least by comparison.

[15] The notion of 'national humiliation' was adopted after the treatment of China in the Treaty of Versailles (1919), which was widely perceived as unfair, with its continuation of Western countries' dominance. The phrase 'century of humiliation' took hold during Japanese occupation (1937–45). It has since been widely adopted in political rhetoric as well as popular culture. Zheng Wang, *Never Forget National Humiliation: Historical Memory in Chinese Politics and Foreign Relations* (New York: Columbia University Press, 2012).

[16] The Boxer Protocol (signed on September 7, 1901) is one of several unequal treaties forced upon China; it was demanded by the Eight-Nation Alliance (Britain, France, the United States, Italy, Austria-Hungary, Russia, and Japan), as well as Belgium, Spain, and the Netherlands following the suppression of the Boxer Rebellion.

[17] Of this generally-accepted estimate of twenty million Chinese deaths during the Second Sino-Japanese War / Second World War, approximately three million were military deaths, eight million were civilians killed by the military, and nine million died from famine and disease. R. J. Rummel, *China's Bloody Century: Genocide and Mass Murder Since 1900* (New Brunswick, NJ: Transaction Publishers, 1991).

[18] Volkan refers to this phenomenon as 'chosen trauma'—a traumatic event utilised for a national political purpose.

[19] China's strong repudiation of criticisms is a key feature of what has been referred to as wolf warrior diplomacy. Shaoyu Yuan, "Tracing China's Diplomatic Transition to Wolf Warrior Diplomacy and Its Implications," *Humanities and Social Communications* 10 (2023): Article 837, https://doi.org/10.1057/s41599-023-02367-6.

[20] Eugen Koh, "The Healing of Historical Collective Trauma," *Genocide Studies and Prevention: An International Journal* 15, no. 1 (2021): 115–33, https://doi.org/10.5038/1911-9933.15.1.1776.

[21] Eugen Koh, "The Impact of Trauma on Peace Processes," *New England Journal of Public Policy* 33, no. 1 (2021): Article 4, https://scholarworks.umb.edu/nejpp/vol33/iss1/4.

[22] "China's Draft Law."

[23] The author worked with the late Stuart Twemlow for several years to establish anti-bullying and violence programs in Australia. His findings and work can be found in Stuart Twemlow and Frank Sacco, *Preventing Bullying and School Violence* (Washington, DC: American Psychiatric Publishing, 2012).

[24] The civil unrest of the Black Lives Matter protests across the US in 2020 was widely publicized to suggest its decline and propagated a message of Chinese ascendancy. See also Oana Burcu and Weixiang Wang, "The View from Beijing on Black Lives Matter: Why Do Black Lives Matter for Beijing?," *Journal of Chinese Affairs* 52, no. 3 (2023): 413–33, https://doi.org/10.1177/18681026231178560.

25 The potency of the civil unrest related to the Black Lives Matter protests illustrates well how a present-day event can be a lightning rod that reactivates and unleashes the pain of unresolved historical trauma; in this case, that of the American Civil War (1861–65), in which some 620,000 men died in battle, which is more than the combined total of all of the wars the United States has fought, and a million more were wounded. This collective trauma is magnified by the legacy of slavery and its continuing impact on the whole society.

26 George W. Bush, "Text of Address to Joint Session of Congress on September 21, 2001," *The Guardian*, September 21, 2001, https://www.theguardian.com/world/2001/sep/21/september11.usa13.

27 ISIS, which stands for the Islamic State of Iraq and Syria, was an extreme fundamentalist organization that controlled about a third of those two countries and reigned with terror from 2014 to 2018. Jessica Stern and J. M. Berger, *ISIS: The State of Terror* (London: HarperCollins, 2015).

28 The war between Ukraine and Russia began with Russia's annexation of Crimea in 2014 and was confined to the Donbas in Eastern Ukraine. Invasion by Russia on February 24, 2022 led to a full-scale war that is continuing. Hamas is an Islamist Palestinian group that took control of the Gaza Strip in 2006; on October 7, 2023, it attacked southern Israel, killing more than a thousand civilians and provoking a relentless response from Israel that by early June 2024, had demolished most of Gaza and killed more than 36,000 civilians.

29 Earl Hopper, *Traumatic Experience in the Unconscious Life of Groups* (London: Jessica Kingsley, 2003).

30 Gustave Le Bon, *The Crowd: A Study of the Popular Mind* (New York: Dover Publications, 2002) (English translation of the original work *Psychologie des foules*, published 1895).

31 *Final Report of the Select Committee to Investigate the January 6th Attack on the United States Capitol*, GovInfo, December 2022, https://www.govinfo.gov/app/details/GPO-J6-REPORT/context.

32 The Cuban Missile Crisis, between October 16 and 28, 1962, was a confrontation between the US and the Soviet Union. It was the closest the Cold War came to a nuclear conflict, when the latter deployed nuclear missiles in Cuba in response to the US installation of nuclear weapons in Italy and Turkey. The film *Thirteen Days* was based on Ernest R. May and Philip D. Zelikow, *The Kennedy Tapes: Inside the White House During the Cuban Missile Crisis* (Cambridge, MA: Harvard University Press, 1997).

33 Sheldon H. Harris, *Factories of Death: Japanese Biological Warfare, 1932–1945, and the American Cover-up* (New York: Routledge, 2002).

34 The rapes and massacres in Nanjing on December 13, 1937 were reported in the international media and were not contested, but China's claims around the scale of what happened continues to be challenged by Japanese revisionists who insist it was only several hundred and at the most a few thousand (not in the hundreds of thousands). The phrase 'Rape of Nanking' was coined and popularized by Iris Chang in her book *The Rape of Nanking: The Forgotten Holocaust of World War II* (New York: Basic Books, 1997). The politics of this popularization of this incident is discussed in some detail in Takashi Yoshida, *The Making of the 'Rape of Nanking': History and Memory in Japan, China, and the United States* (New York: Oxford University Press, 2006).

35 "Interview: Japanese Scholars Say Truth of Nanjing Massacre Undeniable," Xinhua News, December 13, 2017, http://www.xinhuanet.com/english/2017-12/13/c_136822288.htm.

36 Benjamin Valentino, *Final Solutions: Mass Killing and Genocide in the 20th Century*, 1st paperback ed. (Ithaca, NY: Cornell University Press, 2005).

[37] The long list of grievances could begin with the US enforcing unequal trade treaties to allow their sale of opium, the demand of humiliating concessions following the Boxer Rebellion, the betrayal of Chinese contributions to the First World War, the giving of its territories to Japan in the Treaty of Versailles, and deliberately not coming to its aid in when Japan invaded until Pearl Harbor was attacked.

[38] In psychodynamic thinking, symbolic meanings can be known; the emotional significance of an event or experience is often difficult to define and is more extensive in its reach.

[39] Until that point, Taiwan was a small trading outpost of the Japanese in the late fifteenth century, then a Portuguese settlement was established in the sixteenth century, followed by small Dutch and Spanish settlements among a larger indigenous population.

[40] Psychoanalysis distinguishes *fantasy,* a conscious act, from *phantasy,* an unconscious process. In this case, the collective consciousness of the Chinese psyche unconsciously believes that Taiwan is the panacea for their pain and humiliation without needing a rationale for why all will be well when it returns to its motherland.

[41] Kevin Rudd, *The Avoidable War: The Dangers of a Catastrophic Conflict Between the US and Xi Jinping's China* (Sydney: Hachette Australia, 2022), 59–60.

[42] Ibid., 62.

[43] Jon Bateman, "The Fevered Anti-China Attitude in Washington is Going to Backfire," Politico, December 15, 2022, https://www.politico.com/news/magazine/2022/12/15/china-tech-decoupling-sanctions-00071723.

[44] Rudd, *The Avoidable War*, 67–68.

[45] Huiyun Feng and Kai He, eds., *US–China Competition and the South China Sea Disputes* (New York: Routledge, 2018).

[46] Graham Allison, *Destined for War: Can America and China Escape Thucydides's Trap?* (Brunswick, Victoria: Scribe Publications, 2017).

[47] Rudd, *The Avoidable War*, 9.

[48] Ibid., 18.

[49] Ibid., 14.

[50] Contagion commonly refers to the unconscious sharing of an idea, often seen in suicides within a group, especially among adolescents.

EMPLOYING MULTI-AGENT AI TO MODEL CONFLICT AND COOPERATION IN NORTHERN IRELAND

Katherine O'Lone

The University of Manchester

Michael Gantley

CulturePulse; Linacre College, University of Oxford

Justin E. Lane

CulturePulse; Institute of Ethnology and Social Anthropology, Slovak Academy of Sciences

F. LeRon Shults

CulturePulse; Institute for Global Development and Social Planning, University of Agder; NORCE Center for Modeling Social Systems

ABSTRACT

In this article, we outline the development of a multi-agent artificial intelligence (MAAI) model for post-conflict Northern Ireland. We discuss the insights it provides into the primary drivers of conflict and cooperation in the post-Agreement era. Analyses reveal that leading drivers of cooperation in the model are fairness and sadness, while

Katherine O'Lone is a behavioral science fellow in the School of Social Sciences at The University of Manchester.
Michael Gantley is the Chief Project Officer at CulturePulse, a US-Slovak company based in Bratislava.
Justin E. Lane is the Chief Executive Officer of CulturePulse, and a research fellow at the Institute of Ethnology and Social Anthropology, Slovak Academy of Sciences, Bratislava.
F. LeRon Shults is the Chief Research Officer at CulturePulse, a professor at the University of Agder, and a research professor at the NORCE Center for Modeling Social Systems.

This research was supported by a grant from a funder who wishes to remain anonymous. The project was led by the first author while a research fellow at the Woolf Institute.

the main drivers of conflict are related to anxiety and perceived moral authority. We examine these findings in the context of previous computational modeling efforts in Northern Ireland, the social psychological literature on intergroup conflict, and the current geopolitical landscape. We conclude by advocating for the application of this technology as a tool to inform policymaking and address the ethical considerations raised by its use in peacebuilding and reconciliation efforts.

Background

The Good Friday or Belfast Agreement (hereafter the GFA) was signed on April 10, 1998. This historic document marked, for the most part, an end to thirty years of ethno-political violence in Northern Ireland known colloquially as 'the Troubles.' More than 3,000 people were killed and tens of thousands injured. At the time of writing, the international community celebrates the Agreement's twenty-fifth anniversary; rightly fêted as a paradigmatic model of overcoming seemingly intractable conflict, an astonishing feat when one considers that post-conflict peace, on average, lasts only seven years and roughly sixty percent of conflicts reoccur.[1]

However, an agreement is never the end of peacemaking and the resulting peace in Northern Ireland has, by no means, been without difficulties. Political and sectarian threats remain, and more recent issues such as Brexit and ongoing uncertainty surrounding the constitutional future of Northern Ireland jeopardize the relative stability.[2]

In recent years multi-agent artificial intelligence (MAAI) modeling and simulation tools have increasingly been used to address challenges related to intergroup conflict and to explore the conditions for social cohesion and peace within and between human groups.[3] Why have such tools become so popular? Unlike traditional methodologies, MAAI modeling can show the causal links between micro-level behaviors, meso-level interactions, and macro-level emergent social patterns, because what sets it apart from traditional game theoretic agent-based modeling or machine learning techniques is the utilization of psychologically realistic cognitive architectures embedded within realistic social networks. Moreover, it provides stakeholders and change agents with a sort of virtual laboratory, an "artificial society," in which they can test their hypotheses and run scenario simulations before trying them out in the real world.

This is particularly important in regions or countries such as Northern Ireland, where peace and social cohesion are fragile and policy makers must move carefully and wisely.

In this article, we outline how the use of MAAI technology can provide policymakers with a powerful set of digital tools to model and predict both conflict and cooperation. We begin by providing an overview of the emergence of MAAI in policy and highlight its explanatory potential. We discuss previous modeling work on intergroup conflict and reconciliation in Northern Ireland, which provided the foundation for our research. We then outline our methodological approach, including the use of sentiment analysis and the creation of a 'digital twin' to simulate the conditions for social stability (or not) in Northern Ireland with a focus on the implications of removing the 'peace walls.' Finally, we advocate for the use of MAAI in peacebuilding and conclude by addressing some of the ethical concerns that arise from this approach in policymaking.

Computational Simulation and Artificial Societies

To model the complexity of human moral and social behavior within artificial societies, social science has used two approaches.[4] The first, older approach is grounded in evolutionary game theory and has often been used to model phenomena such as the emergence of cooperation in networks or the influence of socio-cognitive biases in the development of social norms.[5] While no doubt useful, the agents in these models lack psychological realism.[6] Arguably, the most policy-relevant issues, such as extremism and the willingness to fight and die for one's group, are shaped by sacred values and specific forms of group alignment rather than rational choice.[7]

The second, more recent approach is MAAI, which creates artificial societies that are populated with agents who are psychologically realistic, complex, and emotionally motivated; they do not always act with rational self-interest. The agents in these models are programmed with algorithms designed to mimic evolved human cognition, such as the tendency to detect intentional forces (e.g., agents) and to protect ritual coalitions in the face of perceived threat.[8] The psychological realism of MAAI models holds extraordinary promise for policymaking and can provide decision-makers with the explanatory power and predictive insights needed to tackle some of the most pressing problems of our age such as environmental threats on human social behavior and the resolution of intergroup conflict.[9]

This approach is arguably the most powerful tool that the social and computer sciences have for linking multi-level factors in the analysis of complex adaptive social systems.[10] A MAAI approach can, for example, explain the emergence of macro-level social risks (such as conflict and the growth of radicalization networks) by "growing" them bottom-up from micro-level agent behaviors (e.g., responses to anxiety, similarities of belief, and perceptions of the violation of key socially shared values) and meso-level interactions (such as interactions taking place between agents in a social network, online or offline).[11] The following analogy is often useful: more than a "snapshot" of correlated variables at a particular time and space, MAAI provides a "video" of longitudinal causal dynamics that can be rewound and played again under different conditions.[12]

MAAI and Policy

Where MAAI is of most use to the policy realm is its ability to construct artificial societies or 'digital twins' of communities and networks where agents interact with one another in ways that potentially affect the values of other agents and their environment, thus giving rise to population-level phenomena. From here, one can adjust the parameters of the digital twin to observe the subsequent individual and population-level effects of implementing new policies within this simulated environment. These digital twins serve as virtual laboratories in which policymakers can explore and discover the conditions under which—and the mechanisms by which—individual and social variables change in the artificial society.[13] However, the true power of this approach lies in its ability to gauge the likely outcomes of interventions in a simulated, low- to zero-risk environment, before their implementation.

The ability of these models to formulate the complexity of human social systems can offer a valuable way to gain insights into some of the most complex policy issues of our time. For example, MAAI has been applied to modeling emotional contagion surrounding COVID-19 and shed light on some of the mechanisms by which misinformation, stigma, and fear spread throughout Scandinavia early in the pandemic;[14] the rise of nationalism and perceptions of threat during the pandemic;[15] the growing secularization of societies;[16] and the integration of Syrian refugees into Dutch society.[17] Recently, policymakers have turned to MAAI and simulation to assist them in addressing the perennially sensitive challenges of predicting and mitigating intergroup conflict and exploring the conditions needed for peace and reconciliation.

Previous MAAI Model of Religious Violence in Northern Ireland

The research outlined in this article was based on a successfully calibrated and validated model developed by two of the authors (F. LeRon Shults and Justin E. Lane) with other colleagues in 2018.[18] This model of mutually escalating religious violence (MERV) was developed with key social psychological theories (e.g., terror management theory, social identity theory, and identity fusion theory) built into the causal architecture to determine the mechanisms underpinning religious, intergroup conflict. This model was validated using data related to the Troubles in Northern Ireland and the 2002 Gujarat riots in India. Both conflicts were extreme, reaching levels of severe physical violence yet taking place on markedly different time scales. Despite this difference, both contexts are examples of what the authors refer to as 'mutually escalating xenophobic anxiety' that led to significant violence and the breakdown of social cohesion.

The model was validated at the individual or 'micro'-level in relation to experimental data from social psychology and at the macro-level—that of the emergent phenomena of concern (here the mutually escalating conflict between two groups)—in relation to data from the conflict in Northern Ireland. Using this data and the insights generated from the key theories, the model highlighted the conditions under which the behavior and the interactions of individual agents can lead to mutually escalating xenophobic anxiety.

The most common conditions for this to occur were a) those in which the size difference between the two groups was not too large and b) that the agents experienced social and contagion hazards at levels of increased intensity that passed their tolerance thresholds. It is under these conditions that agents encounter outgroup members more regularly and perceive them as threats, thus generating mutually escalating xenophobic anxiety.

Methodology

Our more recent investigation into the dynamics of conflict and cooperation in Northern Ireland was conducted in two stages. Initially, we conducted a sentiment analysis that analyzed more than thirteen million news articles (from 1979–2022) related to the conflicts in Northern Ireland, extracting the core psychological and moral dimensions that formed the basis of community tension and conflict. Following this, we employed MAAI techniques to identify the fundamental moral concerns driving both conflict and cooperation. This was achieved by constructing a computational model—a digital twin—that simulates the complex interplay of factors influencing stability, cohesion, and conflict in Northern Ireland.

Sentiment Analysis

News metadata was gathered from GDelt (the largest database of human society ever created).[19] Using a text-analytic system designed by CulturePulse, this data set was coded for more than ninety aspects of culture and psychology such as moral foundations.[20] This coding was done using an artificial intelligence (AI)-powered natural language processing algorithm that matches key linguistic markers drawn from empirical studies of morality and psychology with similar markers found within the text of a news article.

According to moral foundations theory there are (at least) six psychological systems that provide the foundations upon which human cultures then build and develop narratives, moral frameworks, and virtues (care/harm, fairness/cheating, loyalty/betrayal, authority/subversion, purity/degradation, and liberty/oppression). The existence of these foundations is supported by a wealth of cross-cultural empirical and experimental evidence.[21] All six moral foundations described in moral foundations theory are included in this AI system's analysis. In addition, our analysis added tracking for the concepts "forgiveness" and "revenge." Alongside moral foundations, the system also analyzed elements of social values (e.g., friendship, family ties, and race/ethnicity), evolutionary threats such as contagion, predation, and natural disasters, and text patterns such as readability and information entropy.

These data were collected and aggregated on a monthly basis to develop a comprehensive longitudinal data set. The metadata of articles available in GDelt includes specific codes assigned to news reports to categorize the type of events they cover. Our team created a further classification by aggregating these coded events to look not just at the classes of conflict but also at multiple dynamics important to peace and policymaking. Ultimately, the analysis coded all events as either 'conflict,' 'move toward conflict,' 'cooperation,' 'move towards cooperation,' or 'defensive event.' Leveraging these categories and the different moral and socio-psychological dimensions, the AI system is equipped to analyze and identify the underlying factors that influence these events, determining whether they are escalating toward conflict or moving toward peace.

Digital Twin Construction

Digital twin construction relies on the integration of multi-agent AI systems, which simulate the interactions between different agents within a complex system to predict outcomes based on varying inputs and conditions. The conditions can be defined through a mixture of variables and rule interactions as well as by defining the initial conditions of a simulation, which should be matched to the real world as closely as possible. The multi-level approach requires interactions between psychological and social environments, with the social environment being measured either through big-data analysis of media or social media data streams or employing representative survey data. This approach is pivotal in modeling social systems and understanding their stability or susceptibility to change.

The development of digital twins involves a comprehensive analysis of the system being modeled, requiring data sets that capture the nuances of agent behaviors and interactions, often drawn from the psychological, sociological, and historical literature in collaboration with subject matter experts and stakeholders on the ground. Our methodology employs real-time analytics to process and analyze large volumes of data from diverse sources to track themes related to conflict, social cohesion, and societal stability without the need for extensive retraining of AI models. Furthermore, the AI models themselves are designed to be isomorphic in relation to different measures utilized in survey data and psychological studies, facilitating the ability to draw close connections between analyses of large-scale social and historical data sets, social media data, news media, transcripts, surveys, and lab-based studies. This capability is crucial for adapting to the rapidly changing dynamics of social systems and ensuring the validity, accuracy, and relevance of the digital twin.

Results

Sentiment Analysis

Alongside the longitudinal data set of news metadata, a further classification was created by aggregating the coded news events to look not just at the categories of conflict and the multiple dynamics important to peace and policymaking. From this, the AI system analyzed and identified the underlying factors that predict increases in conflict or cooperation. We present the findings below.

Digital Twin Analysis

We started our digital twin analysis by first running the simulation under approximately 138,000 conditions. We then utilized a machine learning technique (based in binary logistic regression) to classify each condition as having outputs that result in conflict or no conflict, in order to better understand what variables are most affecting a context's propensity to result in conflict. We found that the system can classify conditions for conflict with 90.28 percent accuracy (please see Appendix A for a confusion matrix, a measure of the classification accuracy).

From this model, we then looked to find what are the most important features that the system needs to predict conflict (a technique simply known as feature selection). From this, we were able to map the features and rank their importance (see Figure 1). What we found was that the most important features are, by and large, the number of values (in the sense of beliefs and ethical values) being exchanged between agents in the simulation (Num_Values) and how similar or different their beliefs are concerning those values (Cultural_Dissonance_Percent). A graph of the values is presented below.

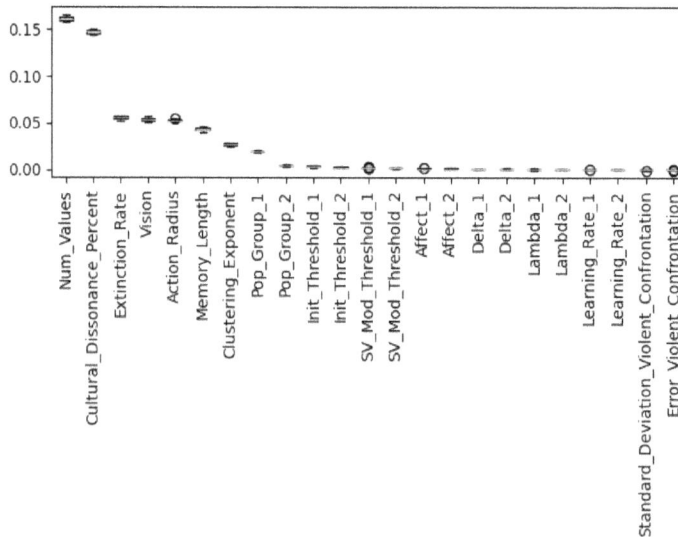

Figure 1. Feature selection: Important features needed by the system to predict conflict. See Appendix B for an explanation of each feature.

Other key variables cover how quickly individuals stop associating negative experiences with the beliefs of others in their environment (Extinction_Rate), how easily they can find others in their environment (Vision), as well as how easily they can interact with those individuals, not just observe them (Action_Radius). This is followed by the Memory_Length, or how far back the memory of each agent in the digital twin goes. In order to simulate how in light of intense emotional experience, there are some things we never forget, the agents in this model also have a form of episodic memory. This simulates the effect of never forgetting—or forgiving—experiences that they might have during a simulation, as in real-world post-conflict contexts.

Discussion of Sentiment Analysis Findings

A quarter of a century on from the Good Friday Agreement what have we found about the mechanisms that influence cooperative and conflict tendencies in Northern Ireland? The results of the sentiment analysis identified sixty features that underlie episodes of cooperation in Northern Ireland and revealed that the biggest driver of conflict was anxiety. The second biggest factor driving conflict was concerns related to the moral foundation of authority. In contrast, the sentiment analysis revealed that the biggest driver of cooperation in Northern Ireland was concerns surrounding the moral foundation of fairness followed by sadness as the secondary driver. We will now discuss each of these psychological and moral drivers in turn.

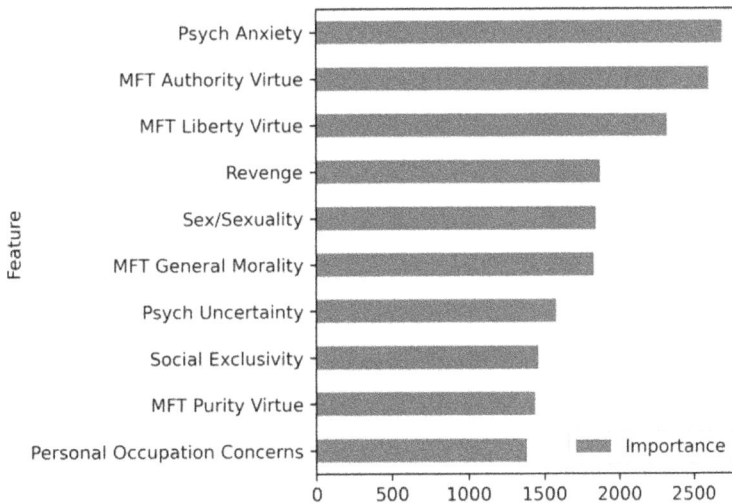

Figure 2. Lead Drivers of Conflict in Northern Ireland. The numbers on the x axis signify importance, with larger numbers signifying greater importance. The features represent anxiety, concerns about moral authority, concerns about violations of liberty, revenge, concerns about sex/sexuality, general moral concerns, psychological uncertainty, concerns about group uniqueness, concerns about violations of moral purity, and concerns about personal/professional resources. According to moral foundations theory (MFT), intuitions about what is moral (or not) rest on at least six psychological foundations (care/harm, fairness/cheating, loyalty/betrayal, authority/subversion, purity/degradation, and liberty/oppression).

Anxiety

The most important feature driving episodes of conflict was anxiety (see Figure 2). This finding corroborates empirical work that demonstrates that anxiety leads to detrimental intergroup relations.[22] Moreover, previous simulation work in Northern Ireland found that episodes of intergroup violence were mostly driven by an increase in the average level of anxiety in the simulated agents over time. One of the most common conditions under which longer periods of mutually escalating anxiety occur are those in which the difference in the size of the hostile groups is not too large. This is particularly relevant to Northern Ireland. When created in 1921, it had a Protestant majority (of approximately two to one) meaning that the Catholic population was the minority group. Over a century, that changed dramatically. Census data from 2021 revealed that for the first time in its history, Catholics outnumber Protestants.[23]

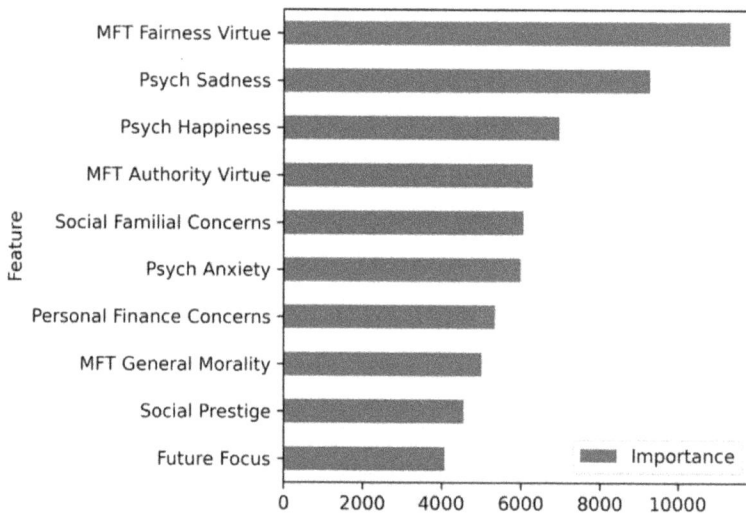

Figure 3. Lead Drivers of Cooperation in Northern Ireland. The numbers on the x axis signify importance, with larger numbers signifying greater importance. The features represent concerns about violations of fairness, sadness, happiness, concerns about moral authority, concerns about family, anxiety, concerns about finance, general moral concerns, concerns about social standing, and concerns about the future.

This is important for several reasons. First, the small size of the difference between the groups (45.7 vs. 43.48 percent) means it satisfies the conditions revealed by Shults and colleagues to be optimal for the escalation of mutual anxiety.[24] Second, the shift from majority to minority status for Protestants (and vice versa for Catholics) will no doubt have a psychological impact. Previous research on projected majority-to-minority demographic shifts has seen increased feelings of threat in members of the once-majority group and a deterioration of positive intergroup attitudes.[25] This demographic shift in Northern Ireland has happened at a time when other political and global events have impacted a strong Protestant or Unionist identity, one that is already alert to threats.[26]

For example, in the aftermath of Brexit, the possibility of a customs border in the Irish Sea has caused enormous controversy; it would psychologically and physically place a hard border between Northern Ireland and the UK, anathema to many Unionists. Moreover, the death of Queen Elizabeth II in 2022 was a seismic change for Loyalists in particular, whose professed allegiance is not to the British government but to the monarchy.[27] With the queen's passing it remains to be seen whether the same emotional attachment to the Crown will endure during the reign of King Charles III.

In addition, close studies of recruitment into Northern Irish paramilitary groups such as the Ulster Volunteer Force have recorded that motivations for enlistment often are rooted in anxiety, although historically it had been an anxiety premised on perceived Irish Republican Army (IRA) threats. So while increased anxieties may lead to resurgences of violence, we cannot expect the same patterns of paramilitarism to repeat in the modern context. The social environment of Northern Ireland and the groups in consideration have changed in how they present themselves publicly, if they present themselves publicly at all.

Authority

The sentiment analysis revealed that discussions in the news around violations of the moral foundation of authority affected the number of episodes of conflict (see Figure 2). This moral foundation evolved in response to our long history of hierarchical and structured societies and in today's world relates to respect for traditions and deference to traditional institutions and authority figures. That these concerns should be driving conflict can also be interpreted in light of the constitutional uncertainty and identity crisis that Northern Ireland is experiencing, particularly from the Unionist perspective. As discussed above, the historical majority identity (e.g., Unionist) is under threat demographically and politically and with that, the legitimacy of traditional authority figures. When a cherished group identity is under threat there is a tendency for members to defend the group and adhere more strongly to shared values and norms.[28] Therefore when authority is perceived to be threatened, this defensive tendency inevitably leads to a breakdown of positive intergroup relations and veers toward conflict. For Unionists, this identity threat is considerable because of the possibility of a border poll in the next decade. If a majority vote to leave the UK, this would lead to a much more pronounced minority status for Unionists; they would be part of a geographically larger united Ireland and exist within a constitutional framework in which both authority and population are not aligned with their social identity.

Fairness

In the twenty-five years since the signing of the Good Friday Agreement, Northern Ireland has, for the most part, remained peaceful. Anecdotal evidence from many of our interlocutors in Northern Ireland, from all sides, emphasizes that although the violence has ended, the signing of the GFA did not address issues surrounding justice and legacy. Now, these dominate the public discourse.[29]

In the social psychological literature, perceptions of injustice or unfairness are often a catalyst to conflict.[30] Our findings suggest that in Northern Ireland, there seems to be a desire for fairness—which moral foundations theory equates with concerns about justice—that is driving and strengthening intergroup relations and moving toward episodes of cooperation (see Figure 3). The importance of careful policy surrounding this feature, given its relevance for cooperation, cannot be understated. State-sanctioned attempts to address the "legacy" of the Troubles have met with a largely hostile reception; the 'Legacy Bill' currently sits in the committee stage in the House of Lords. This bill has been met with hostility from opponents because of a perceived removal of access to justice for victims and relatives of those affected by the Troubles in Northern Ireland. However well-intentioned the bill may have been, it is arguably so unpopular because rather than addressing one of the key drivers of cooperation—issues surrounding fairness—it has done the opposite; people have perceived it as violating fairness concerns.[31]

Sadness

The second largest feature driving cooperation in Northern Ireland is the negative emotion of sadness (see Figure 3). Negative group-based emotions (such as anger) have been previously identified as barriers to reconciliation.[32] In the aftermath of intergroup conflict, all groups collectively experience a set of negative emotions, the most predominant being anger; this presents a significant obstacle to the process of intergroup forgiveness, particularly in Northern Ireland.[33]

However, our results suggest that sadness, a negative emotion, appears to be driving cooperation rather than conflict. The legacy of the conflict hangs heavy over Northern Ireland; it is inevitable that twenty-five years later people look back with sadness and regret at an episode in their history that caused so much suffering. All groups in protracted conflict perceive themselves to have been harmed or suffered wrong at the hands of the other group. This perception of group suffering often comes with the belief that one's group has suffered more than the other, known as 'competitive victimhood' this can lead groups to view their suffering in comparative terms; it is a barrier to reconciliation and cooperation.[34] However, identifying a common or 'inclusive' type of victimhood (i.e., "we are all victims of the conflict") has been shown to facilitate pathways to reconciliation and intergroup cooperation.[35] This 'inclusive victimhood' (i.e., the acknowledgment that everyone has suffered, regardless of ethnic group) and the accompanying sense of sadness could well explain why it is driving a tendency to cooperate in Northern Ireland.

Digital Twin Findings

Number of Values

The result of the feature selection found that the most important features needed by the system to predict conflict were the number of values being exchanged between agents in the simulation and how similar or different their beliefs are concerning those values. This suggests that if there were a large enough set of differing beliefs within a society, there would be ample alternatives to the "sacred values"[36] that tend to trigger conflict and break down intergroup relations. We must be clear that these are not the only variables that influence conflict in the model and certainly not within the real world, however they provide valuable insights for policy makers navigating the complexity of post-conflict societies such as Northern Ireland.

For example, while increasing the number of values in the digital twin produced lower levels of conflict, it would be prudent to avoid increasing the amount of information in an attempt to achieve this, particularly on social media; this can increase anxiety and depression, two core historical triggers elucidated by the initial media analysis in the first stage of the research.[37] As such, one should be cautioned from leveraging social media to flood a discussion with a greater volume of information in the hopes that it would lessen the likelihood of conflict.

'Peace' Walls in Belfast

The first 'peace wall' was put up in Belfast in 1969 and throughout the Troubles, more than thirty miles of walls were erected to prevent outbreaks of violence between Catholic and Protestant communities. The walls leave a permanent physical reminder of Belfast's violent past, yet ironically they were erected as temporary structures.[38] Many scholars, practitioners, and activists argue that their presence maintains and emphasizes sectarian divisions, making salient the perception of outgroup threats between Catholics and Protestant communities.[39] Public attitudes toward the walls have been inconsistent, with no consensus on what to do with them.[40]

In our digital twin simulations, we varied the extent to which segregation factored into the movements of the agents around their environment to simulate the physical barriers created by the peace walls in the real world. Ultimately, the simulations revealed that when it came to whether this segregationist mechanism had an effect on levels of simulated conflict, we found no evidence that it did. This means that in the model, the continuation of the existence of the peace walls had no effect on conflict.

This result may seem at odds with much scholarship and expert opinion on the peace walls. However, a recent report for the Northern Ireland Department of Justice reveals ambivalent public attitudes toward the walls.[41] For example, fifty-eight percent of people living near a peace wall reported that their function was to make the residents feel safe. The results of our digital twin simulations largely correspond to one of the main findings of the report: "it is generally expected that if the peace walls are not removed, life will continue on as normal and it will have little impact on their community."[42]

Ethical Concerns and Implications

Scholars and stakeholders are increasingly concerned, and rightly so, about the ethical implications of all forms of AI.[43] However, the issues surrounding MAAI are particularly complex. Which voices are included in the articulation of the assumptions grounding such policy-relevant models? Who decides which simulation experiments to run? What are the dangers that bad actors will utilize such models to exacerbate conflict rather than promote peace? These are valid concerns. We hope to have shown that Northern Ireland is among those complex contexts where the risks and opportunities are so high that it makes sense to apply MAAI modeling in the pursuit of policies for promoting peace.

We must be clear. We do not suggest that MAAI is a 'magic bullet' for policymakers working in reconciliation and peacebuilding. Nor do we suggest that MAAI is without limitations, or that there are no valid concerns surrounding the potential misuse of such technology. However, given that this technology holds such promise for reconciliation and peace in regions scarred by conflict, it might reasonably be argued to be unethical to not use it.[44]

Transparency of Assumptions

Let us start by highlighting one advantage that MAAI does have: transparency of assumptions. An MAAI approach requires that the assumptions built into the architecture of a formal model are made explicit by the researchers from the beginning, as are the purposes of the simulation experiments. What this does, as Paloutzian and colleagues explain, is to make the ethical dimensions and ramifications of the research transparent, giving them central importance and therefore making it much "less likely that they will be used for malevolence or manipulation."[45]

MAAI as a Collaborative and Ethical Endeavor

For an MAAI approach to be successful, we propose that it must be a multi-level, interdisciplinary, and collaborative approach; one that involves equal input from all stakeholders from the beginning of the process. For example, the insights of subject matter experts or those working 'on the ground' can provide valuable contextual insights that help to calibrate and constrain the model.[46] While MAAI can offer a credible way to model human complex adaptive systems, the technology relies on the knowledge and expertise of others to 'flesh out' the simulated society, which ultimately allows it to be used as a tool to assist decision-making.

Ensuring the ethical use and accuracy of digital twins is paramount, especially when dealing with sensitive topics like religion, diverse communities, and social cohesion.[47] Data ethics and digital trust are foundational to our approach as they guide the moral considerations inherent in collecting, analyzing, and applying data in digital twin constructions. Our research aligns with the ethical frameworks provided by the UK's Centre for Data Ethics and Innovation (CDEI) and the Data Ethics Framework guidelines provided by the UK government, as well as the EU's AI Ethics Guidelines for Trustworthy AI and UNESCO's Recommendation on the Ethics of Artificial Intelligence.

Conclusion

In complex and frequently volatile post-conflict societies, more traditional methods of policymaking and peacebuilding may fall short of addressing the nuanced social and psychological mechanisms that drive communities toward or away from peace. MAAI offers a powerful additional method of testing policy. Our work in Northern Ireland serves as a demonstration of the value of MAAI policy related to conflict and cooperation.

Through the development of a digital twin of Northern Ireland, we have uncovered critical drivers of conflict and cooperation that can assist with the nuanced considerations policymakers must navigate. Our findings suggest that policymakers in Northern Ireland who want to avoid conflict between groups should pay special attention to news events that deal with anxiety and authority, for example. To promote cooperation between groups, policymakers should be mindful of events that evoke a sense of fairness or sadness.

We have also engaged with the ethical dimensions that accompany the deployment of AI in such sensitive contexts. By advocating for transparency and interdisciplinary collaboration, we aim to mitigate potential misuse of this technology. The complexities of modern conflicts and post-conflict societies demand innovative approaches. MAAI, with its ability to simulate and predict the outcomes of various peacebuilding initiatives, stands out as a critical ally in the progress toward enduring peace. Our exploration of its application in Northern Ireland underscores a broader, optimistic narrative for AI's role in peacebuilding.

Appendix

A. Confusion Matrix

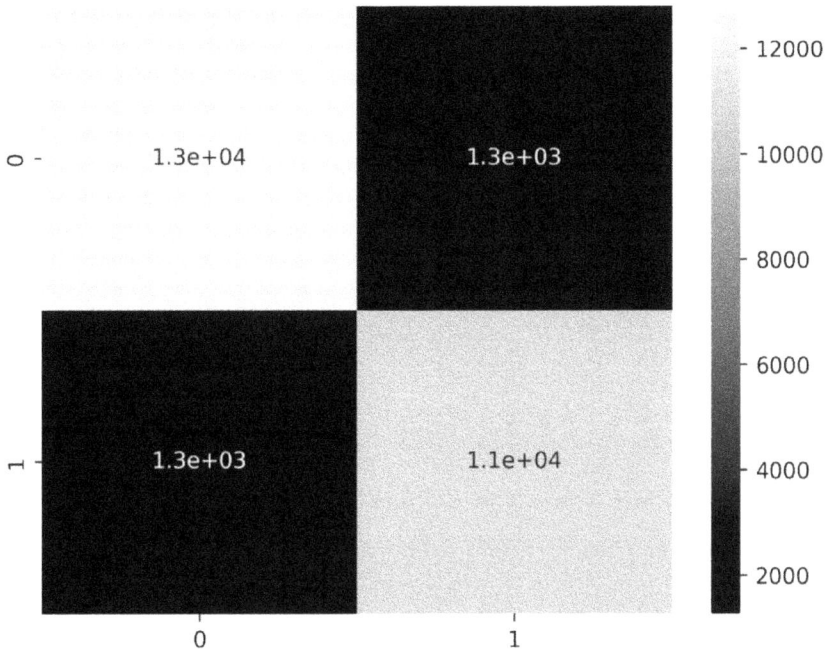

Confusion Matrix: a measure of classification accuracy. The numbers on the right signify the number of misclassifications, or errors, from the model. Having high numbers for the upper left hand (0,0), and lower right hand (1,1), and low numbers for the lower left hand (1,0) and upper right hand (0,1) quadrants is good as it signifies that it correctly classified the data more often than not.

B. Explanation of Features in Figure 1.

Num-values. This is the number of values that are being discussed by agents in the environment. It is similar to how diverse the conversation is conceptually.

Cultural_dissonance_percent. How different the beliefs are between two groups.

Exctinction_rate. This is how quickly agents forget about things that happen in the past.

Vision. How close two agents have to be to observe the actions of others.

Action Radius. How close to two agents have to be in order to interact.

Memory_length. How much information agents remember from the past.

Clustering_exponent. How clustered the network is. More clusters mean more subgroups within the network.

Pop_group_1. Number of people in the first simulated group.

Pop_group_2. Number of people in the second simulated group.

Init_threshold_1. How much energy it takes before an agent takes action.

Init_threshold_2. How much energy it takes before an agent takes action.

Sv_mod_threshold_1. How much emotion is required in group 1 before an experience can create a memory that lasts forever.

Sv_mod_threshold_2. How much emotion is required in group 2 before an experience can create a memory that lasts forever.

Affect 1. How emotional the agents are in group 1 initially.

Affect 2. How emotional the agents are in group 2 initially.

Delta 1. This is related to how agents learn and interact based on emotion.

Delta 2. This is related to how agents learn and interact based on emotion.

Lambda_1. This is related to how agents learn and interact based on emotion.

Lambda_2. This is related to how agents learn and interact based on emotion.

Learning_rate_1. This is related to how quickly agents learn and interact based on emotion.

Learning_rate_2. This is related to how quickly agents learn and interact based on emotion.

Standard_deviation_violent_confrontation. This is the standard deviation for how many violent confrontations are observed in any one time period of the simulation.

Error_violent_confrontation. This is a standard error for how many violent confrontations are observed in any one time period.

Notes

[1] Scott Gates, Håvard Mokleiv Nygård, and Esther Trappeniers, *Conflict Recurrence* (Oslo: PRIO, 2016).

[2] Mary C. Murphy and Jonathan Evershed, *A Troubled Constitutional Future: Northern Ireland After Brexit* (Newcastle upon Tyne: Agenda Publishing, 2022).

[3] F. Leron Shults et al., "A Generative Model of the Mutual Escalation of Anxiety Between Religious Groups," *Journal of Artificial Societies* 21, no. 4 (2018): Article 7, https://doi.org/10.18564/jasss.3840; Todd K. BenDor and Jürgen Scheffran, *Agent-Based Modeling of Environmental Conflict and Cooperation* (Boca Raton: CRC Press, 2018); Raymond F. Paloutzian, Zeynip Sagir, and F. Leron Shults, "Modelling Reconciliation and Peace Processes: Lessons from Syrian War Refugees and World War II," in *Multi-Level Reconciliation and Peacebuilding*, ed. Kevin P. Clemens and SungYong Lee (New York: Routledge, 2021), 225–42.

[4] Saikou Y. Diallo, F. LeRon Shults, and Wesley J. Wildman, "Minding Morality: Ethical Artificial Societies for Public Policy Modeling," *AI & SOCIETY* 36, no. 1 (2021): 49–57, https://doi.org/10.1007/s00146-020-01028-5.

5   Rense Corten, *Computational Approaches to Studying the Co-evolution of Networks and Behavior in Social Dilemmas* (Chichester: Wiley, 2014).

6   Diallo, Shults, and Wildman, "Minding Morality," 51.

7   Nafees Hamid et al., "Neuroimaging 'Will to Fight' for Sacred Values: An Empirical Case Study with Supporters of an Al Qaeda Associate," *Royal Society Open Science* 12, no. 6 (2019): 181585, https://doi.org/10.1098/rsos.181585.

8   Justin E. Lane, *Understanding Religion through Artificial Intelligence* (London: Bloomsbury, 2021); Shults et al. "A Generative Model."

9   F. LeRon Shults and Wesley J. Wildman, "Human Simulation and Sustainability: Ontological, Epistemological, And Ethical reflections," *Sustainability* 12, no, 23 (2020): 10039; Michele Bristow, Liping Fang, and Keith W. Hipel, "Agent-Based Modeling of Competitive and Cooperative Behavior Under Conflict," *IEEE Transactions on Systems, Man, and Cybernetics: Systems* 44, no. 7 (2014): 834–50, https://doi.org/10.1109/TSMC.2013.2282314.

10 F. LeRon Shults, "Simulation, Science, and Stakeholders: Challenges and Opportunities for Modelling Solutions to Societal Problems," *Complexity* (2023): 137500, https://doi.org/10.1155/2023/1375004.

11 Justin E. Lane, "Can We Predict Religious Extremism?," *Religion, Brain & Behavior* 7, no. 4 (2016): 299–304, https://doi.org/10.1080/2153599X.2016.1249923.

12 F. LeRon Shults, "Simulating Supernatural Seeking," *Religion, Brain & Behavior* 9, no. 3 (2019): 262–65, https://doi.org/10.1080/2153599X.2018.1453530.

13 Shults, "Simulation, Science, and Stakeholders."

14 Justin E. Lane et al., "Emotional Contagion in Scandinavia during the COVID-19 Public Health Crisis," PsyArXiv Preprint (2024), https://doi.org/10.31234/osf.io/9e5f7.

15 Josh Bullock et al., "Modeling Nationalism, Religiosity, and Threat Perception: During the COVID-19 Pandemic," *PLoS ONE* 18, no. 4 (2023): e0281002, https://doi.org/10.1371/journal.pone.0281002.

16 Ivan Puga-Gonzalez et al., "The Rise and Fall of Religion: A Model-Based Exploration of Secularisation, Security and Prosociality," in *Advances in Social Simulation: Proceedings of the 18th Social Simulation Conference, 4–8 September 2023* (Cham: Springer, forthcoming).

17 Christine Boshuijzen-van Burken et al., "Agent-Based Modelling of Values: The Case of Value Sensitive Design for Refugee Logistics," *Journal of Artificial Societies and Social Simulation* 23, no. 4 (2020): Articl6 6, https://doi.org/10.18564/jasss.4411.

18 Shults et al., "A Generative Model."

19 https://www.gdeltproject.org/data.html.

20 Jonathan Haidt, *The Righteous Mind: Why Good People Are Divided By Politics and Religion* (New York: Pantheon/Random House, 2012); Jonathan Haidt, "The Emotional Dog and Its Rational Tail: A Social Intuitionist Approach to Moral Judgment," *Psychological Review 108*, no. 4 (2001): 814–34, https://doi.org/10.1037/0033-295X.108.4.814; Jonathan Haidt and Jesse Graham, "When Morality Opposes Justice: Conservatives Have Moral Intuitions That Liberals May Not Recognize," *Social Justice Research* 20 (2007): 98–116, http://dx.doi.org/10.1007/s11211-007-0034-z.

21 Mohammad Atari et al., "Morality beyond the WEIRD: How the Nomological Network of Morality Varies Across Cultures," *Journal of Personality and Social Psychology* 125, no. 5 (2023): 1157–88, https://doi.org/10.1037/pspp0000470.

22 Eran Halperin et al., "Promoting Intergroup Contact by Changing Beliefs: Group Malleability, Intergroup Anxiety, and Contact Motivation," *Emotion* 12, no. 6 (2012): 1192–95, https://doi.org/10.1037/a0028620.

23 Northern Ireland Statistics and Research Agency (NISRA), *2021 Census* (2021).

24 Shults et al., "A Generative Model."

25 Amy R. Krosch et al., "The Threat of a Majority-Minority U.S. Alters White Americans' Perception of Race," *Journal of Experimental Social Psychology* 99 (2022): 104266, https://doi.org/10.1016/j.jesp.2021.104266.

26 James W. McAuley, "Unionism's Last Stand? Contemporary Unionist Politics and Identity in Northern Ireland," *Global Review of Ethnopolitics* 3, no. 1 (2003): 60–74, https://doi.org/10.1080/14718800308405158.

27 David Mitchell, "From Queen Elizabeth to King Charles: How Northern Ireland's Unionists Feel about the Monarchy," *The Conversation*, September 21, 2022, https://theconversation.com/from-queen-elizabeth-to-king-charles-how-northern-irelands-unionists-feel-about-the-monarchy-190997.

28 John Duckitt, "Differential Effects of Right Wing Authoritarianism and Social Dominance Orientation on Outgroup Attitudes and Their Mediation by Threat from and Competitiveness to Outgroups," *Personality and Social Psychology Bulletin* 32, no. 5 (2006): 684–96, https://doi.org/10.1177/0146167205284282; Walter G. Stephan and Cookie White Stephan, "An Integrated Threat Theory of Prejudice," in *Reducing Prejudice and Discrimination*, ed. Stuart. Oskamp (Mahwah, NJ: Lawrence Erlbaum Associates Publishers, 2000), 23–45.

29 Mark Landler, "In Northern Ireland Town, Painful Memories Lie beneath a Fragile Peace," *New York Times*, April 6, 2022, https://www.nytimes.com/2023/04/06/world/europe/northern-ireland-good-friday-peace.html; Charles M. Sennott, "Northern Ireland's Troubled Peace," *The Atlantic,* May 6, 2023, https://www-stage.theatlantic.com/international/archive/2023/05/northern-ireland-unrest-paramilitary-ira-good-friday-agreement/673969/.

30 Yochi Cohen-Charash and Jennifer S. Mueller, "Does Perceived Unfairness Exacerbate or Mitigate Interpersonal Counterproductive Work Behaviors related to Envy?" *Journal of Applied Psychology* 92, no. 3 (2007): 666–80, https://doi.org/10.1037/0021-9010.92.3.666; Samuel Fernández-Salinero and Gabriela Topa, "Intergroup Discrimination as a Predictor of Conflict within the Same Organization: The Role of Organizational Identity," *European Journal of Investigation in Health, Psychology and Education* 10, no. 1 (2019): 1–9, https://doi.org/10.3390/ejihpe10010001.

31 "What Is the Northern Ireland Legacy Bill?" *BBC News*, September 5, 2023, https://www.bbc.co.uk/news/uk-northern-ireland-66648806.

32 Tania Tam et al., "Postconflict Reconciliation: Intergroup Forgiveness and Implicit Biases in Northern Ireland," *Journal of Social Issues* 64, no. 2 (2008): 303–20, https://doi.org/10.1111/j.1540-4560.2008.00563.x; Michal Reifen Tagar, Christopher M. Federico, and Eran Halperin, "The Positive Effect of Negative Emotions in Protracted Conflict: The Case of Anger," *Journal of Experimental Social Psychology* 47, no. 1 (2011): 157–64, https://doi.org/10.1016/j.jesp.2010.09.011.

33 Tam et al., "Postconflict Reconciliation."

34 Masi Noor et al., "When Suffering Begets Suffering: The Psychology of Competitive Victimhood Between Adversarial Groups in Violent Conflicts," *Personality and Social Psychology Review* 16, no., (2012): 351–74, https://doi.org/10.1177/1088868312440048.

35 Nurit Shnabel, Samer Halabi, and Masi Noor, "Overcoming Competitive Victimhood and Facilitating Forgiveness through Re-categorization into a Common Victim or Perpetrator Identity," *Journal of Experimental Social Psychology* 49, no. 5 (2013): 867–77, https://doi.org/10.1016/j.jesp.2013.04.007.

36 Hammad Sheikh, Jeremy Ginges, and Scott Atran, "Sacred Values in the Israeli–Palestinian Conflict: Resistance to Social Influence, Temporal Discounting, and Exit Strategies," *Annals of the New York Academy of Sciences* 1299, no. 1 (2013): 11–24, https://doi.org/10.1111/nyas.12275.

37 Amandeep Dhir et al., "Online Social Media Fatigue and Psychological Wellbeing—A Study of Compulsive Use, Fear of Missing Out, Fatigue, Anxiety and Depression," *International Journal of Information Management* 40, (2018): 141–52, https://doi.org/10.1016/j.ijinfomgt.2018.01.012.

38 Jonathon Byrne, "Peace Walls: 'A Temporary Measure,'" *History Ireland* 17, no. 4 (2009): 43, https://www.historyireland.com/peace-walls-a-temporary-measure.

39 Jack Boulton, "Frontier Wars: Violence and Space in Belfast, Northern Ireland," *Totem: The University of West Ontario Journal of Anthropology* 22, no. 1 (2014): 100–113; Hastings Donnan and Neil Jarman, "Ordinary Everyday Walls: Normalising Exception in Segregated Belfast," in *The Walls between Conflict and Peace, ed.* Alberto Gasparini (Leiden: Brill, 2017), 238–60.

40 John Dixon et al., "When the Walls Come Tumbling down': The Role of Intergroup Proximity, Threat and Contact in Shaping Attitudes towards the Removal of Northern Ireland's Peace Walls," *British Journal of Social Psychology* 59, no. 4 (2020): 922–44, https://doi.org/10.1111/bjso.12370.

41 Ipsos MORI Northern Ireland, *Public Attitudes to Peace Walls: 2019 Findings* (2020).

42 Ibid., 7.

43 European Parliamentary Research Services (EPRS), *The Ethics of Artificial Intelligence: Issues and Initiatives* (2020).

44 Nigel Gilbert et al., "Computational Modelling of Public Policy," *Journal of Artificial Societies and Social Simulation* 21, no. 1 (2018): Article 14, https://doi.org/10.18564/jasss.3669.

45 Paloutzian, Sagir, and Shults, "Modelling Reconciliation and Peace Processes," 237.

46 Shults and Wildman, "Human Simulation and Sustainability."

47 F. LeRon Shults and Wesley J. Wildman, "Ethics, Computer Simulation, and the Future of Humanity," in *Human Simulation: Perspectives, Insights, and Applications*, ed. Saikou Y. Diallo et al. (Heidelberg: Springer, 2019), 21–40; F. LeRon Shults and Wesley Wildman, "Artificial Social Ethics: Simulating Culture, Conflict, and Cooperation," in *SpringSim '20: Proceedings of the 2020 Spring Simulation Conference* (2020): Article 38.

BROTHERS AND SISTERS FROM ANOTHER MOTHER— PROMOTING INTER-CULTURAL UNDERSTANDING, CONFLICT REDUCTION, AND SOLIDARITY AMONG PARTNER FORCES IN THE SAHEL

Alain Tschudin

International Centre of Nonviolence, Durban University of Technology; Stellenbosch University; University of Cambridge

James Smith

International Centre of Nonviolence, Durban University of Technology

ABSTRACT

The dynamics of war have changed markedly from conventional battlefield kinetic encounters to unconventional sub-threshold or asymmetric warfare, with combatants using new tactics and emergent technologies to gain a comparative advantage over their adversaries. In the face of such developments and mindful of globalized extremist challenges, we propose that fresh innovations should be encouraged with respect to the conventional training of international and African partner forces tasked with teaming

Professor Alain Tschudin is Director of the International Centre of Nonviolence (ICON), Durban University of Technology, South Africa. He is a Research Fellow in the Centre for the Study of the Afterlife of Violence and the Reparative Quest at Stellenbosch University and Senior Research Associate, St Edmund's College, University of Cambridge. James Smith is a Cultural Understanding Consultant and Human Security Advisor and a graduate student in the International Centre of Nonviolence at Durban University of Technology.

We are grateful to Dr. Simóne Plug for valuable input on our draft manuscript.

up to engage security threats in the Sahel region. Accordingly, this article promotes a contemporary peacebuilding approach using a transformative, dialogical methodology that focuses on the promotion of greater inter-cultural understanding between local security forces and their external allies. We suggest that such an intervention is cost-effective, sustainable, adaptable, and replicable, insofar as it builds unity and shared understanding, and reduces direct and indirect violence (e.g., green-on-blue casualties and resentment toward different troops). It increases motivation and strengthens solidarity in the field to help partners work toward shared goals and enhanced operational effectiveness, which in turn results in conflict reduction and a more sustainable peace.

The critically acclaimed film, *Tirailleurs*[1] tracks the forced enlistment of a father and son from West Africa in the French campaign during World War I. Those watching the original French language version as non-first language speakers might activate subtitles to assist in understanding. It is surprising, therefore, that when the voice of the protagonist commences, no subtitles come up. One might be forgiven for thinking that there is a bug in the system. Reaching for the non-responsive controls, if one does not speak Fulani, one might feel disorientated and thrown by the goings on in the opening scenes. In the absence of understanding the words, one is forced to gain information from observing human interactions, gestures, landscapes, and floral and faunal context.

The resultant chaos is intentional on the part of the director and proves immensely insightful. This is great cinema, for it corrals the viewer into empathizing with the enlisted father, who cannot speak French. Much like the viewer's helpless fumbling around to find the subtitles, he wanders around the encampment in a state of alienation, asking fellow African soldiers if anyone can speak his language, often to a frosty and mocking reception. One can imagine his angst at being forced into a context that he cannot decipher, relying on translation via interpreters for his survival and that of his young son, the latter being his priority. It is dramatically ironic, therefore, that the son, who is in the same infantry section, but who can speak French, is embraced by French officers and promoted for valor in the same contacts, while his father, the de facto hero, is marginalized.

The film encapsulates the esprit de corps of military solidarity as it explores the complexity of cultural pluralism in combat. Nobody escapes unscathed. Much like the subtitles of a film, a lingua franca among partner forces is mission critical in terms of preventing antagonism and partner-on-friendly fire, and beyond that, to promoting solidarity, such as between African and international partner forces in the Sahel.

This anecdote speaks directly to the topic of this article. Communicative limitations and resultant miscommunications in operational theaters can increase tensions, exacerbating divisions that lead to non-cooperation, resentment, an escalation in conflict, violence, and even death. Both authors have been to war; one as a humanitarian deployed in emergency coordination during active conflicts and the other as a soldier and officer in battlefield contacts. Both have worked on extremist movements in Africa and have experienced the opportunity cost of inattentiveness to inter-cultural communication and understanding.[2] Accordingly, this article seeks to offer a transformative approach to building relations between African and international partner forces such as those of the United Nations (UN), North Atlantic Treaty Organization (NATO), EU, UK, and US through dialogue and mutual understanding that will contribute to remedying the issue of their sustained cooperation and conflict reduction at a systemic level in the Sahel.

The Changing Character of War in the Anthropocene

The opening two decades of the twenty-first century have forced humanity to face up to some dramatic changes. Increasing concerns over human actions during the Anthropocene and their deleterious, irreversible consequences for life on Earth reached a crescendo at the 2022 climate meeting of the United Nations.[3] If the bleak prognosis has anything to offer humanity, it is the certain knowledge that we are living in a changing world, burdened with significant costs of conflict.[4] As the world changes, the nature of human activity and enterprise adapts and changes with the dynamic and fluid environments facing us.[5]

The context of war and peace appears to be no different. Classical definitions of war still hold sway; war still involves contention by force (see Cicero); it can still be regarded as a relation between states (Jean-Jacques Rousseau), although today it often involves non-state actors and, to paraphrase Carl von Clausewitz, it remains defined as the continuation of politics by other means. Although force in contemporary times can manifest in terms that are radically different from those of the ancients (consider the reference to new technology below), the violent and belligerent nature of war remains constant, as does the non-violent and harmonious nature of peace.[6] However, the dynamics violently propelling us in one direction, or gently nudging us in the other, have changed.

Almost twenty years ago, Hew Strachan pointed out that "getting to the heart of war is both less and more complex: less because the nature of war probably changes less over time than does its character (a point derived from Clausewitz), more because defining the nature of war is a complex, inter-disciplinary process. Philosophy is not a bad place to begin."[7] Strachan argues that with the second invasion of Iraq in 2003 and the so-called "war on terror," certain sea changes became apparent in the character of contemporary war. He notes that their underlying causes remain traditional (ethnicity, religion, statehood) with regional more than global roots, concluding that "if war remains an adversarial business whose dynamics create their own consequences, which can themselves be unpredictable, its nature cannot change." Using the challenges identified both in Iraq and Afghanistan, he points out that policy "has to adapt to the changing character of war, so that its aspirations remain in step with war itself and with what war can actually deliver."[8]

Changes to the character of war arise, in no small part from the rapid onset of the fourth industrial revolution and boom in technology. In *What It Is Like To Go to War*, Karl Marlantes, a decorated Marine officer, Vietnam veteran, and alumnus of the University of Oxford and Yale University, puts it as follows:

> It is bad enough that we send our youth off to fight our wars ill prepared for the spiritual and psychological consequences of entering combat. Add to this the fact that combat is becoming increasingly intermingled with the ordinary civilian world. With cell phones, Facebook, Twitter, air travel, and remoted controlled weaponry, the battlefield is less clearly defined and the bloody consequences of what modern weapons do can be completely masked. Consider the bomber crews that fly from the United States and back to bomb Iraq or Libya, telling their spouses and kids they'll be gone a little longer than usual that day... Imagine the psychic split that must ensue from bringing in death and destruction from the sky on a group of terrorists... and then driving home from the base to dinner with the spouse and kids.[9]

Akin to this, Grégoire Chamayou, in *Drone Theory*, argues that "in many respects, the drone dreams of achieving through technology a miniature equivalence to that fictional eye of God."[10] However, as he argues, drones are not merely about panoptical surveillance but about lethal enforcement strikes, or what he refers to as "annihilation." Citing the fear, insecurity, and terror unleashed on recipient communities, he proposes that drones effectively traumatize populations who are subjected to a constant state of hypervigilance, uncertainty, and stress over the prospects of being struck.[11]

Cautioning against heavy-handed state interventions, Kim Hudson and Dan Henk note that, "from the earliest beginnings, violence and coercion have been features of the human condition," while the contemporary difference is that, "much of the new security thinking reflects a profound pessimism about the willingness or ability of individual states to realise a comprehensive liberal security vision."[12]

What has changed are the dynamics of a globalized society in the throes of the so-called fourth industrial revolution, coupled with the advance of the military-industrial complex. This is accompanied by the backsliding of all things liberal, which coincides with what Edward Luce describes as the retreat of Western liberalism as we advance toward the third decade of the third millennium.[13] In light of this, a plethora of authors refer to alternatives such as "adaptive peacebuilding," "developmental peace," the "sustaining peace agenda," and the "perpetual peacebuilding" paradigm.[14]

Ours represents an intentional attempt to promote peace, albeit within a context of conflict and protracted violence. To achieve our aim, we invoke the old Aristotelian maxim favored by scholastic philosopher Thomas Aquinas, "one and the same is the knowledge of opposites."[15] We will argue that in the face of war, advancing knowledge that promotes peace is critical and, moreover, that efforts to reduce conflict and promote lasting peace and harmony in the Sahel will rely largely on shared communications between African and international partner forces. Regrettably, as Christian Peterson et al. point out in their introductory chapter of *The Oxford Handbook of Peace History*, "many scholars prefer to 'play war' by producing more scholarship about the components of war than the dynamics of peace."[16] It is thus that we enter the realm of peace studies.

Peace Studies Gloss: Emergence Out of Twentieth Century Conflict and Twenty-first Century Evolution

The discipline of peace studies largely arose out of the post–World War II milieu, gaining momentum as the Cold War ensued. More specifically, within this area of studies, Oliver Ramsbotham et al. track the historical emergence of conflict resolution, noting its transfer from corporate and community contexts to civil and international conflicts and its uptake in the 1950s and 1960s in response to the existentialist threat posed by nuclear proliferation and superpower posturing.[17]

They suggest that while the 1970s on into the 1980s were characterized by the non-proliferation of nuclear weapons, alternative dispute resolution, and protracted social conflicts such as that witnessed in Israel and Palestine,

> By the 1980s, conflict resolution ideas were increasingly making a difference in real conflicts. […] In the Middle East, a peace process was getting under way in which negotiators on both sides had gained experience both of each other and of conflict resolution through problem-solving workshops. In Northern Ireland, groups inspired by the new approach had set up community relations initiatives […] In war-torn regions of Africa and South-East Asia, development workers and humanitarian agencies were seeing the need to take account of conflict and conflict resolution as an integral part of their activities.[18]

By comparison, Ramsbotham et al. note that the 1990s largely focused on reconstruction, after the fall of the Berlin Wall, with increasing democratization in former totalitarian states (such as apartheid South Africa) on the one hand and genocidal crimes against humanity on the other, such as that witnessed in Bosnia and Rwanda.

They note that as the singular global conflict of the Cold War diminished, internal conflicts along ethno-religious, linguistic, and self-deterministic fault lines erupted, leading to mercenary and militia violence against civilian populations. Simultaneously, major world leaders espoused peace and conflict resolution, with related development funding initiatives, while fresh challenges arose from non-state conflicts, the hegemony of limited Western methods, and the applicability of cold-war conflict models to post–Cold War contexts.[19]

Hence, despite some pessimism raised toward the end of the twentieth century, the first decade of the third millennium largely commenced with an optimism about the prospects of globalization and world peace, ushering in the so-called "liberal peace" model.[20] However, just as the cosmopolitan approach to building and sustaining peace was coming to the fore, the attack on the Twin Towers at the World Trade Center in New York and attempted attack on the Pentagon on September 11, 2001 proved to be a seismic moment that bifurcated the paths ahead.[21] The response to 9/11 triggered the so-called global war on terror, with radicalization both to the left and to the right.

While we in the academy were teaching about international humanitarian law and the emerging doctrine of the responsibility to protect (R2P), the United States and its allies unleashed an infraction upon the sovereignty of the state of Iraq, claiming as justification the still unsubstantiated claim of the presence of weapons of mass destruction. As the theater of military operations expanded into Afghanistan, newly emerging information and communications technology (ICT) and social media enabled the Arab Spring, which commenced with uprisings in Tunisia that rapidly spread across the Middle East and North Africa (MENA). This tinderbox ignited neighborhood revolutions of the people against totalitarian and authoritarian rulers and was perhaps most visible in the Syrian conflict, which escalated into all-out war.

The demise of R2P coincided with the NATO airstrikes on Libya, which were seen as a dramatic overreach and undermining of advances in regional and sub-regional peacebuilding, such as that observed through the African Union and the Economic Community of West African States (ECOWAS).[22] With the abandonment of principles such as subsidiarity and solidarity within geopolitical responses to conflict and violence, and the increasing skepticism about the West, Northern partners soon began to lose credibility, opening up spaces for alternative entrants to the fray. These included groups such as the Russian paramilitary Wagner Group and increasingly Islamic extremists such as Al-Qaeda, the Islamic State of Iraq and the Levant (ISIL), and related terror groups.

One might argue that the death knell of liberal peacebuilding was the abrupt, chaotic, and catastrophic withdrawal of allied forces from Afghanistan in 2021. After two decades of intense international involvement, the citizens of that country were all but abandoned to their fate at the hands of the Taliban, who had made it abundantly clear in advance that they would not respect the norms of international law. Blatant violations of women's and children's rights, and those of minorities, make it clear that liberal democracy has sounded the retreat.

In its place, we are confronted with aggressive and totalizing territorial contestation and expansion, such as evidenced by Russia in Ukraine, for example, and the turn to conservative, nationalistic, and right-leaning governance in traditional democracies. All of this, undoubtedly, has been exacerbated by the global COVID-19 pandemic, which has reversed developmental advances, caused economic recession, and resulted in a world of uncertainty accompanied by angst, in light of the accelerating crisis surrounding climate change and planetary integrity.

In effect, this gloss over the arc of peace studies over the last eighty years suggests that the first decade of the twenty-first century saw increasing skepticism around the notions of conflict management and resolution, with critical interrogation suggesting that the resumption of hostilities and recurring triggers might have been underestimated in the wave of enthusiasm around positive developments in global society at the end of the twentieth century.

Having witnessed the waning enthusiasm for modernist views on upwards and onwards progress, in a post-structuralist milieu, unfolding from the mid-1990s much more sensitivity toward the ebb and flow of conflict ensued.[23] Accordingly, instead of seeing the process of conflict resolution as a tick-box exercise, Johan Galtung suggests the following: "By *peace* we mean the capacity to transform conflicts with empathy and creativity, without violence; a never-ending process."[24] From the early 2000s, increasing attention was paid to the nuanced difference in approach between conflict resolution and conflict transformation, whereby some practitioners, such as Hugh Miall, Oliver Ramsbotham, and Tom Woodhouse sought to promote extensions between the two, while others such as John Paul Lederach saw clear differences.[25]

As Ramsbotham et al. point out,

> This broad view of conflict transformation is necessary to correct the misperception that conflict resolution rests on an assumption of harmony of interests between actors, and that third-party mediators can settle conflicts by appealing to the reason or underlying humanity of the parties. On the contrary, conflict transformation requires real changes in parties' interests, goals or self-definitions. These may be forced by the conflict itself, or may come about because of intra-party changes, shifts in the constituencies of the parties, or changes in the context in which the conflict is situated. Conflict resolution must therefore be concerned not only with the issues that divide the main parties but also with the social, psychological, and political changes that are necessary to address root causes.[26]

Our colleague Geoff Harris, writing on war, conflict, and peacebuilding in Africa, regards conflict as inevitable and defines it as an "incompatibility of needs and interest between individuals and groups," noting that it can be ignored or managed, resolved and "albeit not commonly, transformed." On his reading, "conflict transformation concerns the relationship between the parties and is likely to involve truth, justice, mercy, forgiveness and reconciliation."[27] He notes how a lack of responsiveness to conflict can spill over into direct violence or other indirect or less obvious forms such as structural or cultural violence (cf. Galtung).

Finally, authors such as Nicholas Ross and Mareike Schomerus remind us of the ongoing gap between policy and practice.[28] Despite the signaling of reform in the United Nations and notable efforts by various UN agencies, this remains challenging for the sustainable implementation and promotion of peace.[29]

Transformative Learning and Ecosystems Theory

Given the theoretical evolution of peace studies as a whole, and mindful of the shift in nuance within applied conflict studies from management and resolution to transformation, it is possible to discuss the approach adopted by the International Centre of Nonviolence (ICON) at the Durban University of Technology, South Africa. ICON engages the study of conflict and violence, along the spectrum from negative peace, often known as "the silencing of the guns" or "the absence of violent conflict" to positive peace, whereby notions such as reconciliation, restoration, lasting social harmony and sustained well-being are explored. The very action of moving from negative to positive peace entails transformation. ICON undertakes this work both in contexts of direct violence and indirect violence.

As such, ICON's work embraces two complementary theoretical paradigms, namely transformative learning and ecosystems theory. The notion of transformative learning hinges on the relationship between encouraging critical reflection, and the nexus between directed thought and applied action. Efforts in this area were pioneered by Jack Mezirow.[30]

For Mezirow, a defining condition of being human is that we have to understand the meaning of our experience. For some, any uncritically assimilated explanation from an authority figure will suffice. But in contemporary societies we must learn to make our own interpretations rather than act on the purposes, beliefs, judgments, and feelings of others. Facilitating such understanding is the cardinal goal of adult education. Transformative learning develops autonomous thinking.[31]

Picking up on Mezirow,[32] Christopher Blundell et al. note that, "frames of reference, which form through experience, are used to categorize experiences and interpret new information," becoming "the basis for habits of mind, which are broadly orientating ways to think, feel and act."[33] Such frames of reference are powerful influencers of behavioral change and can be applied from intra-individual through to societal levels or systems.

As Periklis Pavlidis recognizes, the active shaping by human beings of their living conditions, as well as the conscious transformation of social relations, are closely connected with the critical distancing from the surrounding prevailing reality, with the understanding of its internal contradictions and therefore, with the perception of the potential and prospects of its evolution. Cultivation, therefore, of our ability to think dialectically, concerns not only our thought but our practical activity as well.[34]

To this end, we adopt a transformative approach within the following conceptual frame, namely ecosystems theory as initiated by Urie Bronfenbrenner and subsequently developed.[35] He suggested that human development is significantly influenced by the interactions that the individual being shares with their surrounding physical and social ecology, as evidenced within and across four systems: micro, meso, exo, and macrosystems. Initially, Bronfenbrenner developed his theory with children and was concerned with their self-other interactions on ontogenesis, but now it is applied to diverse contexts to assist with adaptive and optimal development across the lifespan.

Galtung, likewise, refers to four levels of organization of "the human condition" (micro, meso, macro, and mega), noting that the center of gravity of societies shifts over time from a closed to an open approach to being. Referring to four stages, he argues for a shift from intolerance to tolerance, then to dialogue, and finally to *mutual learning*, which in his opinion, "holds the key to the future."[36] Indeed, with efforts to curb extremisms, which themselves at base level reflect a societal reversal, namely, a lack of dialogue, lack of tolerance, and return to intolerance, serious attention must be invested to advance mutual learning between African and international partner forces.

Thus framed, we can move to discuss how such an approach to the reduction of conflict and violence can be enabled by undertaking a process of transformative learning, within a relevant setting, as informed by our suggested approach, namely conducting it within a systems context. Effectively, this entails promoting the notions of tolerance, dialogue, and mutual learning for transformation at the individual, small group, larger group, and collective levels. For this we shall shortly turn to a discussion of the promotion of inter-cultural understanding among partner forces in the Sahel.

First, however, it is helpful to consider Robert Scales's theory of four world wars, which aptly reinforces the need for attentiveness to the changing dynamics of war: the

First World War was the chemist's war, the second was the physicist's war, the third (or Cold War) was the information theorist's war, and the fourth will be the behavioral scientist's war.[37] He writes:

> World War IV will cause a shift in the classical centers of gravity from the will of governments to the perceptions of populations. Victory will be defined more in terms of capturing the psycho-cultural rather than the geographical high ground. Understanding and empathy will be important weapons of war. Soldier conduct will be as important as skill at arms. Culture awareness and the ability to build ties of trust will offer protection to our troops more effectively than body armor.[38]

Recognizing this keystone of culture, Francois Vreÿ, Abel Esterhuyse, and Thomas Mandrup suggest that despite military culture being critically important for military effectiveness, it has been neglected due to three primary factors, namely negative perceptions of armed forces, dated literature, and largely external sources with little African input.

They cite the South African Defence Force (SADF) Military Dictionary, which defines culture as, "the accumulated total of a group's knowledge, skills, beliefs, traditions and artefacts, usually related to a period of time," noting that, irrespective of how it plays out, military culture "directs, shapes, informs and provides the context to every single military action, whether of an organizational or operational nature, and irrespective of how big or small such action is. There is a direct link between military culture and those factors which ensure success."[39]

Mindful of the decisiveness of culture and the key importance of promoting empathy and understanding through cultural awareness and building relationships that are based on trust, we now approach the topic of African and international partner forces that engage extremisms in the Sahel.

Understanding Partners' Cultures in the Fight Against Extremism

The recent withdrawal of French and European forces from Mali, after nine years on Operation Barkhane, and the suspension by the Nigerien junta of the US Nigerien Accord allowing a US presence in Niger, has dangerous ramifications for countering violent extremist organizations (C-VEOs), the prevention of human trafficking, the protection of civilians, defending women's rights, setting the security conditions for jump-starting economies, and defeating exploitative corruption in the Sahel as a whole.[40]

Military juntas have taken advantage of the gaps left by inept and corrupt leaders and replaced quasi democracies, autocracies, and oligarchies with military rule and sought new partners including mercenary organizations and allies that are less "rules based," are content to ignore human rights, and do not encourage democratic rights values.[41] Little has changed with concessions from mining and mineral rights being renegotiated with alternative competitors such as the Russian mercenary company Wagner Group and private military or security companies that have started taking over the training of Sahel security forces with little or no emphasis on human rights, justice pathways, countering human trafficking, and gender and child protection concerns.[42]

What is evident, in cases such as the failure of the G5 Sahel coalition against jihadist insurgencies, is that Sahelian counter-extremism missions fail not because of a lack of tactical successes against the adversaries but rather due to a lack of understanding of the politics, economics, social group dynamics, sensitivities, beliefs, and values of the partner forces and the countries' populations.[43] Where one Western or international partner force fails, another is soon ready to fill the gap and exploit the opportunity to attack the former in the information space, especially if there is an easy and particularly emotive and sensitive historical counter-imperialist narrative that detracts from the juntas own inability to deal with the problem of violent extremism, economic decline, political instability, and human rights transgressions.[44]

It is critical for us to understand why international partnerships are either successful, enduring, and persistent or fail from the onset or even before they begin. Commanders, planning teams, and operators who will interact on the ground, whether that is in training or on operations, must understand that operational risks including those to mission, reputation, and life, lie within the clear understanding of each other's cultures, histories, developmental ecosystems, and overall needs and desired end states. Without this understanding, the partnership will not endure because the frictions that exist between cultures will be exacerbated by stresses of training and combat.

The Grave Error of Paternalism in Partnerships

The international partner forces must learn an alternative, more informed and empathetic style of diplomacy at every level, from strategy to tactics. This is necessary to avoid taking what is viewed by African partners as "a meddling, patronising, imperial or colonial approach," one to which the post Françafrique (France's sphere of economic, political, and military influence in its former colonies) countries are particularly sensitive.[45] This is especially reinforced because many Malians continue to live with the system's negative impacts to their economy, political autonomy, and local development. This particular anti-French and wider anti-"imperialist," read Western, sensitivity has been exploited and exacerbated by effective misinformation and disinformation campaigns, narratives, and information products by organizations such as Wagner Group and Russia's Africa Corps. Popular anti-colonial and anti-imperialist narratives are easy to propagate with populations looking conveniently to history to explain or blame the current complex situations on the past. These narratives have been used effectively by juntas and Chinese and Russian information operations to mobilize urban and rural unrest and protests against French, US, and European interests and reputation in the Sahel. An appropriate response does not necessitate being "hyper" alert to sensitivities, but rather turns on being situationally and culturally aware, empathetic, trained, and educated. Such a response avoids getting into situations that allow these sensitivities to manifest or where adversaries, actors, and competitors exploit a simple "demonization" narrative among a receptive marginalized and often impoverished audience.[46]

Critical to this is an understanding of the differences between international forces that largely consist of northwestern European and North American individualist personnel interacting with highly collectivist Sahelian partner forces. Misunderstandings of this social group phenomenon are often the underlying cause of frictions, especially when culturally northwestern individualists who make up a significant proportion of peace keeping, peace support, and peace enforcement "coalitions of the willing" cannot understand why collectivists do not lead, make decisions, manage people and equipment, plan, or conduct operations in the same way that Westerners do.

For individualist partner forces there is no desire to keep the social grouping or community happy at the expense of output, transparency, fairness, and efficiency, whereas the collectivist Sahelians must ensure that their collective, ethnicity, tribe, clan, or family support each other, even when transparency, efficiency, and output are adversely affected. It is extremely difficult for international armies and security forces, who base their "measurement of effect" on "output," to adapt their thinking to building relationships first. It takes considerable understanding, empathy, and behavioral change to manage and develop ways, means, and ends to deal with this dichotomy.

The Art of Understanding

The challenge of training Europeans and Americans to understand and to empathize with African partners is not insurmountable, but takes considerable development of the individual, team, and collective knowledge of the eco-behavioral ecosystems within which Sahelian partner forces develop, the civilian population's struggles and aspirations, the lenses through which the people see their history, politics, their economic constraints, their social groups and networks of influence, their beliefs and values, and their physical, psychological, and information environment.[47] Westerners must be taught how to develop high context communication skills or less direct and more meaningful implied verbal and nonverbal communication to foster a deeper understanding of the Sahelian partners' implied communication rather than relying on the more explicit communication so typical in NATO and UN security forces and armies.

This approach requires an interest in the individual and collective experiences of the Sahelian partner and an understanding of the completely opposite ecosystems of the people with whom they are partnering. Both parties must be taught how to manage the relationship and its associated behavioral dimensions and idiosyncrasies to prevent frictions. Creating training and education solutions that give both partners the knowledge, skills, experiences, and behaviors is challenging. More importantly, providing a viewpoint or lens similar to one's colleagues on the local or international partner force remains a difficult task both in terms of understanding each other's complex development as well as the politics, economics, social groups, networks, interests, and positions that affect the current operation. Both partners need to understand how each other's environment and immediate settings from family, education, and external influences have shaped the broader cultural values, laws, customs, and sensitivities.

Where Europeans and Americans want to take the lead and direct, they need to step back and allow the Sahelian partner to lead and make their own decisions while facilitating their progress against the insurgents, rather than fighting the insurgency for them. European and US governments must analyze the mistakes of Vietnam, Afghanistan, and now the Sahel and understand that the speculative model of trying to establish a proxy force based on European or American militaries and police forces may be flawed from the outset. Despite the common colonial experience of many African countries, the overarching raison d'être of these forces was the protection of the state, and this has remained unchanged since decolonization.

Doctrinally these forces remain the same with little change to structure, training, discipline, and attitudes toward the civil population and civic institutions. The Sahelian security model was designed to protect the few from the masses and not the masses from a complex insurgency. Little has been done to develop the methods of leadership, management, command, and control. Creating carbon copies of international armies that have long developmental histories as expeditionary forces supported by sophisticated command, control, logistics, planning, and intelligence will fail at the first hurdle if solely attempting to advance the core military business of operations in the absence of consideration of Sahelian social structures, politics, economics, beliefs, and values.

"Reading the room"—Communicating in the High Context

One of the most difficult transformative approaches to building trust between partners is understanding how different partners communicate and reflect, whether that is in the "low context" explicit style typical of Western partners who get straight to the point or talk about business or solutions, or in the "high context" implied style, relying on body language, gestures, non-verbal cues, storytelling, and understanding status and hierarchical relationships so typical of Sahelian partners. US and European military personnel tend to get "straight to the point" and concern themselves with the facts of the matter known in the military as the BLUF or "bottom line up front" and the tangible output, desired effect, or product of a conversation. Westerners especially want to understand exactly what they need to do or get from the partner to solve a problem or understand an issue as quickly as possible and move on. Often international partner forces ignore the surrounding context, principals, history, and associated events in the past, which they see as superfluous to the issue at hand, looking only to the future and how to plan for the next situation.

There exists, within Western military theories of strategy, the Lykke strategy model, namely that everything can be solved quickly, expeditiously, and that the "ends (objectives), ways (concepts) and means (resources)" are clear.[48] This is not the case with many Sahelian partners for whom context, significant events, history, the internecine relationships of extended kith, kin, and influence are not only important but shape the current situation and the future. Without understanding this alternative perspective and context and acknowledging the importance of it to Sahelian partners, Western forces and governments will continue to misunderstand the intricacies of diplomacy and negotiation in a meeting with Sahelian partners where nothing is heard or said, but everything is implied and understood.

These two styles of communication mean that neither understands why the other either places so much emphasis on explicit information, or why the other implies what the desired end state is and leaves critical information unsaid. Unless the detail between the lines is comprehended by interpreters on both sides, it is difficult to understand what the other partner really means or wants from the relationship. This can prove to be detrimental to an enduring and persistent relationship where neither fully understands what the other values and believes in, or knows what their position and interests are.

Clearly the stress of conflict, political interests, and the fight for resources exacerbates the situation, making the pursuit of effective cooperation even more fragile especially when the ends are different. A good example of this is illustrated by the French experience in Mali. While the French end state was to contain, disrupt, or defeat the extremist threat to France's interests, the Malian government (especially individuals in control of resources and mining concessions), intended merely to limit the extremists' freedom of action and influence over their interests. Their ability to control those resources and create the conditions to enable them to generate personal wealth without interference was the end state, not necessarily the defeat of the extremists.[49] This quickly brought them into conflict with one another, where the French intended to train the Malians to act as a proxy force capable of containing the insurgency according to French doctrine, rather than promote the needs of the Malians, which were often diametrically opposed.

This inability to understand what either partner wanted in terms of objectives, output, or "ends" meant that in the high context world of the Sahel, where relationships are built on interpersonal trust, Malian military personnel valued enduring personal relationships with high context communication, while the French valued the ability of the Malians to produce the "solution" that they wanted the partner to deliver, before any relationship was built. Neither was able to meet the other's needs, as neither understood what was required from the relationship and the end state. This would have a significant effect in the breakdown of the relationship and worse still, the pursuit of a peace. The civilian populations caught in between the factions would suffer the most from the breakdown.

Protecting Civilians, Women, Peace, and Security

Undoubtedly gender-based violence, sexual exploitation, and abuse is not solely committed by VEOs and has been perpetuated by armed forces, security forces, and non-governmental organizations (NGOs) alike. International partner forces must develop a clear understanding of how Sahel partner forces perceive violence against civilians and "win over," train, and educate sensitively the Sahel partner force, against illegal, unacceptable, and unprofessional military behavior. The difficulty lies in understanding what the tolerance threshold is for violence and illegal, unacceptable behavior, adjusting perceptions and educating against violence against civilians and women, while developing the partner forces' mindfulness of international humanitarian law (IHL).

The challenge to the international partner is how to train and educate the African partner force to champion women, peace, and security and to develop gender mainstreaming in their organization, conduct of planning, training, and operations, and diversifying their personnel to ensure that they engage with women affected by conflict.[50] This is a difficult task especially when one considers that some cultures are more conservative in their approach to the emancipation and inclusion of women in the military and security forces. International partner forces must train their personnel and the partner force to understand and plan for the reality of gender issues in their mission.[51]

Unlike their own Western economies, international partner forces may encounter an African civilian population that may be at risk purely by carrying out their daily economic and domestic practices and pattern of life. Adults and children (and especially women and girls) are more vulnerable to the threat of extremist violence purely because their more traditional agrarian and domestic roles (traveling long distances, unguarded to collect water and firewood, going to school alone, attending markets or working in fields) makes them easy targets and exposes them to risk from gender-based violence, sexual abuse, intimidation, kidnapping, and ethnic targeting.

At the strategic, operational, and tactical levels, planners must consider the African gender perspective if they are to have a positive effect on stemming human rights violations. At the strategic level, planners must analyze the operational value of having a diverse gender range sewn into the force to be deployed, especially in countries where the female population is greater than the male population and more vulnerable to gender targeting. The presence of female officers and soldiers provides the force with the ability to train and operate alongside women in the partner force and to adapt to engage with, protect, and interact with the female population as well. Women as a force multiplier cannot be underestimated. Victims of gender-based violence and conflict-related sexual violence are anecdotally less likely to approach male soldiers than they are female soldiers.

The UN Security Council (UNSC) has specifically mandated UN peacekeeping operations and signatories to UNSC Resolution 1325 to address conflict-related sexual violence (CRSV). Along with other mission substantive entities, the military component is responsible for proactively preventing CRSV, deterring perpetrators, protecting civilians, especially women and children, and neutralizing potential, impending, and ongoing CRSV threats.

To facilitate peacekeepers, police, and the military in carrying out these mandated tasks, the UN-CRSV Specialized Training Materials (STM) package was developed. These materials familiarize militaries with the concept of CRSV, clarify roles and responsibilities, and equip them with the required tools to proactively address CRSV in their operational environment. It is the international partner's responsibility, as a signatory, to engage with the African partner force (some of whom are signatories themselves) and provide training through these packages to educate, prevent, deter, report, and manage the response to CRSV.

Cultural Training against Strategic Failure

There is little evidence to suggest that Western forces spend sufficient time educating, training, and teaching their people at various levels, from the strategic "big government" top-level state departments, foreign affairs, diplomatic corps, national security, international policy, and operations departments down to the lowest tactical level soldier, to truly understand partners. The exception to the rule is characterized by deep subject matter experts who have had the experience of living in the country and learning the language and culture themselves.

Country and cultural knowledge, communications skills, behaviors, and experiential learning can all be delivered to some extent in an academic and practical environment, however teaching empathy with the partner force, understanding their ecosystems, education, how they learn, what they value, and their perspectives on others is critical to strategic, operational, and tactical success and must be learned over time and "on the job."

That said even the "on the job" learning remains unmonitored, unevaluated, and unexploited. As an example, the failure of the Afghan National Army to prosecute a successful campaign against the Taliban post the withdrawal of US and multinational forces from tactical and operational responsibility suggests the following. Irrelevant of how carefully designed a strategy is, and how effective coalition forces are at the operational and tactical level, if a dependency on an external international partner force exists, it will never change a culture, but only a few behaviors and less so transfer any significant ability to carbon copy the organization and its outputs. Moreover, it will damage the host nation's ability to conduct its own C-VEO response using its own resources and methods.

The example remains extant for the Sahelian model, where setting up a partner force supported by an inordinate amount of financial backing, technology, equipment, capability, and capacity that the local partner force cannot replicate, teaches false and unsustainable lessons to the international forces providing the assistance and sets up the partner force for inevitable failure.

"Wargaming" versus "Peacegaming" the Consequences

Fundamental to understanding a Sahelian partner force's culture is spending time researching their motivations, interests, networks, influence, perceptions of what they need in terms of training, conduct of operations, and "what good looks like." What the Sahelian partner "needs" and what the international forces assess is required for them in terms of "outputs" are often at loggerheads with each other. Negotiating the "middle ground" is key to success. How one achieves this often requires practicing with international forces and if possible, the Sahelian partner force in a tabletop exercise or "wargame" of scenarios with injects of disruptive activity, negotiation, frictions, or events that the international force would not anticipate or understand but that are common to the partner force's culture, upbringing, levels of education, sensitivities, or lenses of experience.

Lessons learned from previous iterations of similar operations and training exercises like Exercise Flintlock should be used to shape the wargaming event.[52] The aim is to inoculate both the international forces and the Sahelian partner forces, desensitize them and practice for occurrences that would normally cause friction and explore means, tools, methods, and strategies to overcome these issues. Conducting this sort of simulation of friction in a game while breaking down barriers, creating understanding, and building rapport is better than doing it "live" in the training or operational environment where the risks are higher and the possibility of both divorcing themselves from working with the other more damaging.[53]

Economy, Corruption, and Patronage

Evidence suggests that the conflict in the Sahel is firmly rooted in complex social, historic, economic, climate, agricultural, and political frustrations of the populations of the Sahel and not in easily recited violent extremist ideological reasons, which are popular in France, Europe, and the US.[54] Successful C-VEO strategies require a more holistic approach rather than a unilateral military solution, with analysis of the source of the conflict indicating that the fight for resources is a greater "push pull" factor in causing the conflict than religion alone.[55]

In the Sahel where resources are limited, marginalized communities are economically repressed, agriculture is failing, and people are unable to generate income to sustain a living, especially as they are excluded from rentier patronage and a corrupt system based on mining and mineral extraction and the associated services. Inevitably VEOs fill the gap and provide economic alternatives as well as forms of social mobility, whether that consists of trafficked women and girls, slaves, cattle, camels, weapons, food, fuel, or drugs. In Europe and the US, graft, corruption, nepotism, and patronage are seen as undermining to a free and fair economy, while in the Sahel systems they may be the only means by which some are able to sustain their families where little economic activity and welfare exists.[56]

Interfering in Sahelian economic practices of corruption, patronage, and nepotism, especially around services and contracts that support international forces' camps and sustainment may have the opposite effect and turn the population against international forces irrespective of how good the intentions are. Sensitive and alternative ways and means to spread resources and opportunities without encouraging corruption must be practiced, with commensurate education imparted to international partner forces to avoid any cultural frictions over sensitive economic practices that negatively impact host nation soldiers' families financially.

Awareness of the economic desperation of Sahelians and the system is imperative to a sensitive approach to activities that could further undermine economic stability. Treating the symptoms of conflict, i.e., the violence associated with VEOs, does nothing to address the real underlying causes, which sit firmly in the economic sphere. It is important for international partner forces to understand that their role, within this conflict, is a stabilizing factor but not the solution, without which, real economic growth cannot be jump-started and sustained.

Conclusion

This article has advocated for the critical necessity of inter-cultural understanding between international partner forces and African forces engaging extremist threats in the Sahel. After some preliminary engagement on the changing character of war in the current era and the emergence of contemporary peace studies out of war and post-conflict reconstruction, the notion of transformative learning was advanced and located within ecosystems theory, for the purpose of conflict reduction and advancement of peace.

As has been discussed in the case of the Sahel, culture, strategy, and success are intricately and decisively intertwined. To ignore this is to risk jeopardizing human lives. Understanding Sahelian partners' sensitivities, their complex socioeconomic and political struggles, and the deadly intricacies of the C-VEO conflict remains one of the most complex challenges facing African and international partner forces. This is especially the case in the absence of significant investment in culturally sensitive training and education.

Indeed, training can mitigate the risk of cultural faux pas and may prevent some frictions, but ultimately it is the responsibility of the international and host nation partner forces to build rapport, knowledge on each other's unique styles of leadership, contextual communication, and management of both people and material. Without a deeper understanding of people and the conflict dynamics and context by each and every actor from the strategic to the tactical, any foray into the region is inevitably on a path to failure.

Accordingly, Hudson and Henk propose that

> Military education emphasizes critical times and places at which concentrated effort can be directed to achieve decisive results – the tactician's schwerpunkt. The

challenge here is to broaden perspectives to apply this expertise to decisive results involving diverse communities of actors in a culturally complex environment – to seek a social schwerpunkt, the outcome of which is human well-being, harmonious human relations in general and productive civil-military relations in particular. Of particular value would be senior security-sector officials able to visualize and pursue ends as broad as self-sufficient societies able to peacefully resolve internal differences with mutually advantageous linkages to the wider international community.[57]

This social *schwerpunkt*, cross-cultural competence, rests on a significant challenge, namely "the expectation that security-sector personnel successfully perform their duties in circumstances of significant cultural complexity that include differing organizational cultures and members of different nationalities and people-groups… rendered more complex by world-view differences often encountered within larger societies, reflecting differences of religious belief, class, generation, gender and similar factors."[58] To address this, perspective-taking, suspended judgment, and 'cultural filtering' of verbal and non-verbal communications across cultural boundaries is required.

In all of this, they propose, as do we, that relationship-building is mission critical. If you want peace, prepare for a mutual understanding of the other, which socially, economically, and ethically represents a much better longer-term investment than preparing for war or for the related costs of conflict.[59]

To advance this pressing endeavor, the last word of the current article but opening move of the way forward is provided by the recently deceased Professor Johan Galtung on the importance of relationality to peace culture and the measure of our humanity:

> Violence and war, conflict, and peace, all have one thing in common: they are relational. Violence takes place between perpetrator and victim, war between belligerents, conflict between goals held by actors and by implication between actors, peace between actors, as a peace structure, with a peace culture. The actors may be individuals or collectivists; either way, the basic measure of peace is what happens to human beings, the extent to which their basic needs and basic rights are met. *Homo mensura*: man is the measure of all things (Protagoras).[60]

Notes

1 Mathieu Vadepied, dir., *Tirailleurs* (Unité-Korokoro-Gaumont-France 3 Cinema-Mille Soleils-Sypossible Africa, 2022), 109 min.

2 James Smith, "Understanding African Partner Forces' Culture in the Fight against Extremism," in *Extremisms in Africa: Volume 3*, ed. Alain Tschudin et al. (Johannesburg: Bookstorm, 2020), 177–199; Alain Tschudin et al., eds., *Extremisms in Africa: Volume 1* (Johannesburg: Fanele, 2018); *Volume 2* (Johannesburg: Tracey McDonald, 2019); *Volume 3* (Johannesburg: Bookstorm, 2020).

3 See Antonio Guterres, "Secretary-General's Remarks to High-Level Opening of COP27," 27th Conference of the Parties to the United Nations Framework Convention on Climate Change (COP27), Sharm el-Sheikh, Egypt (November 7, 2022), https://www.un.org/sg/en/content/sg/speeches/2022-11-07/secretary-generals-remarks-high-level-opening-of-cop27.

4 Dominic Rohner, "How to Curb Conflict: Policy Lessons from the Economic Literature," in *New Paths and Policies towards Conflict Prevention: Chinese and Swiss Perspectives*, ed. Courtney J. Fung et al. (London: Routledge, 2021), 54–59.

5 See Jean Chrysostome Kiyala and Norman Chivasa, eds., *Climate Change and Socio-political Violence in Sub-Saharan Africa in the Anthropocene: Perspectives on Peace, Security and Sustainable Development*, The Anthropocene: Politik—Economics—Society—Science (APESS 37) (Cham: Springer Nature, 2024).

6 Note however the evolving understanding of weapons of war; for example, the inclusion of rape as a weapon of war following the International Criminal Tribunal for Rwanda (ICTR). See ICTR, The Prosecutor v. Jean-Paul Akayesu, ICTR-96-4-T, Trial Chamber 1, September 2, 1998, available on https://unictr.irmct.org/.

7 Hew Strachan, *The Changing Character of War* (Oxford: Europaeum, 2007), 9–10.

8 Ibid., 31.

9 Karl Marlantes, *What It Is Like to Go to War* (London: Atlantic Books, 2012), 18–19.

10 Grégoire Chamayou, *Drone Theory*, trans. Janet Lloyd (St Ives: Penguin, 2015). 37.

11 Ibid., 45.

12 Kim Hudson and Dan Henk, "Strategising in an Era of Conceptual Change: Security Institutions and the Delivery of 'Security' in the 21st Century," in *On Military Culture: Theory, Practice and African Armed Forces*, ed. Francois Vreÿ, Abel Esterhuyse, and Thomas Mandrup (Cape Town: UCT Press, 2013), 1, 6.

13 Edward Luce, *The Retreat of Western Liberalism* (Washington, DC: Atlantic Monthly Press, 2017).

14 Cedric De Coning, "Adaptive Peacebuilding," *International Affairs* 94, no. 2 (2018): 301–17, https://doi.org/10.1093/ia/iix251; Rachel F. Madenyika and Jason G. Tower, "Introduction: Understanding Conflict Prevention in the Shifting Global Context," in *New Paths and Policies towards Conflict Prevention: Chinese and Swiss Perspectives*, ed. Courtney J. Fung et al. (London: Routledge, 2021), 1–12; Yin He, "A Tale of Two 'Peaces': Liberal Peace, Developmental Peace and Peacebuilding," in Fung et al., *New Paths and Policies*, 47; Björn Gehrmann, "How to Sustain Peace: A Review of the Scholarly Debate," in Fung et al., *New Paths and Policies*, 15; Thania Paffenholz, "Perpetual Peacebuilding: A New Paradigm to Move Beyond the Linearity of Liberal Peacebuilding," *Journal of Intervention and Statebuilding* 15, no. 3 (2021): 367–85, https://doi.org/10.1080/17502977.2021.1925423.

[15] Aristotle, Metaphysics.

[16] Christian P. Peterson et al., "Introduction: The Search for Global Peace: Concepts and Currents in 21st Century Peace History Scholarship," in *The Oxford Handbook of Peace History*, ed. Charles F. Howlett et al. (Oxford: Oxford University Press, 2023), 1.

[17] Oliver Ramsbotham, Tom Woodhouse, and Hugh Miall, *Contemporary Conflict Resolution*, 4th ed. (Cambridge: Polity, 2016), 7–11.

[18] Ibid., xvi.

[19] Ibid.

[20] Francis Fukuyama, *The End of History and the Last Man* (New York: Free Press, 1992); Michal Natorski, "The Liberal Peacebuilding Approach: Debates and Models," in *The European Union Peacebuilding Approach: Governance and Practices of the Instrument for Stability* (Frankfurt: Peace Research Institute Frankfurt, 2011), 3–7, http://www.jstor.org/stable/resrep14480.4.

[21] Tom Woodhouse and Oliver Ramsbotham, "Cosmopolitan Peacekeeping and the Globalization of Security," *International Peacekeeping* 12, no. 2 (2005): 139–56, https://doi.org/10.1080/01439680500066400.

[22] John W. Dietrich, "R2P and Intervention after Libya," *History and Social Sciences Faculty Journal Articles*, Paper 86 (2013), https://digitalcommons.bryant.edu/histss_jou/86.

[23] See Johan Galtung, "Conflict Resolution as Conflict Transformation: The First Law of Thermodynamics Revisited," in *Conflict Transformation*, ed. Kumar Rupesinghe (New York: St. Martin's Press, 1995), 51.

[24] TRANSCEND Mission Statement in Johan Galtung and Dietrich Fischer, *Johan Galtung: Pioneer of Peace Research* (Heidelberg: Springer, 2013), 129.

[25] See Johannes Botes, "Conflict Transformation: A Debate over Semantics or a Crucial Shift in the Theory and Practice of Peace and Conflict Studies," *International Journal of Peace Studies* 8, no. 2 (2003): 1–27; Hugh Miall, Oliver Ramsbotham, and Tom Woodhouse, *Contemporary Conflict Resolution* (Cambridge: Polity Press, 1999); John Paul Lederach, *Preparing for Peace: Conflict Transformation across Cultures* (New York: Syracuse University Press, 1995).

[26] Ramsbotham, Woodhouse, and Miall, *Contemporary Conflict Resolution*, 4th ed., 198.

[27] Geoff Harris. "Armed Conflict in Africa in the 21st Century," in *The Elgar Companion to War, Conflict and Peacebuilding in Africa*, ed. Geoff Harris (Cheltenham: Edward Elgar, 2024), xi.

[28] Nicholas Ross and Mareike Schomerus, "Donor Support to Peace Processes: A Lessons for Peace Literature Review," ODI Working Paper 571 (2020).

[29] See for example, Alain Tschudin, *Strengthening the Capacity of African Countries to Design and Implement Policies That Promote the Nexus between Peace, Humanitarian Work, Development and Human Rights for an Accelerated Implementation of the SDGs* (New York: United Nations Office of the Special Adviser on Africa, 2022).

[30] Jack Mezirow had been influenced, in turn, by Thomas Kuhn's paradigm, Paulo Freire's notion of conscientisation, and Jürgen Habermas's domains of learning.

[31] Jack Mezirow, "Transformative Learning: Theory to Practice," *New Directions for Adult and Continuing Education* 1997, no. 74, (Summer 1997): 5–12.

[32] Jack Mezirow, "Learning to Think Like an Adult," in *The Handbook of Transformative Learning: Theory, Research, and Practice*, ed. Edward W. Taylor and Patricia Cranton (San Francisco: Jossey-Bass, 2012), 73–95.

33 Christopher Blundell, Lee Kar-Tin, and Shaun Nykvist. "Moving beyond Enhancing Pedagogies with Digital Technologies: Frames of Reference, Habits of Mind and Transformative Learning," *Journal of Research on Technology in Education* 52, no. 2 (2020): 178–96, https://doi.org/10.1080/15391523.2020.1726235.

34 Periklis Pavlidis, "Critical Thinking as Dialectics: A Hegelian-Marxist Approach," *Journal for Critical Education Policy Studies* 8, no. 2 (2010): 74–102.

35 Bronfenbrenner was a Russo-American developmental scientist, influenced profoundly by Lev Vygotsky's socio-cultural theory and Kurt Lewin's behaviorism theory. Urie Bronfenbrenner, "Ecological Systems Theory," in *Annals of Child Development* 6 (1989): 187–249; Steven C. Hertler et al., " Urie Bronfenbrenner: Toward an Evolutionary Ecological Systems Theory," in *Life History Evolution: A Biological Meta-Theory for the Social Sciences* (Cham: Palgrave Macmillan, 2018), https://doi.org/10.1007/978-3-319-90125-1_19.

36 Johan Galtung, "Peace Studies and Conflict Resolution: The Need for Transdisciplinarity," *Transcultural Psychiatry* 47, no. 1 (2010): 30.

37 Robert H. Scales, "Clausewitz and World War IV," *Military Psychology* 21, no. sup1 (2009): S23–35, https://doi.org/10.1080/08995600802554573.

38 Ibid.

39 Francois Vreÿ, Abel Esterhuyse, and Thomas Mandrup, eds., *On Military Culture: Theory, Practice and African Armed Forces* (Cape Town: UCT Press, 2013), xv–xvi.

40 Isabelle King, "How France Failed Mali: The End of Operation Barkhane," *The Harvard International Review*, January 2023, https://hir.harvard.edu/how-france-failed-mali-the-end-of-operation-barkhane/; Ikechukwu Uzoma, "In Shifting US Ties with Niger and Africa, Focus on Human Rights and Democracy to Strengthen Partnerships," Just Security, April 8, 2024, https://www.justsecurity.org/94380/us-niger-coup-human-rights-democracy/; King, "How France Failed Mali."

41 Paul Stronski, "Russia's Growing Footprint in Africa's Sahel Region," Carnegie Endowment for International Peace, February 28, 2023, https://carnegieendowment.org/2023/02/28/russia-s-growing-footprint-in-africa-s-sahel-region-pub-89135.

42 Riza Kumar, "The Wagner Group in the Central Sahel: Decolonization or Destabilization?," *The Counter Extremism Project*, webinar, February 28, 2024, https://www.counterextremism.com/video/cep-webinar-violent-extremism-and-terrorism-sahel-riza-kumar.

43 Catherine Nzuki, "The Cost of Paternalism: Sahelian Countries Push Back on the West," Centre for Strategic and International Studies (CSIS), March 21, 2024, https://www.csis.org/analysis/cost-paternalism-sahelian-countries-push-back-west.

44 Ibid.

45 Ibid.

46 Ibid.

47 C. Chen and Y. Tomes, "Culture and Adolescent Development," *Online Readings in Psychology and Culture* 6 (2006): 4.

48 Arthur F. Lykke Jr., "Defining Military Strategy," *Military Review* 69, no. 5 (May 1989): 2–8.

49 Jorden de Haan and Aly Diarra, "Building Peace by Formalizing Gold Mining in the Central Sahel," Africa Up Close (blog), Wilson Center, May 25, 2023, https://www.wilsoncenter.org/blog-post/guest-contributor-building-peace-by-formalizing-gold-mining-in-the-central-sahel.

50 "Addressing Conflict-Related Sexual Violence: An Analytical Inventory of Peacekeeping Practice," UNIFEM, United Nations Department of Peacekeeping Operations, UN Action against Sexual Violence in Conflict, 2010, https://www.unwomen.org/sites/default/files/Headquarters/Attachments/Sections/Library/Publications/2012/10/WPSsourcebook-04D-AddressingSexualViolence-en.pdf.

51 "Pre-Deployment Training," United Nations Peacekeeping Resource Hub, https://peacekeepingresourcehub.un.org/en/training/pre-deployment.

52 Kit Klarenberg, "Exercise Flintlock: US Military Training in Africa Backfires," Al Mayadeen, August 2, 2023, https://english.almayadeen.net/articles/analysis/exercise-flintlock:-us-military-training-in-africa-backfires.

53 Montgomery McFate, "The Military Utility of Understanding Adversary Culture," *Joint Force Quarterly*, no. 38 (2005): 42–48.

54 Signe Marie Cold-Ravnkilde and Boubacar Ba, "Unpacking 'New Climate Wars': Actors and Drivers of Conflict in the Sahel," Danish Institute for International Studies (DIIS), 2022, https://pure.diis.dk/ws/files/5417749/Actors_and_drivers_conflict_Sahel_DIIS_Report_2022_04.pdf.

55 Serge Michailof, "The Social and Economic Roots of The War in The Sahel," WillAgri, 2020, https://www.willagri.com/wp-content/uploads/2020/02/Dossier-Willagri-03-20-EN-1.pdf.

56 Matthew Steadman, "Crisis in the Sahel: Why Tackling Corruption in Defence and Security Is Essential to Securing Peace," Transparency International, February 19, 2020, https://ti-defence.org/sahel-conflict-boko-haram-mali-niger-burkina-faso-defence-corruption.

57 Hudson and Henk, "Strategising in an Era of Conceptual Change," 16.

58 Ibid., 19.

59 Peter Knoope, "Between Rhetoric and Reality: Strategic Approaches to Counter-Terrorism," in *Extremisms in Africa: Volume 1*, ed. Alain Tschudin et al. (Johannesburg: Fanele, 2018), 9–35; Madenyika and Tower, "Introduction," 3.

60 Galtung, "Peace Studies and Conflict Resolution," 140.

UNDERSTANDING THE INDIRECT STRATEGY MOMENT IN GLOBAL AFFAIRS

Kumar Ramakrishna

S. Rajaratnam School of International Studies, Nanyang Technological University

ABSTRACT

This article argues that policymakers need to better grasp what can best be understood as the "indirect strategy moment" in global affairs. It explains what is meant by indirect strategy in the classical strategic thought, before analyzing how indirect strategy has already been applied in the post-Cold War era. The article will then illustrate how indirect strategy is being applied in the cyber, social media, and telecommunications domains, before arguing that adopting "indirect strategy lenses" appears to be rather important in order to better frame current and ongoing geostrategic developments across a range of issues and domains. A recurring theme is that in this indirect strategy moment, the line between peace and war has been increasingly blurred.

Kumar Ramakrishna is a professor of National Security Studies, the Provost's Chair in National Security Studies, and Dean of the S. Rajaratnam School of International Studies, Nanyang Technological University, Singapore. This article represents a substantive reconceptualization and reworking of the author's "Enter the Age of Csywar: Some Reflections on an Emergent Trend," New England Journal of Public Policy 34, no. 2 (2022): Article 5, https://scholarworks.umb.edu/nejpp/vol34/iss2/5.

More than two years after the Russian invasion of Ukraine in February 2022, it seems that the prospect of an end to the fighting remains as dim as ever. More than that, the threat of escalation through the use of nuclear weapons has, worryingly, also emerged.[1] That being said, it is important to note that the current conflagration is somewhat an anomaly in the context of what had transpired over the past decade. Ever since the initial intervention in eastern Ukraine in March 2014 by Russian troops in unmarked uniforms—the so-called "little green men"[2]—most analysts have argued that low-key "hybrid conflict" has been the norm in the long standoff between Moscow and Kyiv. Hybrid conflict broadly refers to the methods and tools used by individual state or non-state actors to pursue their objectives, spanning the conflict continuum from disinformation to cyber war, energy supply disruption, and traditional warfare.[3] Moscow had in fact been engaging in hybrid conflict with Ukraine since the 2014 intervention.[4]

Thus far, it seems clear that Russian president Vladimir Putin's decision to switch to an outright "special military operation" in February 2022 has not yielded the desired outcome of a Ukrainian military and political capitulation. Instead US intelligence assessments in late 2023 suggested that Russia had "lost a staggering 87 percent of the total number of active-duty ground troops it had" before the invasion, as well as "two-thirds of its pre-invasion tanks."[5] Against such a backdrop, it is not far-fetched to imagine that a ceasefire between Kyiv and Moscow might eventually ensue. Putin may then revert to his previous and relatively far more cost-effective hybrid warfare playbook as the main means to secure his geopolitical objectives vis-à-vis Kyiv.[6] In fact, while NATO governments warned in January 2024 of a possible Russian military attack in five to eight years, in the lead up to such an outcome, NATO remains fully cognizant that the Russian Federation is unlikely to shy away from targeting NATO member states with "sophisticated hybrid strategies, including political interference, malicious cyber activities, economic pressure and coercion, subversion, aggression and annexation" as well as "coercive military posture and rhetoric."[7] Hybrid warfare thus remains highly relevant. More fundamentally, it points to the importance of indirect strategy in global geostrategic competition.

This article develops its argument in the following fashion. It will first briefly explain what is meant by "indirect strategy" in the classical strategic thought. This will be followed by an analysis of how indirect strategy has already been applied in the post-Cold War era. The article will then further examine how indirect strategy has been applied in the cyber, social media, and telecommunications domains, before ending off with a concise analysis as to why adopting "indirect strategy lenses" appears to be rather important in order to better frame current and ongoing geostrategic developments across a range of issues and domains, from economic and technological de-risking to the preservation of domestic socio-political cohesion in the face of foreign influence campaigns by hostile state actors. A recurring theme, as we shall see, is that in this indirect strategy moment, the line between peace and war has been increasingly blurred.

Indirect Strategy Explained

In his classic *Introduction to Strategy* (1963), the French military strategist Andre Beaufre (1902–1975) argued that in the direct mode of warfare, military force plays the decisive role; in the indirect mode, military force plays a secondary role. The theory and practice of indirect strategy is not new. The fifth-century BCE Chinese strategist Sun Tzu emphasized the importance of avoiding the enemy's strengths and attacking his weaknesses instead.[8] The best strategy, according to Sun Tzu, was to "win without fighting."[9] In other words, the ability of a state to impose its will on the adversary without relying excessively on military power represented the "acme of skill."[10] This basic concept of avoiding adversary strength and attacking his weakness represents the essence of indirect strategy.

The US military acronym DIME—diplomatic, informational, military, and economic elements of state power—helps illustrate the point.[11] If a state decides upon a direct application of DIME, then the military instrument would be preponderant, with the other instruments in support. Conversely, in an indirect application of DIME, the non-kinetic instruments— diplomatic, economic, and informational—would be preponderant in the total strategic response, with the military instrument playing a calibrated supporting role.

Indirect Strategy in the Post-Cold War Era

Beaufre observed that in the Cold War (1945–1990) environment of mutual nuclear deterrence between the superpowers, indirect strategy was very important and "not the direct strategy's adoption of material force."[12] In the post-Cold War era, the continuing imperative to avoid outright confrontation between nuclear-capable great powers, and the understandable reluctance of major peer-competitors of the US to directly engage the latter militarily on the conventional front, has resulted in strategic innovation that prioritizes indirect strategy. Hence, in his book *Battlegrounds,* H. R. McMaster argues that Russia has—since the breakup of the Soviet Union—engaged in so-called hybrid "new-generation warfare" that seeks to avoid direct military confrontation with the West, seeking instead to "disrupt, divide and weaken societies" regarded as competitors.[13] In essence, Russian strategists, declaring that the very "rules of war" have evolved, noted that nonmilitary instruments of achieving political and strategic objectives have grown and, in many cases, have exceeded military force in their effectiveness.[14] Chinese military strategists have similarly argued that modern warfare has evolved and now involves "using all means, including armed force or non-armed force, military and non-military, and lethal and non-lethal means to compel the enemy to accept one's interests," and that the many "new battlefields" could include environmental, financial, trade, cultural and legal forms of warfare.[15] Russian and Chinese thinking share the core idea of avoiding Western military strengths and attacking its weaknesses—the essence of indirect strategy.

Indirect Strategy Today

At the current time, indirect strategy is being applied in the cyber, social media, and telecommunications domains, among others.

Cyber Domain

John Carlin in *Dawn of the Code War* observes that the expansion of internet connectivity has rendered national critical infrastructure—water, electricity, communications, and banking—as well as our private information more vulnerable.[16] One result: hostile state actors could mount devastating cyberattacks on a target state's vulnerable, digitally interconnected homeland and cripple it, while bypassing the massed strength of the latter's conventional armed forces. For instance, when Russian forces invaded the Republic of Georgia in 2008, Georgian websites were hit by botnet-mounted distributed denial-of-service (DDoS) attacks in one of the earliest examples of hybrid warfare.[17] This massive cyberattack not only disrupted key government websites, it deprived the Georgian authorities of the ability to communicate with the outside world.[18] To be sure, cyberattacks have been used by all sides for years now. For instance, in December 2023, Iran's oil minister blamed "outside interference" for disrupting seventy percent of the country's approximately 33,000 gas stations nationwide. The minister added that while 1,650 stations remained operational, others were "forced to operate their pumps manually."[19] An Israel-linked hacker collective called Predatory Sparrow claimed responsibility for the cyberattack, which was in retaliation for Iranian support of Hamas and other militant groups in the context of the current Israel-Hamas war in Gaza following the October 7, 2023 Hamas mass-casualty terror attacks in Israel.[20]

Social Media Space

Meanwhile, as Jacob Helberg asserts in *The Wires of War*, another way that a hostile state may seek to sidestep the military forces of a target state and target the latter's weaker spots, is via intervening in the latter's national social media space. Helberg calls this the "front-end battle," whereby foreign governments attempt to "shape what we think and feel by manipulating the information we consume."[21] While during the Cold War both the United States and the Soviet Union attempted to use media ranging from leaflets to radio broadcasts to shape perceptions in each other's geographical spheres of influence, as Helberg points out, social media has "dramatically transformed the front-end war," deluging audiences with a flood of information, making the distinction between truth and falsehood "infinitely harder to assess."[22] For their part, Peter W. Singer and Emerson T. Brooking likewise warn in their book *LikeWar* that a hostile state, by learning how to manipulate opinion within the target state, can foster "political and social polarization" in the latter—again without a shot being fired—in other words, a classic indirect strategic move.[23] In fact Singer and Josh Baughman argue that the Chinese People's Liberation Army regards so-called "cognitive warfare" to be "on par with the other domains of warfare like air, sea, and space," and Chinese planners believe this indirect strategic maneuver to be the "key to victory—particularly victory without war."[24] They point to Chinese influence operations increasingly using AI where machine learning is employed to "mine user emotions and prejudices to screen and target the most susceptible audiences, and then quickly and intensively 'shoot' customized 'spiritual ammunition' to the target group."[25] The overall aim is to is to weaken the target state indirectly by exploiting its social media space to "'fuel the flames' of existing biases and manipulate emotional psychology to influence and deepen a desired narrative" that serves the interests of the hostile, intervening state.[26] As in the cyber domain, deliberate influence operations that seek to manipulate the national social media space of a target state is increasingly commonplace. For instance, it is now known that former

US president Donald Trump directed the Central Intelligence Agency to "launch a clandestine campaign on Chinese social media" led by a "small team of operatives who used bogus internet identities to spread negative narratives" about Beijing while deliberately "leaking disparaging intelligence to overseas news outlets."[27]

Telecommunications Domain

One of the ongoing criticisms of the widely popular social media app TikTok is that under Chinese national security laws, Chinese big tech firms like ByteDance, which owns TikTok, are obligated to, if so required, ensure that user data—even that of citizens of other countries—is made available to Beijing, despite privacy concerns.[28] For instance, it was found out that China-based employees of ByteDance have been able to repeatedly access private data about US TikTok users, prompting former president Trump to threaten to ban the app in the United States.[29] Ultimately, despite TikTok's public assurances that it is making the effort to "cordon off access to the most sensitive details about Americans that exist on TikTok's servers," it has been acknowledged that in the final analysis, it's their system, as the underlying telecommunications architecture is built in China.[30] In a wider sense, it is notable that China has also begun to seek greater influence over the future versions of the internet, with a view to shaping its development as a means of commerce, communications, and even conflict.[31] This is highly significant from an indirect strategy vantage point, because as Helberg argues pithily, by capturing control of the core layer of the Internet, "you control everything" and can therefore more readily bypass the massed armed strength of the target state, and instead, attack its societal soft underbelly.[32]

In this respect, China's not often obvious quest to dominate the backend architecture of the internet is noteworthy. By 2020, the leading telecommunications firm Huawei dominated about 30 percent of the global market share in telecommunications equipment, while making significant progress toward the goal of capturing the emerging market in fifth-generation communications networks.[33] These networks, known as 5G, which are a hundred times faster than 4G in speed of information transfer, are potentially transformative in the context of the rapidly emerging global internet of things—"the vaguely defined network of millions of internet-linked devices."[34] From an indirect strategic perspective, dominating the lucrative 5G market confers huge advantages: a hostile-state linked telecommunications firm that builds and runs a nation's 5G network will have little trouble, according to Robert Spalding, "stealing and mining all the data on that network: all the academic papers and research, all engineering and business plans, all the photos, emails, and text messages."[35] Additionally, if needed, a hostile state could, through such indirect control of a target state's 5G network, potentially not merely access, but delete and manipulate data as well.[36] More ominously, some analysts warn that in a conflict, a hostile state could even "weaponize" the 5G technology managed by an affiliated network by, for instance, directing self-driving cars into crowds or flying drones into the flight path of commercial aircraft.[37]

That being said, a sense of perspective is in order, as not all countries are ready for the mass adoption of 5G technology. For instance, analysts argue that Southeast Asia is not likely to become an important global market for 5G in the short to medium term.[38] Moreover, while some states like Malaysia allowed Huawei to participate in its 5G rollout, Vietnam opted to develop its own 5G technology, and Singapore granted 5G contracts to Nokia and Ericsson. While Indonesia has been open to buying Chinese telecom equipment, partly due to its relatively low cost and support for capability development, Indonesian cybersecurity officials are aware of the possible risks associated with its use."[39] The upshot of the preceding analysis of indirect strategy in the strategic telecommunications domain is simple. Data, as Helberg argues, can arguably be seen as the "new oil" and information the "most contested geopolitical resource" sought after by many states.[40] He states that "the strategic significance of data and information is increasingly stretching beyond the realm of intelligence collection and into the realm of political influence and control."[41]

At a more fundamental level, this discussion of indirect strategy as operationalized in the cyber, social media, and telecommunications spheres, shows one way that the line between war and peace in contemporary warfare is increasingly blurred.[42]

Adopting Analytical Lenses Appropriate for Navigating the Indirect Strategy Moment in Global Affairs

A key implication of the foregoing analysis is that adopting "indirect strategy lenses" appears to be rather important in order to frame current and ongoing geostrategic developments across a range of issues and domains.

De-risking Viewed Through an Indirect Strategy Lens

A first set of lenses relates to the increasingly pertinent issue of economic and security *de-coupling* or *de-risking*. Simply put, de-coupling, the older term, suggests a "radical separation," while de-risking, which was coined in the financial sector, essentially means "curbing risks while avoiding a clean break."[43] In the context of US-China geopolitical competition, practitioners and analysts have recently argued that full de-coupling from China would be highly impractical, as it is the world's largest manufacturer of goods and the biggest trading partner of a majority of countries. Beijing would thus have the edge if other countries were forced to pick sides. In any case, current economic interlinkages between the US and China may actually serve as a check on Chinese global unilateralism. Hence, the more modest notion of selective de-risking has been increasingly mooted.[44] From my perspective, quite apart from the arguments for economic, technological, and security self-reliance, de-risking is arguably also another way in which countries could seek to indirectly weaken the national capabilities and potentials of peer-competitors without recourse to costly armed conflict. This can be illustrated in the case of semiconductors and rare earth metals.

Semiconductors

Much has been made of US-Chinese strategic competition for control of the manufacturing supply chains for semiconductors and high-performing microchips that are critical for everything from artificial intelligence to cell phones.[45] From an indirect strategy perspective, a state that is able to dominate the global supply chain for such critical chips would be able to indirectly weaken a peer-competitor's national capabilities. This is likely one factor why in mid-2023, at the urging of the US, the Netherlands—where ASML, a leading manufacturer of chipmaking machinery resides—imposed export restrictions on such technology, a move that analysts argue targets China.[46] ASML produces equipment that is used by the Taiwan Semiconductor Manufacturing Company Limited (TSMC),[47] the Taiwanese firm that produces an estimated 90 percent of the world's highly advanced semiconductors and supplies global technology giants like Apple and Nvidia. Significantly, TSMC has also invested in a second semiconductor plant in the US state of Arizona, in addition to one in Japan under its subsidiary the Japan Advanced Semiconductor Manufacturing, Inc. (JASM).[48] In addition, the US passed the CHIPS and Science Act in August 2022, which authorizes fifty-two billion USD to boost domestic semiconductor manufacturing.[49] The bottom line? Washington appears to be coordinating with its allies and partners to ensure that China—whose own semiconductor industry is significantly less advanced—would be unable to dominate this vital global industry.[50]

Rare Earth Metals

Indirect strategy lenses are also helpful in analyzing developments in the equally important domain of rare earth metals. If China is lagging behind in semiconductor manufacturing, it is a different story in the rare earth metals case. To illustrate, China produces 80 percent of the world's gallium and 60 percent of germanium, which are needed to produce chips and significantly, have military applications.[51] In July 2023, in response to the imposition of chip technology export restrictions by the US, Japan, and the Netherlands, Beijing announced curbs on the export of gallium and germanium. As one analyst argued, China's posture was a case of "if you won't give us chips, we won't give you the materials to make those chips."[52] To be sure, China "accounts for 63 percent of the world's rare earth mining, 85 percent of rare earth processing, and 92 percent of rare earth magnet production."[53] Such rare earth alloys and magnets that China produces are crucial components in firearms, missiles, radars, and stealth aircraft.[54] US military night vision goggles also require Chinese specialty metals as a critical component.[55] Furthermore, China remains the "only country in the world that's developed the capacity to cover the entire value chain of 17 rare earth elements" and has "developed the advantages in not just technology, but also waste management."[56] Chinese technical advantages in and ensuing domination of the global supply chain for rare earth metals, in short, is another illustration of how a state could indirectly weaken the national capabilities of its peer-competitors without recourse to costly armed conflict. In sum, a state that dominates strategically critical supply chains and resources—while systematically and deliberately denying such advantages to peer-competitor states—can gradually impose its geopolitical will and undermine its adversaries without the need for direct military confrontation, another example of the indirect strategic emphasis on avoiding adversary strength and targeting its weaknesses instead.

Indirect Strategy Across the Hybrid Conflict Spectrum

It is important to reiterate the earlier point that indirect strategy lenses are important if we are to make sense of how the line between peace and war has increasingly been blurred. Examples abound, if one were to just observe carefully. For example, experts allege that Chinese maritime vessels have been deliberately cutting underwater internet cables linking the Matsu islands to the main island of Taiwan, to compromise the latter's internal communications connectivity—a crucial requirement for the island's national security, and a shrewd example of a hybrid, indirect approach.[57] As another example, Russia, the world's biggest wheat exporter, could weaponize food exports to undermine its wheat-dependent strategic competitors if it should decide to.[58] Once again: the essence of indirect strategy is to avoid adversary strength and target his weaknesses instead.

In the case of Southeast Asia, moreover, Chinese state-backed hackers have been reported to be "incredibly active" in targeting government and military targets in member states of the Association of Southeast Asian Nations (ASEAN), and have "quietly compromised" them by exfiltrating sensitive information.[59] It was reported that in 2023 that a Chinese hacker collective called Stately Taurus "compromised a Philippine government agency for five days," around the same time as "clashes between the two countries' ships in the South China Sea."[60] That the Philippines has a "soft underbelly" in its cyber sector is attested to by the fact that more than 60,000 user accounts were compromised in the third quarter of 2023, meaning that the Philippines was "among the world's thirty most-attacked countries."[61] Philippine officials have bemoaned the fact that they lack sufficient numbers of "cyber warriors" to shore up this vulnerable sector, thereby inviting indirect approaches by hostile state actors that seek to avoiding Manila's military strengths and to exploit its cyber weaknesses instead.[62]

It cannot be overstated that indirect strategy lenses are vitally useful in helping states anticipate how hostile actors could seek to undermine them from within by disrupting social and political cohesion. Observers have noted that Russian state-backed social media manipulation of socio-political fault-lines within neighboring states have included the exploitation of ethnic tensions and historical revisionism in Estonia, culture and religion in Georgia, political polarization in Poland, and anti-migrant sentiment in the Czech Republic.[63] In 2023, the New Zealand government warned publicly about the "targeting" of its "diverse ethnic Chinese communities by groups and individuals linked to China's intelligence arm."[64] Incidentally, Singapore, where the current writer hails from, shares with New Zealand concerns about foreign influence operations. It is no secret that militarily the well-trained and well-equipped Singapore Armed Forces have a well-established reputation as a potent deterrent against direct military aggression.[65] Hence, in this indirect strategy moment, potential adversaries would likely explore more cost-effective, indirect, hybrid approaches to shrewdly and subtly impose their will upon globalized, multicultural states like Singapore, even during peacetime. One way would certainly be through foreign influence operations aimed at spreading disinformation, false narratives, and outright falsehoods to undermine trust between Singaporeans and their government.

It is little wonder that the Singaporean government in recent years has tried to shore up domestic socio-political cohesion through legislation such as the Protection from Online Falsehoods and Manipulation Act 2019 (POFMA). Passed in June 2019, POFMA "helps protect the Singapore public against online harm by countering the proliferation of online falsehoods," through "correction directions which require recipients to insert a notice against the original post, with a link to the Government's clarification."[66] The idea is that the "clarification sets out the falsehoods and facts for the public to examine, without the original post being removed," so that readers "can read both the original post and the facts, and decide for themselves what is the truth."[67] More recently, under the newer Foreign Interference (Countermeasures) Act 2021 (FICA), Singaporean individuals delivering speeches, interviews, or written articles that promote the political interests of a foreign entity would be legally required to "make yearly disclosures to the authorities of political donations of $10,000 or more that he has received and accepted, and declare his foreign affiliations and any migration benefits."[68] The rationale behind the relatively calibrated FICA law is to send the signal that Singapore remains open to foreign business—but not foreign interference.[69]

Concluding Observations

Singapore is world-renowned for being a highly cosmopolitan, religiously and culturally diverse, and stable society.[70] Yet a scan of the angry statements circulated on social media platforms frequented by Singaporeans in the wake of the outbreak of the highly destructive Israel-Hamas conflict in Gaza, suggests that domestic socio-political fault-lines remain a potential weakness that hostile state actors or even transnational terrorist groups could exploit via indirect means, through orchestrated social media campaigns.[71] This is precisely why analyst Ajit Mann is correct in reminding us more generally that "dominating the narrative space should be a national security priority," as that is where "non-state actors fight best" and "foreign governments have proven effective in waging war against us without implementing kinetic force."[72]

In the final analysis, in this indirect strategy moment in global affairs, states need to conceive of far more than merely kinetic threats. As this article has suggested, while some state actors may prioritize armed force to attain their objectives—such as

Russia in the case of Ukraine since February 2022—more often than not, the indirect strategic approach of avoiding target state strength and attacking its weaknesses is increasingly being adopted, whether one thinks about Russian new-generation warfare or the Chinese "three warfares"—public opinion warfare, psychological warfare, and legal warfare.[73] In fact, it is clear that many other states, including the US, have become more aware of the indirect strategic approach and have at times adopted it themselves, ranging from influence operations to economic, technological de-risking aimed at undermining the longer-term national capabilities of peer-competitors. In this era of hybrid conflict and indirect strategy, as Sean McFate argues, there is increasingly "no such thing as war or peace – both co-exist, always."[74] It thus behooves national security practitioners, analysts and even the general public, to better grasp how their nation-states could be shrewdly undermined by subtle, not immediately obvious, non-kinetic, indirect strategic approaches. In this indirect strategy moment in global affairs, in short, as the old saying goes: "You may not be interested in war, but war is interested in you."[75]

Notes

1 Guy Faulconbridge and Lidia Kelly, "Putin Warns the West: Russia Is Ready for Nuclear War," *Reuters*, March 14, 2024, https://www.reuters.com/world/europe/putin-says-russia-ready-nuclear-war-not-everything-rushing-it-2024-03-13/.

2 Vitaly Shevchenko, "'Little Green Men' or 'Russian Invaders'?," *BBC News*, March 11, 2024, https://www.bbc.com/news/world-europe-26532154.

3 Tarik Solmaz, "'Hybrid Warfare': One Word, Many Meanings," *Small Wars Journal*, February 25, 2022, https://smallwarsjournal.com/jrnl/art/hybrid-warfare-one-term-many-meanings.

4 David Kilcullen, "Russia's War in Ukraine Is Complex and Probably Underway," *UNSW Newsroom*, February 4, 2022, https://www.unsw.edu.au/newsroom/news/2022/02/russia-s-war-in-the-ukraine-is-complex-and-probably-already-unde.

5 Katie Bo Lillis, "Russia Has Lost 87% of Troops It Had Prior to Start of Ukraine War, according to US Intelligence Assessment," *CNN*, December 13, 2023, https://amp-cnn-com.cdn.ampproject.org/c/s/amp.cnn.com/cnn/2023/12/12/politics/russia-troop-losses-us-intelligence-assessment/index.html.

6 Mason Clark, "Russian Hybrid Warfare," *Institute for the Study of War*, September 2020, https://www.understandingwar.org/report/russian-hybrid-warfare.

7 Nicholas Camut, "Putin Could Attack NATO in '5 to 8 Years,' German Defense Minister Warns," *Politico*, January 19, 2024, https://www.politico.eu/article/vladimir-putin-russia-germany-boris-pistorius-nato; "Countering Hybrid Threats," *North Atlantic Treaty Organization*, March 7, 2024, https://www.nato.int/cps/en/natohq/topics_156338.htm.

8   Mark R. McNeilly, *Sun Tzu and the Art of Modern Warfare* (New York: Oxford University Press, 2015).

9   Ibid.

10 "Sun Tzu, c. 400–320 BC, Chinese General and Military Theorist," in *Oxford Essential Quotations*, 5th ed., ed. Susan Ratcliffe (New York: Oxford University Press, 2017), https://www.oxfordreference.com/display/10.1093/acref/9780191866692.001.0001/q-oro-ed6-00010536;jsessionid=A8B662CCA1AC9B0F64BD7BADAD9E5E02.

11 Steven Aftergood, "Strategy: Directing the Instruments of National Power," *Federation of American Scientists*, April 30, 2018, https://fas.org/publication/strategy-jcs/.

12 Tim Kumpe, "Andre Beaufre in Contemporary Chinese Strategic Thinking," *Military Strategy Magazine* 5, no. 2 (Spring 2016), https://www.militarystrategymagazine.com/article/andre-beaufre-in-contemporary-chinese-strategic-thinking/.

13 H. R. McMaster, *Battlegrounds: The Fight to Defend the Free World* (New York: Harper, 2020), 40–41.

14 Molly K. McKew, "The Gerasimov Doctrine: It's Russia's New Chaos Doctrine of Political Warfare. And It's Probably Being Used on You," *Politico*, September/October 2017, https://www.politico.com/magazine/story/2017/09/05/gerasimov-doctrine-russia-foreign-policy-215538/.

15 David Barno and Nora Bensahel, "A New Generation of Unrestricted Warfare," *War on the Rocks*, April 19, 2016, https://warontherocks.com/2016/04/a-new-generation-of-unrestricted-warfare/.

16 John P. Carlin, with Garrett M. Graff, *Dawn of the Code War: America's Battle against Russia, China and the Rising Global Cyber Threat* (New York: Public Affairs, 2018), 42.

17 Ibid., 158.

18 Nina Jankowicz, *How to Lose the Information War: Russia, Fake News, and the Future of Conflict* (London: I. B. Tauris, 2020), 60–61.

19 Daryna Antoniuk, "Iran Confirms Nationwide Cyberattack on Gas Stations," *The Record*, December 19, 2023, https://therecord.media/iran-cyberattack-gas-stations-israel.

20 Ibid.

21 Jacob Helberg, *The Wires of War: Technology and the Global Struggle for Power* (New York: Avid Reader Press, 2021), 52.

22 Ibid., 52–53.

23 P. W. Singer and Emerson T. Brooking, *LikeWar: The Weaponization of Social Media* (New York: Houghton Mifflin Harcourt, 2018), 126–27.

24 Josh Baughman and Peter W. Singer, "China's Social-Media Attacks Are Part of a Larger 'Cognitive Warfare' Campaign," *Defense One*, October 17, 2023, https://www.defenseone.com/ideas/2023/10/chinas-social-media-attacks-are-part-larger-cognitive-warfare-campaign/391255/?oref=defense_one_breaking_nl.

25 Ibid.

26 Ibid.

27 "Trump Launched Covert Influence Operation against China," *CNA*, March 15, 2024, https://www.channelnewsasia.com/world/former-us-president-donald-trump-launched-covert-cia-influence-operation-against-china-4197016.

28 Emily Baker-White, "Leaked Audio from 80 Internal TikTok Meetings Shows That US User Data Has Been Repeatedly Accessed from China," *BuzzFeed News*, June 18, 2022, https://www.buzzfeednews.com/article/emilybakerwhite/tiktok-tapes-us-user-data-china-bytedance-access.

29 Ibid.

30 Ibid.

31 Baughman and Singer, "China's Social-Media Attacks."

32 Helberg, *Wires of War*, 145.

33 McMaster, *Battlegrounds*, 141.

34 Bill Geertz, *Deceiving the Sky: Inside Communist China's Drive for Global Supremacy* (New York: Encounter Books, 2019), 167.

35 Robert Spalding, with Seth Kaufman, *Stealth War: How China Took Over While America's Elite Slept* (New York: Portfolio/Penguin, 2019), 114.

36 Helberg, *Wires of War*, 155.

37 Spalding, *Stealth War*, 114.

38 Manoj Harjani and Gatra Priyandita, "What's Next for 5G in Southeast Asia?," *The Strategist*, October 30, 2023, https://www.aspistrategist.org.au/whats-next-for-5g-in-southeast-asia/.

39 Ibid.

40 Helberg, *Wires of War*, 157.

41 Ibid.

42 Christopher Woody, "NATO's Top Officer Says We're Living with 'a More Blurred Line between Peace and War'—Thanks to New Russian Tactics," *Business Insider*, September 19, 2018, https://www.businessinsider.com/nato-jens-stoltentberg-world-faces-blurred-line-between-peace-and-war-2018-9.

43 Agathe Demarais, "What Does 'De-Risking' Actually Mean?," *Foreign Policy*, August 23, 2023, https://foreignpolicy.com/2023/08/23/derisking-us-china-biden-decoupling-technology-supply-chains-semiconductors-chips-ira-trade/.

44 Ibid.

45 Helberg, *Wires of War*, 239-–240.

46 Arjun Kharpal, "Netherlands, Home to a Critical Chip Firm, Follows U.S. with Export Curbs on Semiconductor Tools," *CNBC*, June 30, 2023, https://www.cnbc.com/2023/06/30/netherlands-follows-us-with-semiconductor-export-restrictions-.html.

47 Ibid.

48 Diksha Madhok, "World's Largest Chipmaker TSMC to Build a Second Factory in Japan," *CNN*, February 7, 2024, https://edition.cnn.com/2024/02/07/tech/tsmc-taiwan-japan-second-factory-intl-hnk/index.html.

49 Makena Kelly, "Biden Signs $280 Billion CHIPS and Science Act," *The Verge*, August 9, 2022, https://www.theverge.com/2022/8/9/23298147/biden-chips-act-semiconductors-subsidies-ohio-arizona-plant-china.

50 Gregory C. Allen and Emily Benson, "Clues to the U.S.-Dutch-Japanese Semiconductor Export Controls Deal Are Hiding in Plain Sight," *Center for Strategic and International Studies*, March 1, 2023, https://www.csis.org/analysis/clues-us-dutch-japanese-semiconductor-export-controls-deal-are-hiding-plain-sight.

51 Annabelle Liang and Nick Marsh, "Gallium and Germanium: What China's New Move in Microchip War Means for the World," *BBC News*, July 31, 2023, https://bbc.com/news/business-66118831.

52 Ibid.

53 Lara Seligman, "China Dominates the Rare Earths Market. This U.S. Mine Is Trying to Change That," *Politico*, December 14, 2022, https://www.politico.com/news/magazine/2022/12/14/rare-earth-mines-00071102.

54 Ibid.

55 Helberg, *Wires of War*, 98.

56 Derrick A. Paulo, Tang Hui Huan, Allister D'Souza, and Chubby Jayaram Singh, "China Is King of These Critical Metals. The Battle over Their Supply Has Ensnared Southeast Asia," *CNA*, November 19, 2023, https://www.channelnewsasia.com/cna-insider/china-critical-metals-rare-earths-southeast-asia-ev-battery-3928246.

57 "Chinese Ships Cut Internet of Taiwan's Outlying Islands," *CNA*, March 8, 2023, https://www.channelnewsasia.com/asia/taiwan-china-ships-cut-internet-outlying-islands-3333376.

58 David Fickling, "Russia Can Turn Food into a Weapon in Future Crises," *The Print*, March 1, 2022, https://theprint.in/opinion/russia-can-turn-food-into-a-weapon-in-future-crises/852952/.

59 Matt Burgess, "China Is Relentlessly Hacking Its Neighbors," *Wired,* February 28, 2023, https://www.wired.com/story/china-hack-emails-asean-southeast-asia/.

60 "Philippines Turns to Hackers for Help as US Warns of China Cyberthreat," *Straits Times*, January 8, 2024, https://www.straitstimes.com/asia/se-asia/philippines-turns-to-hackers-for-help-as-us-warns-of-china-cyber-threat.

61 Ibid.

62 Ibid.

63 Jankowicz, *How to Lose the Information War*, 198.

64 "China Opposes New Zealand's Accusations of Foreign Interference," *CNA*, August 11, 2023, https://www.channelnewsasia.com/world/china-opposes-new-zealand-accusations-foreign-interference-3693411.

65 Samuel Chan, "Developing Singapore's Next-Generation Military," *East Asia Forum*, January 2, 2021, https://eastasiaforum.org/2021/01/02/developing-singapores-next-generation-military/.

66 "POFMA Office," March 27, 2022, https://www.pofmaoffice.gov.sg/.

67 Ibid.

68 Jean Iau, "Line Crossed under Foreign Interference Law When People Promote Foreign Political Interests: Experts," *Straits Times*, February 4, 2024, https://www.straitstimes.com/singapore/line-crossed-under-foreign-interference-law-when-people-promote-foreign-political-interests-experts.

69 Ibid.

70 "Building a Multicultural Singapore," *SG101*, n.d. https://www.sg101.gov.sg/social-national-identity/multicultural/. This is an official Singapore government agency website.

71 Mathew Mathews and Hazim Zulfadhli, "In Discussing Israel-Hamas Conflict in Singapore, Upholding Social Harmony Is Key," *Today*, March 6, 2024, https://www.todayonline.com/commentary/commentary-discussing-israel-hamas-conflict-singapore-upholding-social-harmony-key-2376716.

72 Ajit Mann, "How We Must Battle Weaponized Narrative Wielded by Our Enemies," *Homeland Security Today*, November 23, 2020, https://www.hstoday.us/subject-matter-areas/counterterrorism/how-we-must-battle-weaponized-narrative-wielded-by-our-adversaries/.

73 Peter Mattis, "China's 'Three Warfares' in Perspective," *War on the Rocks*, January 30, 2018, https://warontherocks.com/2018/01/chinas-three-warfares-perspective/.

74 P. K. Mallick, "Sneaky Wars," *Indian Strategic Knowledge Online*, May 22, 2023, https://indianstrategicknowledgeonline.com/web/Final%20Mcfarlet.pdf.

75 Amol Dethe, "You May Not Be Interested in War, but War Is Interested in You," *BFSI*, February 26, 2022, https://bfsi.economictimes.indiatimes.com/news/you-may-not-be-interested-in-war-but-war-is-interested-in-you/89840730.

COPING WITH THE COMPLEXITY OF THE CHANGING CHARACTER OF WAR: TOWARD A NEW PARADIGM OF ADAPTIVE PEACE

Cedric de Coning

Norwegian Institute of International Affairs

ABSTRACT

The world has entered a period of heightened geopolitical instability that is compounded by climate change and the emergence of new technologies. The number of conflicts and related deaths are increasing. Dramatic failures in Afghanistan and elsewhere show that the mainstream approach to peace and conflict is no longer effective. The aim of this article is to contribute to re-thinking peace and security in two ways. First, by explaining why trying to influence complex social change process with a determined-design approach is self-defeating. Second, by introducing adaptive peace theory as a normative and functional approach to ending violent conflicts and sustaining peace in specific contexts, that is aimed at navigating the complexity inherent in trying to nudge societal change processes toward peace, without causing harm.

Dr. Cedric de Coning is a research professor in the research group on peace, conflict, and development at the Norwegian Institute of International Affairs (NUPI). He is also a senior advisor for the African Centre for the Constructive Resolution of Disputes (ACCORD) in South Africa.

The collapse of the internationally backed government in Afghanistan in August 2021 made for dramatic news, but it also forced the international peace and security community to recognize that they must seriously reflect on the effectiveness of the theories of change they have employed to try to bring about peace and stability in places such as Afghanistan, the Balkans, the Middle East, and Africa. These interventions represent highly concentrated international efforts to build state and social institutions according to predetermined international best practices and standards, in some cases backed by large peacekeeping or other military forces. However, despite billions of dollars spent, these international efforts have failed to transform the underlying drivers of violent conflict in these places. As a result, it is today increasingly less clear what types of problems, if any, could be resolved through such international peace and security efforts.[1]

Some argue that this is due to the changing character of war, and that as a result, our methods for ending wars and managing conflict have become outdated.[2] In this article I will pursue a different line of inquiry. Instead of focusing on the changing character of war theory, I will argue that an additional reason why the international peace and security community's efforts have failed, has to do with the shortcomings of the mainstream approach and related methodology that this community has employed to try to make, keep, and build peace in societies that experience conflict. I will explain this mainstream approach and why it is problematic in the next section, but in short, it is a determined-design approach, i.e., the outcome and theory of change is predetermined. I focus on the need to change the way we understand conflict as well as our approach to sustaining peace.

Donella Meadows argued that when influencing a complex system, having an effect on higher order system factors like principles and rules is more effective than influencing lower order factors like stocks and flows.[3] In her system of levels of influence, the second highest order of influence is having an effect on the paradigm of the system, and the most influential level is changing your own paradigm, i.e., your own underlying understanding and approach to the system in question. My aim with this article is to contribute to the larger process that is underway to re-think international peace and security by helping the peace research, policy, and practitioner community understand the shortcomings of the determined-design paradigm, and to introduce adaptive peace theory as an alternative method for making sense of conflicts and an approach to supporting societies in their efforts to sustain their own peace.

I will build my argument by first explaining how I understand and use peace and what I mean by the changing character of war and peace. I will argue that in the current geopolitical context, adapting our understanding and approach to peace is not only relevant, but urgent. I will then introduce complexity theory and employ it to explain why we need a theory of peace that is designed to cope with, rather than attempt to gain control over, the uncertainty inherent in sustaining peace. Last, I introduce adaptive peace theory as a new approach to and method for understanding and influencing peace processes.

Sustaining Peace

In this article I use peace in its broadest possible framing to include all policy instruments aimed at conflict management, conflict resolution, or conflict transformation, as well as bringing about stability, ensuring security, and making, keeping, and building peace. I use sustaining peace as a concept that implies that there are always some pockets or elements of peace in a society, even amidst violent conflict, and that the purpose of peacebuilding is to increase and expand this peace, while also safeguarding and protecting the peace that exists

Peace is an ambiguous concept that can mean different things for different people, but in the context of this article, a society that effectively constrains direct and structural violence, and that is self-governed by social institutions that promote social justice, as understood by the society in question, would be regarded as more peaceful than a comparable society where this is not the case. This concept of peace combines what Johan Galtung referred to as negative peace (absence of violence) and positive peace (presence of social justice).[4] On a spectrum of more or less peaceful, violence between states is today rare, but violence among interest and identity groups remains a challenge in many countries. The overall number of conflicts, and their victims, has declined since the end of the Cold War, but over the last decade this trend has been reversed and is now increasing.[5]

The puzzle that peace studies grapple with is threefold. First, how can societies prevent violent conflict and sustain peace. Second, where violent conflict is occurring, how can societies end war and transition toward peace. Third, what can external actors like the United Nations, the African Union, or international non-government organizations do to assist these processes.

Peace manifests in a specific socio-ecological context. I will most often refer to societies, but when I do, I use society in the broadest possible and most inclusive way, implying households, villages, communities, states, and communities of states or regional and international organizations. I understand society as a social system that is emergent from a patterned network of relationships that constitute a coherent whole that exists between individuals, groups, and institutions.[6] I also recognize that societies are embedded in ecologies and that all social systems are also social-ecological systems.

The Changing Character of War and Peace

Séverine Autesserre has coined the term Peace Inc. for what can be thought of as the peace industry, i.e., those researchers, policy makers, and practitioners that make a living out of international peace and security.[7] The critical school in peace and conflict studies argues that in our contemporary condition, Peace Inc. understands its role as transferring Western liberal norms and institutional models that sustain peace in the West, to societies affected by conflict, in the belief that adopting these norms and institutions will help them to end conflict and sustain peace.[8] The underlying paradigm that informs Peace Inc.'s understanding and approach is that international peace and security experts have the agency to analyze a conflict and identify its causes, design interventions based on international knowledge and best practices, and then execute these interventions through instruments such as peacekeeping and aid, with a high likelihood of success. Peace Inc. thus has a predetermined value system, a belief that it has the agency to end wars and introduce peace and has the organizations and instruments needed to act on its values and beliefs. When results have been unsatisfactory, evaluators have rarely been tasked with reviewing the underlying theory of change. Instead, the focus has been on poor implementation, insufficient resources, or local spoilers.[9]

The subjects in this paradigm are seen as passive, or at best their agency to act on their own is weak. When left to themselves they are fragile, poor, and conflict prone. They therefore need external help to maintain their stability and guidance to build their nations and states. They are thus framed as recipients or beneficiaries of international peace, security, and development assistance.

One reason why this dominant determined-design approach is so resistant to change is because most international peace work has been financed through official development assistance (ODA). Donors, and their parliaments, prefer theories of change that posit a linear cause and effect relationship between the volume and quality of ODA invested in a particular society affected by conflict, and its impact on peace.[10] I will explain why their expectations are unrealistic, but I recognize that their interest in achieving a positive return on their investment is not unreasonable. It is unrealistic because, as I explain in the next section, the very act of intervening in another society with the intent to bring about a predetermined effect desired by a donor nation or external peacebuilder, undermines the ability of that society to achieve and sustain a self-sustainable peace on its own. It is thus a self-defeating aim. If donor agencies cannot free themselves from providing support framed in ways that are conditioned on norm transfer and linear theories of change, then freeing peacebuilding from its ODA yoke may be one of the steps needed to break free from the determined-design paradigm and to decolonize Peace Inc.

Another reason why there is so much structural inertia that prevents a move away from a determined-design approach is because a lot of effort has been invested in professionalizing mediation and peacebuilding over the last two decades. As a result, much of the international effort to improve the effectiveness and sustainability of Peace Inc. has been inward looking. For example, the effort to improve mediation outcomes has primarily focused on the role of the mediator, rather than on, for example, enhanced understanding of the interests, behaviors, and relationship dynamics among the parties to a conflict. Because the dominant focus has been on the mediator, and the international standards and expectations they have to meet, rather than on the realities and context-specific drivers of conflicts, the result has been that many peace processes, and the agreements they generate, resemble each other.[11] This is not because many of the conflicts the international community have mediated over the last decades have suffered from the same causes and drivers, but rather because the mediators all have to comply with the same international standards and are guided by the same guidance and toolkits. The motive behind professionalizing international mediation and peacebuilding is perfectly understandable and reasonable, but it has produced a top-down determined-design approach to international mediation.

It is thus not surprising that there is a growing gap between how Peace Inc. makes sense of and acts to bring about peace, and how ordinary people experience conflict and international mediation and peacebuilding. For people in Afghanistan, the Democratic Republic of the Congo, or Somalia, most of the international effort has had little tangible effect on their everyday lived experience of conflict or peace.[12] Peace Inc. has been slow to recognize this gap, but the peace research community identified it two decades ago and has vocally criticized what they call the liberal peace model.[13] In response, the academic literature has experienced a local turn, i.e., a focus on studying and understanding conflict and peace from the bottom up, rather than from the top down.[14] Hybrid peace proponents have also pointed out that in reality, peace processes generate complex outcomes.[15] Peace Inc. needs the consent, compliance, and cooperation of national and local actors and thus needed to make compromises to accommodate the local. Local actors on the other hand need international recognition and support, and thus needed to make compromises to accommodate their relationship with the international.

However, despite these criticisms, Peace Inc. has been resistant to change, and it is perhaps only now—spurred by the dramatic failure of the American-led Western intervention in Afghanistan—that a wider recognition is emerging among the policy and practitioner community that there is an urgent need to re-assess how they have understood and tried to influence peace.

This recognition of the need to re-think how we understand peace comes at a critical time. We are living in a period of great uncertainty and risk. The human species faces the possibility of extinction if we are unable to significantly change the ways in which our civilization is destroying our ecosystem. At the same time, the geopolitical balance of power is in flux as we transition from a unipolar world order into some kind of polycrisis.[16] Historically such transitions are characterized by tension, competition, and mistrust and thus a come with a heightened risk of conflict. The conflicts in Afghanistan, Iraq, Libya, and Syria have intensified the scope and speed of the transition. Since the fall of Kabul two new major conflicts—the Russian war on Ukraine and the Israeli attempt to defeat Hamas by going to war with the Palestinian people—further risk local, regional, and international escalation. Our collective anxiety has been further exacerbated by fast-paced technological developments, including the emergence of artificial intelligence, that have radically changed the way we generate and process information and communicate, with significant implications for the interconnectedness of the world as well as increased risks for the social cohesion of our societies. All of these developments, separately and even more so when compounded, can further increase the risk of conflict, depending on how we—as individuals, societies, states, and international organizations—choose to respond.

We are thus living in a period of significant uncertainty, and this increases the risk of social and economic upheaval that can be harmful for human security and can trigger violent conflict. International, regional, national, and local capacities to prevent and manage conflict will thus be critical to sustain peace during the coming decades. However, our collective failure to resolve several major conflicts over the last few decades have triggered the need to reconsider whether our understanding of peace and our theories of change for sustaining peace are still fit for purpose. There is thus an urgent need to review and adapt our collective understanding of what peace means in the context of the changing character of war brought about by the compounding effects of the changing global order, climate change, and new technological developments.

Uncertainty, Unpredictability, and Irreproducibility

As the experiences in Afghanistan and elsewhere have demonstrated, it is not possible to undertake a project, for example a community violence reduction initiative in Iraq or security sector reform in Somalia, and predict the outcome with any certainty. Nor can we use a model that has performed relatively well, for instance the Truth and Reconciliation Commission in South Africa or Northern Ireland's Good Friday Agreement, and repeat it elsewhere with the expectation that it will produce the same result.

This uncertainty, unpredictability, and irreproducibility are characteristics of complex system behavior, not a result of insufficient knowledge or inadequate planning or implementation.[17] Complexity theory describes the characteristics and functions of a particular type of holistic system that has the ability to adapt and that demonstrates emergent properties, including self-organizing behavior. Such systems emerge and are maintained by the overall system-level effects of the dynamic and non-linear interactions of its elements. Interactions between elements are based on the information available to them locally and the results of their interaction with their environment, as well as on the modulated feedback they receive from the other elements in the system.[18]

One way to highlight the unique characteristics of complex systems is to contrast them with complicated systems. A complicated system can potentially be fully understood and predicted, provided sufficient information is available. Designing, building, and launching a rocket into space is highly complicated, but once it is mastered, the same process can be repeated with a reasonable degree of certainty and predictability. In contrast, social systems are complex, meaning they continuously adapt and self-organize based on non-linear positive and negative feedback dynamics. As a result, it is not possible to replicate the design elements that contributed to the relative successful outcomes achieved in one peace process in another context with the expectation that it will produce the same result.[19] This is why the study of peace and conflict have to integrate an understanding of how complex adaptive systems function under stress and adapt to change, and why determined-design, linear cause and effect theories of change should be reserved for rocket science.

International peace efforts have long suffered from an engineering inspired model that international experts have the agency to diagnose a conflict, plan, and execute a linear-causal step-by-step peace intervention that can 'build' peace and 'fix' failed states.[20] States are, however, comprised of complex social systems that differ in fundamental ways from structures like bridges that can be built from a plan, or mechanical systems that can be fixed if they break down. Because social systems are complex, they continuously adapt and self-organize, and they are thus constantly building and fixing themselves.

If we apply these insights from complexity theory to how we make sense of conflict and peace, we will recognize that ending a violent conflict and sustaining peace are not problems that can be solved by a specific time-bound external intervention. Peace emerges and is sustained over time through the dynamic interaction of numerous self-organizing processes. It is not a static state of equilibrium or harmony that can be obtained and then preserved. In complexity theory terms we can say that peace does not have a stopping rule. Sustaining peace is a continuously evolving process that can never be finally attained.[21] However, the level of peace attained in a given context (time and space) can generate a meaningful working level of everyday peace for the society involved. We can compare societies and conclude that, for example, contemporary Norway is more peaceful than the United States, or that Zambia is more peaceful than its neighbor the Democratic Republic of the Congo. And while we are aware that these comparisons are only valid for a limited period of time, we can learn from them and identify characteristics and indicators that can help us to make more consistent and systematic comparisons. For example, the Global Peace Index has identified indicators that can help us understand why some societies are more peaceful than others.[22] Such indicators can never tell the full story, but we can use them to trace elements of the dynamic processes that result in some societies becoming more or less peaceful over time.

If ending wars and building peace is so uncertain, unpredictable, and complex, how then can peacebuilders meaningfully contribute to ending wars or sustaining peace? One would need an approach to social transformation that is designed to cope with the uncertainty, unpredictability, and irreproducibility inherent in complex social change processes. In the next section I will introduce one such approach, namely adaptive peace theory.

Adaptive Peace Theory

Adaptive peace theory is a normative and functional approach to ending violent conflicts and sustaining peace in a specific context. It is aimed at navigating the complexity inherent in trying to nudge societal change processes toward peace, without causing harm. Adaptive peace theory is a conscious effort to decolonize peacebuilding by moving away from an approach based on predetermined values, models, and standards selected by those power structures that dominate Peace Inc. Instead, the focus is on empowering the agency of the affected communities and societies to learn from their own attempts to sustain peace.

Adaptive peace theory is based on four premises: first, a recognition that social systems are ontologically complex. That implies that the behavior of social systems is highly dynamic and non-linear. As a result, it is not possible to make sense of or predict specific future behavior of such systems using deductive theoretical approaches based on the past behavior of similar systems, or even the same system in a different context. That also means that one cannot attempt to influence the behavior of such systems using pre-planned linear cause and effect theories of change, and realistically expect that it will produce a predetermined outcome. Instead, making sense of these systems, and attempting to influence them, requires an inductive epistemology that generates and continuously adapts knowledge through a concerted effort to learn from context-specific and iterative attempts to purposefully engage with the system. One can summarize this approach to knowledge generation as learning from doing and doing from learning. This adaptive approach to developing and continuously revising the knowledge that emerges from the process of acting and learning is what the 'adaptive' in adaptive peace theory refers too.

Second, understanding social systems as complex implies a recognition that they emerge, evolve, and are sustained by the self-organizing effects of the relationships between the elements that make up the system, which in social systems are individuals, groups, and institutions. The elements respond to the information that they have locally and that they gain from their relationship with others, and this generates negative and positive feedback loops that ultimately self-organize the overall behavior of the system. This process of continuous adaptation is vital to the health of any society just as evolution is vital to the survival of any species and ecosystem. Insights derived from how self-organization maintains and transforms complex systems suggest that for peace to become self-sustainable, resilient social institutions that promote and sustain peace need to emerge from the active participation of the society in the process of sustaining peace, including reflecting on and learning from both successes and failures. From a conflict management perspective, self-organization refers to the processes and devices a society uses to sustain peace, i.e., the overall ability to manage its own tensions, pressures, disputes, crises, and shocks without relapsing into violent conflict.[23] For peace to be self-sustainable a society needs to have a network of mutually reinforcing institutions that can manage disputes peacefully. Peacebuilding is thus essentially about stimulating and facilitating the capacity of societies to sustain peace themselves, i.e., to assist a society to develop a sufficiently robust and resilient network of social institutions so that it can self-organize and evolve peacefully, despite social competition, environmental stress, and unexpected shocks.

Third, recognizing societies as complex, emergent, and self-organizing implies a recognition that peace is not something that can be imposed or administered by an external peacebuilder or a mediator.[24] Peace is a continuously emerging process that is generated and sustained by the active participation of the society in sustaining its own peace.[25] The people affected by, and involved in, any given conflict situation are thus the critical knowledge holders who have the primary agency to make and sustain their own peace. The empowered agency of the people involved is critical for the effectiveness and sustainability of any peace initiative.[26] Initiatives to prevent or manage conflict or to sustain a peace process must emerge and evolve from a collaborative and experiential process in which the people affected by the conflict have the agency to direct the process. This also implies that the peace process must be context and time specific and helps to explain why peace processes based on standards and norms exported from elsewhere have usually been less effective and unsustainable. External peacebuilders can support and stimulate the process, but the critical agency needs to emerge from the social institutions of the affected communities or societies. The robustness and resilience of the self-organizing capacity of a society determine the extent to which it can withstand pressures and shocks that risk a (re)lapse into violent conflict. Peacebuilding should thus be about safeguarding, stimulating, facilitating, and creating the space for societies to develop robust and resilient capacities to self-organize peacefully.

Fourth, complex systems exist and function in relationship to other systems. The boundaries between systems are porous. As a result a system can be influenced by developments elsewhere in the larger system-of-systems that they may not have control over. For example, a society in Somalia whose livelihood depends on livestock may be affected by climate change that has its origins elsewhere in the larger global socio-ecological system. The society in Somalia can attempt to adapt to the effects of climate change, but it cannot control or influence climate change itself. This implies that in addition to the indigenous factors within a given system that are ordered through the self-organizing process of that system, there are also exogenous factors that influence any given system. Peacebuilding also involves building relationships and networks with partners in other systems that may have an effect on your own system's ability to sustain its peace. Through these relationships peacebuilders can form networks of change that can try to influence the behavior of the international peace and security system across local to global scales. Social systems are thus always embedded in other systems, or have sub-systems, and these vertical relationships also influence the ability of a given system to sustain its peace.

External peacebuilders represent exogenous interests, and while their aim may be to support sustaining peace in a given context as both a local and global good, they need to understand their positionality vis-à-vis the system they are trying to influence and factor that into their role in the peacebuilding process. They, knowingly or unknowingly, represent the values and interests of their host systems and the systems that fund their work. In many cases there may be shared values and interests, but that should not be assumed. Similarity can easily hide isomorphic mimicry or other subtle but important differences.[27] The relationships between external peacebuilders and the societies they support thus need to be carefully managed. External peacebuilders can assist the process of sustaining peace, but if they interfere too much—if they start to direct the process and attempt to control the outcomes to serve their interests—they will disrupt the feedback processes critical for self-organization to emerge and to be sustained. This typically happens when peacebuilders attempt to engineer the process in order to generate predetermined outcomes desired by their host system or the system that funds their work.[28] Trying to control the outcome produces the opposite of what peacebuilding aims to achieve; it generates dependence, it undermines self-sustainability, and it can prolong instability.[29] That is why, as I pointed out earlier, determined-design peace and aid is self-defeating. State and social institutions develop resilience through iterative trial and error over generations. Too much filtering and cushioning slows down and inhibits these feedback processes. Every time an external peacebuilder 'solves a problem' it denies internal social institutions an opportunity to learn from doing, including learning from failing. Getting it wrong and trying again stimulates the learning and adaptation processes necessary for social institutions to develop and become robust. Too much external interference distorts these system dynamics. For example, a stabilization dilemma emerges when an international peace operation is so effective in providing stability that the ruling political elites such as government officials, business leaders who influence the government, and institutions that hold power in the system, have little incentive to invest in the political settlements necessary to bring about self-sustainable peace.[30]

From Theory to Practice: The Adaptive Peace Methodology

The methodology that adaptive peace theory employs to make sense of and influence complex social systems can be summarized in three iterative steps: assess, act, and adapt.[31] The assess step consists of the affected people making sense of the situation that their community or society finds itself in, historically, holistically, and from multiple or pluralistic perspectives and methodologies. This can be a spontaneous process or it can be facilitated by peacebuilders. Making sense of the present and past usually also leads to envisioning or imagining alternative futures over the longer, medium, and short-term.

The act step consists of identifying actions that can start to change the drivers that are causing the conflict and that can contribute to bringing about those imagined futures. As adaptive peace theory recognizes that it is not possible to pre-design a causal path that can bring about a desired future state, the methodology is inductive and experiential. One element of the adaptive approach is variety; as the outcome is uncertain, one must experiment with a variety of initiatives across a spectrum of probabilities. The theory of change that informs each alternative needs to be clearly understood so that one can assess and learn from the effects it generates in each time and context-specific iteration.

The adapt step consists of a process that enables learning and selection; one has to actively monitor and evaluate the effects of the initiatives undertaken by paying close attention to the feedback they generate. The adaptive peace methodology thus requires an active participatory decision-making process that reflects on an learns from the feedback generated by past actions, to make decisions to stop those initiatives that perform poorly or have negative side effects, while those that show more promise can be further adapted to introduce more variety, or can be scaled-up to have greater impact.

As the socio-ecological environment within which the system functions is continuously evolving, the three steps need to form an iterative process that facilitates continuous evolution and adaptation. Any effect achieved is temporary and subject to new emerging dynamics. To summarize, in order to sustain peace amid complexity and uncertainty, the adaptive peace methodology generates actions that are intended to bring about and sustain peace, multiple initiatives are undertaken simultaneously, assessed, and adapted in a continuous and iterative process of purposeful inductive learning from doing and doing from learning.

The adaptive peace methodology is scalable from local programs to national campaigns or to international operations and strategic frameworks.[32] At the operational and strategic levels this implies an iterative and collaborative process of reviewing conflict analysis and theories of change, and adapting planning in an ongoing process of institutional learning.[33] The approach can be applied to a wide range of peace efforts, for example a mediation process between states or an initiative to manage a resource shared between communities.

Lessons from Applied Adaptive Peace Experiences

In order to assess some of the underlying pathways of the adaptive peacebuilding approach, the Japan International Cooperation Agency (JICA) undertook a research project in partnership with the author. The project analyzed context-specific, participatory, and adaptive approaches to peace across a number of countries and policy contexts, based on the experiences and outcomes of peace interventions in the recent past. The case studies included Colombia, Mozambique, Palestine, Syria, and Timor-Leste, which represent different conflicts in Africa, Asia, Latin America, and the Middle East, and involve a diverse range of peacebuilding actors and different types of peace processes and conflict situations.[34]

The research project found that when context-specific approaches to mediation and peacebuilding empower local agency, it is a key element that influences the self-sustainability of peace processes.[35] Context-specific peacebuilding in this context refers to bottom-up or homegrown approaches to achieving and sustaining peace based on local or national cultural, historical, and political understandings of peace. It differs from approaches to peace where the values and concept of peace are imported from elsewhere. The people affected by the conflict determine the ideas or content, priorities, and values, and the peacebuilding process is aimed at (and limited to) facilitating a participatory process that helps to strengthen or generate new social institutions through local and national ownership and leadership. The research found that that there is a link between the extent to which a peace initiative is context-specific and adaptive, and the level of self-sustainability attained.

This empirical evidence is consistent with adaptive peace theory that posits that the capacity for self-organization in a complex system, such as a society affected by conflict, has a direct bearing on its social cohesion, resilience, and adaptive capacity. The implication is that investing in strengthening the self-organizing capacity of communities and societies—in other words, helping them to strengthen their social institutions and social networks—will help build the resilience, adaptive capacity, and social cohesion they will need to prevent or recover from conflict, and to consolidate, further grow, and sustain the levels of peace that they have been able to achieve.

The overall finding of the research project, based on results of the case studies that provided the empirical basis for the research, was that context-specific and adaptive approaches to peacebuilding—ones that invest in people and encourage the active participation of affected communities—are more effective than top-down and determined-design approaches because they stimulate the emergence of local social institutions that work to promote and sustain peace.[36]

Conclusion

The aim of this article is to contribute to the larger process that is underway to re-think international peace and security by helping the peace research, policy, and practitioner community understand the shortcomings of the dominant determined-design approach, and to introduce adaptive peace theory as an alternative method for making sense of conflict and an approach to supporting societies in their efforts to sustain their own peace.

Re-thinking how we make and sustain peace is urgent, as we are now in a period of increased geopolitical instability, compounded by climate change and new technologies. As a result of these developments and a range of related factors, the number of conflicts and related deaths are increasing while the mainstream approach to peace and conflict is no longer effective. There is thus an urgent need to review and adapt our collective understanding of what peace means, and how to achieve and sustain it, in the context of the changing character of war.

International peace efforts have long suffered from an engineering inspired model. I have used complexity theory to show that states and societies are complex social systems that differ in fundamental ways from structures like bridges, or mechanical systems that can be fixed if they break down. Because social systems are ontologically complex, they continuously adapt and self-organize, and they are thus constantly building and fixing themselves.

I then introduced adaptive peace theory as a normative and functional approach to ending violent conflicts and sustaining peace in a specific context. Adaptive peace is aimed at navigating the complexity inherent in trying to nudge societal change processes toward peace, without causing harm. The 'adaptive' in adaptive peace theory refers to the inductive methodology of developing and continuously revising the knowledge that emerges from the process of acting and learning.

Peace is an emerging process that is generated and sustained by the active participation of the society. The people affected by, and involved in, any given conflict situation are thus the critical knowledge holders who have the primary agency to make and sustain their own peace.

External peacebuilders can assist the process, but if they interfere too much—if they start to direct the process and attempt to control the outcomes to serve their interests—they will disrupt the feedback processes critical for self-organization to emerge and to be sustained. Trying to control the outcome produces the opposite of what peacebuilding aims to achieve; it generates dependence and it undermines self-sustainability.

For peace to be self-sustainable a society needs to have a network of mutually reinforcing institutions that can manage disputes peacefully. Peacebuilding should thus essentially be about stimulating and facilitating the capacity of societies to sustain peace themselves. The resilience of a society determines the extent to which it can withstand pressures and shocks that risk a lapse into violent conflict. Peacebuilding should thus be about safeguarding, stimulating, facilitating, and creating the space for societies to develop robust and resilient capacities to self-organize peacefully.

Notes

1   Oliver P. Richmond, *After Liberal Peace: The Changing Concept of Peace-Building*, RSIS Commentary no. 272 (Singapore: S. Rajaratnam School of International Studies, 2016).

2   Mary Kaldor, *New and Old Wars: Organized Violence in a Global Era* (Cambridge: Polity, 1999).

3   Donella Meadows, *Leverage Points: Places to Intervene in a System* (Hartland: The Sustainability Institute, 1999).

4   Johan Galtung, "Violence, Peace, and Peace Research," *Journal of Peace Research* 6, no. 3 (1969): 167–91.

5   Anna Marie Obermeier and Siri Aas Rustad, *Conflict Trends: A Global Overview, 1946–2022* (Oslo: PRIO, 2023).

6   Niklas Luhmann, "The Autopoiesis of Social Systems," in *Essays on Self-Reference* (New York: Columbia University Press, 1990), 1–20.

7   Séverine Autesserre, *Peaceland: Conflict Resolution and the Everyday Politics of International Intervention* (Cambridge: Cambridge University Press, 2014).

8   Oliver P. Richmond, "The Problem of Peace: Understanding the 'Liberal Peace,'" *Conflict, Security & Development* 6, no. 3 (2006): 291–314.

9   Ashraf Ghani and Clare Lockhart, *Fixing Failed States: A Framework for Rebuilding a Fractured World* (New York: Oxford University Press, 2009).

10 Pablo Yanguas, *Why We Lie About Aid: Development and the Messy Politics of Change* (London: Zed Books, 2018).

11 Cedric de Coning, Ako Muto, and Rui Saraiva, eds., *Adaptive Mediation and Conflict Resolution: Peace-Making in Colombia, Mozambique, the Philippines, and Syria* (London: Palgrave Macmillan, 2022).

12 Roger Mac Ginty, *Everyday Peace: How So-Called Ordinary People Can Disrupt Conflict* (Oxford: Oxford University Press, 2021).

13 Roland Paris, *At War's End: Building Peace after Civil War* (Cambridge: Cambridge University Press, 2004).

14 Thania Paffenholz, "Unpacking the Local Turn in Peacebuilding: A Critical Assessment towards an Agenda for Future Research," *Third World Quarterly* 36, no. 5 (2015): 857–74.

15 Roger Mac Ginty, "Hybrid Peace: The Interaction between Top-Down and Bottom-Up Peace," *Security Dialogue* 41, no. 4 (2010: 391–412.

16 Edgar Morin and Anne Brigitte Kern, *Homeland Earth: A Manifesto for the New Millennium* (Gresskill: Hampton Press, 1999).

17 Emery Brusset, Cedric de Coning, and Bryn Hughes, eds., *Complexity Thinking for Peacebuilding Practice and Evaluation* (London: Palgrave Macmillan, 2016).

18 Paul Cilliers, *Complexity and Postmodernism: Understanding Complex Systems* (London: Routledge, 1998).

19 Cedric de Coning, "Insights from Complexity Theory for Peace and Conflict Studies," in *The Palgrave Encyclopedia of Peace and Conflict Studies*, ed. Oliver Richmond and Gëzim Visoka (London: Palgrave Macmillan, 2020).

20 Charles T. Hunt, "Complexity Theory," in *United Nations Peace Operations and International Relations Theory*, ed. John Karlsrud and Kseniya Oksamytna (Manchester: Manchester University Press, 2020), 195–216.

21 Thania Paffenholz, "Perpetual Peacebuilding: A New Paradigm to Move Beyond the Linearity of Liberal Peacebuilding," *Journal of Intervention and Statebuilding* 15, no. 3 (2021): 367–85.

22 The Global Peace Index is an annual report produced by the Institute for Economics & Peace (IEP) that measures the relative position of nations' and regions' peacefulness. The reports can be seen at Vision of Humanity, accessed March 30, 2024, https://www.visionofhumanity.org/resources/?type=research.

23 Cedric de Coning, "From Peacebuilding to Sustaining Peace: Implications of Complexity for Resilience and Sustainability," *Resilience* 4, no. 3 (2016): 166–81.

24 Adam Day and Charles T. Hunt, "A Perturbed Peace: Applying Complexity Theory to UN Peacekeeping," *International Peacekeeping* 30, no. 1 (2023: 1–23.

25 Oliver P. Richmond, "Peace Formation and Local Infrastructures for Peace," *Alternatives: Global, Local, Political* 38, no. 4 (2013): 271–87.

26 Cedric de Coning and Linnéa Gelot, "Placing People at the Center of UN Peace Operations," IPI Global Observatory, May 29, 2020, https://theglobalobservatory.org/2020/05/placing-people-center-un-peace-operations/.

27 Lant Pritchett, Michael Woolcock, and Matt Andrews, "Capability Traps? The Mechanisms of Persistent Implementation Failure" (Working Paper 234, Center for Global Development, 2010).

28 Mie Roesdahl, Jasper Peet-Martel, and Sweta Velpillay, *A Global System in Flux: Pursuing Systems Change for Locally-Led Peacebuilding* (Copenhagen: Conducive Space for Peace, 2021).

29 Ben Ramalingam, *Aid on the Edge of Chaos: Rethinking International Cooperation in a Complex World* (Oxford: Oxford University Press, 2014).

30 Cedric de Coning, "How Not to Do UN Peacekeeping: Avoid the Stabilization Dilemma with Principled and Adaptive Mandating and Leadership," *Global Governance: A Review of Multilateralism and International Organizations 29, no.* 2 (2023): 152–67.

31 Cedric de Coning, "Adaptive Peacebuilding," *International Affairs* 94, no. 2 (2018): 301–17.

32 Gearoid Millar, "Toward a Trans-scalar Peace System: Challenging Complex Global Conflict Systems," *Peacebuilding* 8, no. 3 (2020): 261–78.

33 Daniel Forti, *UN Peacekeeping and CPAS: An Experiment in Performance Assessment and Mission Planning* (New York: International Peace Institute, 2022).

34 More information on this research project is available on the website of the JICA Ogata Sadako Research Institute for Peace and Development: https://www.jica.go.jp/english/jica_ri/research/peace/20190401-20220331.html.

35 De Coning, Muto, and Saraiva, *Adaptive Mediation and Conflict Resolution.*

36 Cedric de Coning, Ako Muto, and Rui Saraiva, eds., *Adaptive Peacebuilding: A New Approach to Sustaining Peace in the 21st Century* (London: Palgrave Macmillan, 2023).

MUSCAT, MADRID, ULSTER, AND THE HOLY LAND: THE MEDRC MODEL OF ENVIRONMENTAL PEACEBUILDING IN A REVIVED MIDDLE EAST PEACE PROCESS

Ciarán Ó Cuinn

MEDRC

ABSTRACT

Mandated to assist the Middle East peace process through environmental diplomacy, MEDRC, the last surviving institution of that process, has survived through an institutional and operational approach to conflict resolution separate from the rest of the process. Understanding its transferable approach is important in fields of environmental diplomacy and conflict resolution not only in the context of combating transboundary climate and environmental threats but of using these threats as entry points into a peace process. As the international community grapples with the need for a credible solution to the intractable conflict in Israel and Palestine, the MEDRC approach has implications for the process design of a revived and reformed Middle East peace process. The aim of this article is to present for the first time the detailed elements of the MEDRC Model and underpinning Conflict Resolution Process Guidelines, and to examine implications for environmental peacebuilding in general and a for a revived Middle East peace process.

Ciarán Ó Cuinn has been the Center Director of MEDRC since 2013 and is a specialist in international relations and conflict resolution. Previously he worked on the Irish peace process as principal ministerial policy adviser at Ireland's Department of Foreign Affairs, Department of Justice, and Department of Communications, Marine and Natural Resources. The views expressed in this article are his own and do not necessarily represent those of his institution and official role.

M EDRC is a multilateral international organization, headquartered in Muscat, Oman and mandated to assist the Middle East peace process through environmental diplomacy.[1] Established in 1996 out of the multilateral Middle East peace process, known the Madrid Process, it is all that remains of that effort. It has succeeded in retaining the support and cooperation of all parties to the conflict because of an approach to conflict resolution entitled the 'MEDRC Model.' This multilateral institutional model, based on equality and balance, is unique in the context of the Middle East peace process and the wider field of environmental peacebuilding.

The MEDRC Model is designed to be transferable to benefit states seeking to use transboundary environmental issues in the service of the peace process. In the context of the Middle East peace process it can be regarded as an alternative approach to the Abraham Accords, in placing Palestinian inclusion and agency at its core alongside all other member states. More immediately, the approach has the potential to influence and improve a revived Middle East peace process where it offers a practical and proven operational framework to underpin high-level diplomatic initiatives such as a revived Arab Peace Initiative or any variation on the Madrid Process.

The article will trace the development of the model and its potential future utility in the process design of a revived Middle East peace process. This has implications for the resolution of other intractable conflicts and for future work on environmental diplomacy where greater understanding of the potential links between environment-related projects and peace is necessary.[2]

Muscat

The MEDRC institution is headquartered in Muscat, in the Sultanate of Oman, and its processes are inspired by the Omani tradition of dialogue and diplomacy. Based on concepts of *shura* (consultation), *'ijmae* (consensus), and *sablah* (council), the tradition emphasizes long-term, normative processes built around balance, resilience, and equality as a basis for social cohesion and peaceful international relations.[3] Its roots and practice are millennia deep and rooted in its unique geography, trade, and diversity.

The Sultanate of Oman sits where the Indian Ocean meets the Gulf and where Iran meets Arabia. Shaped by a geopolitical reality quite different from the rest of the Gulf Cooperation Council (GCC), with the vast majority of its coastline facing into the Indian Ocean and Gulf of Oman, the Sultanate historically looked outward to the Indian Ocean as much as to the interior of the Arabian Peninsula and the Levant.[4]

Occupying this diverse regional and inter-regional contact zone, the Sultanate has developed a sophisticated system of balances and counterbalances between the various forces that cut through its neighborhood.[5] Distinctive in the Arab world in its non-Ottoman past and its unique Ibadi identity, Oman is religiously tolerant, its jurisprudence and avowedly anti-sectarian stance emphasizing the values and principles of mediation, social equality, and equality before the law.[6]

Arguably, the clearest and most accessible insight into the workings of this Omani approach lie not in the field of diplomacy, but in the Omani *falaj* system of water management. In an arid desert environment, water is the most immediate and precious prerequisite for life. The system for distribution of water is an elemental social system that shapes and defines society, culture, and state.

Oman's system of water management is based around a resilient system for equitable distribution. In simple terms, the *falaj* system is the means of sharing water from an aquifer, spring, or wadi among a community. It involves a canal dug into the ground to carry water by gravity to villages and farms. Each water shareholder receives the flow of water for a length of time rather than by volume. The length of time depends on the area of land owned and the contribution to the construction of the *falaj* system. During dry periods the flow will be low, but the time share will remain the same, leading to equity among irrigators.[7]

This system of water management has been inextricable from the social and economic structure that has permitted it to function successfully and largely unchanged for centuries.[8] It can be considered a hydro-political system that has become a social contract deeply rooted in religious principles.[9]

The *falaj* system then, has been a significant factor in defining and shaping Oman's socioeconomic structure and community relations.[10] As with the international relations of Oman, it is part of a tradition that favors long-term balance and normative processes around equality and resilience over short-term zero-sum outcomes. In international relations Oman's traditions have long been recognized as showing how 'balancing interests, tolerance toward differences, and a determined search for mutual benefits can open international doors and keep them open, even during conflict.'[11] Today, trusted by Iran, the United States, and Saudi Arabia alike, Oman holds to its long tradition of diplomacy through consultation, consensus, and council.[12]

The concepts of balance, symmetry, and resilient systems in peace processes or diplomacy are obviously not unique. The role of inclusion, participation, and mitigating asymmetry is a central part of peacemaking.[13] The Irish peace process operationalized balance through concepts such as the role of British and Irish governments as 'joint guarantors.' It was also evident in the concept of 'coequal partnership' between parties, and in particular between first and deputy first ministers. Similarly, the concept of 'parity of esteem,' was conceptually central to the success of the Irish peace process at individual, community, and regional levels.[14] Similar to Oman, these are not formal legal codices but have created a positive set of norms that underpin a resilient positive peace based on balance, in place of 'negative peace, based on structural violence, a hierarchy of humanity, or even Carthaginian destruction.[15]

What sets Oman apart however, is the extent to which these values and principles of balance, social equality, and equality before the law, evident across national and international policy and practice, are deeply ingrained in national culture.[16] The Omanis are known as *Ahl al Shura*, People of Consultation, for a reason.[17] This unique culture was very much in evidence in the establishment of MEDRC.[18]

Madrid

The Madrid Process brought the Omani approach into first contact with the formal structures of the Middle East peace process, with the convening of the Madrid Peace Conference in 1991. In the shadow of the first *intifada* and end of the Cold War and the first Gulf War, the US and USSR issued letters of invitation stating that the negotiations would proceed on the basis of UN Security Council Resolution 242 of November 22, 1967 that incorporated the principle of trading land for peace.[19] The process would have two tracks:

- a bilateral track between Israel and Syria, Jordan-Palestine respectively, launched in Madrid on October 30, 1991 and,
- a multilateral track, launched in Moscow on January 28, 1992, involving the Palestine Liberation Organization (PLO), Israel, and thirteen Arab governments in multilateral working groups focused on i) water, ii) refugees, iii) economic development, iv) the environment, v) arms control, and regional security.[20]

Opening the Madrid Conference, Prime Minister Shamir of Israel ruled out land for peace. This set the tone for the bilateral track where the parties restated fixed positions. Madrid did open the door however to the Oslo Accords agreed between the PLO and Israel in 1993 and 1995 respectively.[21] These would come to replace Madrid as the bilateral Israel-Palestine track in the Middle East peace process.[22]

The multilateral track was attended by thirty-six parties. First and foremost, the multilaterals were to provide a supportive framework for the bilateral negotiations; the latter were the crux of the peace process.[23] The process then was theoretically balanced, with Arab parties stating that progress in the multilateral process was dependent on progress in the bilaterals.[24]

In that context, Oman participated actively in the Multilateral Working Group on Water Resources, keenly aware of the diplomatic, regional, and technical importance of water. Addressing Oman's role in the talks in 1995, Oman's current foreign minister, Sayyid Badr bin Hamad Al-Busaidi, then under-secretary at the Foreign Ministry, referred to the lessons of the *falaj* approach to water needs of the region and to the vision of MEDRC.[25] In June of 1995 US vice president Al Gore and Omani foreign minister Yusuf bin Alawi bin Abdallah released a joint US-Oman communiqué confirming that each would fund the establishment of MEDRC and inviting others to join.[26]

The following month, a joint meeting of the Multilateral Working Groups on Water Resources and the Environment met in Amman, Jordan and noted, in a the press statement of the gavel-holder that, "the United States and Oman announced that each would commit 3 million dollars to establish the Middle East Desalination Research Centre in Muscat, Oman. The center is a concrete manifestation of regional cooperation created through the multilateral peace process."[27] By that stage the balancing Israel-Palestine track, the Oslo process, was already weakening with negotiations between the PLO and Israel consistently undermined by Likud, the settlers, and Hamas.[28]

Peace Process Collapse

The Israeli rejection of Oslo in the May 1996 election and the subsequent backtracking of the Benjamin Netanyahu government, coupled with a spiral of mutual violence, ended any possibility of balance between the tracks.[29] The widespread perception of the demise of Oslo then rendered the balancing multilateral track diplomatically and politically inoperable.

The last meeting of the Multilateral Working Group on Water Resources was held in Hammamet, Tunisia in May 1996. The final press statement of the gavel holder, while optimistically noting that the multilateral track was intended to complement and support the bilateral negotiations, stated that several of the group's members had pledged a total of fifteen million dollars in support of MEDRC.[30] MEDRC then, was born into a political and diplomatic crisis when launched formally in December 1996.

As an international organization its membership was limited to states and other international organizations. An international establishment agreement set out its core mandate, to assist the Middle East peace process, and was signed by the initial member states: Oman, the United States, Japan, Israel, and Korea. It then concluded a headquarters agreement with the Sultanate of Oman. Under this agreement, MEDRC was recognized as a diplomatic mission with the standard diplomatic protections offered to its headquarters seat. Oman and the United States would jointly chair. All initial members provided a matching three million dollars and, in the initial decade of its operations, MEDRC issued calls for proposals for research into desalination technologies across the Middle East and North Africa.

Sustained by the initial core funding, its concrete institutional status, and its focus on technical desalination research at the outset, MEDRC survived. A crucial sustaining factor during these years was hope of a rebirth of the Israel-Palestine track in the form of the 2000 Camp David Summit, the Quartet Roadmap, and ongoing state building activities in Palestine. In that context, Palestine and Jordan joined in 2002.

By the end of the 2010s however, the lack of a credible Israeli-Palestinian track and the failure of all other multilateral initiatives brought MEDRC to an increasingly precarious state. The organization began concerted efforts between 2009 and 2013 to broker joint training and dialogue between the parties in the water sector, and in particular to aid the delivery of the Central Gaza Desalination Plant, but without significant success.

The collapse of the Israel-Palestine track was reflected in the state of dialogue and joint action around water between the Israeli and Palestinian sides. This was not surprising; the water conflict between Palestine and Israel is inseparable from the broader political context and the roots of the conflict.[31] Article 40 of the Oslo II Accord replicated and codified the occupation-era status quo in the West Bank and allocated eighty-seven percent of the West Bank's transboundary groundwater yield to Israel with just thirteen percent to the Palestinians.[32]

Under Oslo II, in the West Bank only water systems that had previously 'related solely to Palestinians,' and were 'held by the military government and Civil Administration,' would be transferred to the Palestinian Authority, with all other systems, including those for settlements, remaining under Israeli control.[33] For Gaza, an enclave territory too small to have sufficient natural water resources for its large refugee population and thus, a built-in dependency on Israel, full responsibility was handed to the Palestinian Authority.[34] This was, and remains, the essential shape and status quo on the issue of water relations between Israel and Palestine.

By early 2014, against the backdrop of the failed peace talks organized by US Secretary of State John Kerry, MEDRC had more or less contracted completely and member states led by the joint-chairs agreed to a rethink and new strategy. Relying on external balance, in the form of an Israel-Palestine track that no longer existed, had become untenable. A new approach, separate from the existing process design of the Middle East peace process, was required.

Ulster

The new strategy took inspiration from the balanced Omani tradition and the similar practices underpinning the Irish peace process. In the absence of a balancing external Israel-Palestine track, MEDRC had to create one internally. Building on its efforts between 2009 and 2013, the core focus of the organization became Palestinian-Israeli conflict resolution. A MEDRC trilateral program would focus on Israel-Palestine issues. This MEDRC chaired process would involve Palestine, Jordan, and Israel and support, where possible, dialogue, negotiations, and joint activities using water and the environment as an entry point. A MEDRC bilateral Palestine program would see MEDRC support the water, environmental, and state building activities of the Palestinian side. A small technical bilateral program with Jordan would exist also.

The new processes and programs were normative; no matter what the political situation outside, in MEDRC, the parties, at a minimum, would meet and engage as absolute multilateral equals. Using the approach of the Irish peace process, member states would be joint owners, joint guarantors, and coequal partners of MEDRC and its processes. This allowed member states without diplomatic relations to share ownership of the institution and recognize one another as such.

Strategically, equality and balance, including between the core parties of the peace process, became the bottom line. Operationally, a commitment to parity of esteem and the concept of an 'overtly balanced outcome' became central to all MEDRC actions.

Encompassing the new strategy was a new mandate: "to be a model organization for states seeking to use transboundary environmental issues in support of a peace process."[35] This mandate allowed MEDRC to look beyond the process design constraints and path dependency of the Middle East peace process.

The new mandate empowered MEDRC to work on the basis of best practice in terms of conflict resolution, public management, peacebuilding, and environmental diplomacy. It served also to enable it to seek to fill the lacuna in agency around multilateralism in environmental and water diplomacy.[36]

Since 2014, MEDRC has conducted its activities in line with the new transferable model approach, outlined below.

The MEDRC Model

Similar to the *falaj* model, the MEDRC Model should be imagined as a resilient system in balance.[37] It is built on an insistence on equity and symmetry. The external political environment is the flow. The MEDRC Model takes that flow and creates peacebuilding actions based on a political framework of equality and parity of esteem. It can accommodate various strategies and aspects of conflict resolution using water, environmental diplomacy, and peacebuilding activities.[38]

The model is transferable. It is designed to be used by states to establish similarly resilient multilateral centers in any transboundary conflict using any transboundary environmental issue as an entry point to support a peace process or improved relations. Beyond the environment, the approach could be used to create a resilient institutional underpinning for any final status area of negotiation in an established peace process. It does not wait for or depend on conflict ripeness but expands and contracts in line with the flow of the political situation. The approach is iterative or adaptive.

In 2020 MEDRC began a project funded by the German Federal Foreign Office entitled *Using Transboundary Environmental Issues in the Service of a Peace Process*. As part of that project, independent external consultants conducted a review of this model and found that MEDRC was the only such multilateral organization doing such track one work and that the model was transferable to other conflicts using other transboundary environmental issues. Under this project MEDRC disseminates the model to governments engaged in peace process activities. The central institutional and operational elements of the replicable model are outlined next.

The MEDRC Model: Multilateral Centers to Support Peace Processes

In practice the MEDRC Model is an institutional multilateral framework based on equalizing contact between the core parties to a conflict. It is a set of diplomatic practices and a resilient institutional core, together proposed under the term "multilateral center." The approach is not rigid or prescriptive. Different cultures, conflicts, and capacities must shape any successful intervention. In that context, the following are general guidelines for the establishment and operation of a MEDRC Model multilateral center.

Engaging the Core Parties to a Conflict

The process of engaging the core parties to a conflict and securing their agreement to participate will vary depending on the conflict. In an established political track this can begin via a confidence building measure. In more intense conflicts it can be seen as an initial diplomatic contact group activity that later institutionalizes. In conflicts where contact and cooperation are limited by narrow treaty agreements, it can be used as a way to broaden dialogue. In an established peace process, establishing a variation of the model on each of several final status issues would also be of benefit.

Selecting a Transboundary Environmental Issue of Joint Concern

The multilateral center should have a broad peace process mandate and a secondary environmental mandate focused on a transboundary environmental issue of joint concern to the parties to the conflict. This environmental mandate area should not be so narrow that it limits dialogue. In an established political track, the issue might be a final status issue, such as water. In an early or less structured process, the issue might be a less contentious topic. The mandate may be expanded in due course, reflecting the flow of the political environment.

MEDRC was initially mandated to focus on desalination, then water, and from 2022 on, all transboundary environmental issues including climate change. This 'creeping mandate' approach facilitates the iterative and pragmatic approaches to peacebuilding and underpins resilience.

Involving Surrounding States

As an international organization, the multilateral center should aim to attract member states in addition to the conflict parties. The role of supporting states is to ensure and strengthen adherence to multilateral norms and to help bring diplomatic balance to potential disparities between core parties. They also provide financial support as core institutional funding or project support. Prospective member states may be geographic neighbors, states with a historic interest or role in the conflict, or states with an interest in conflict resolution, development cooperation, or the policy focus.

MEDRC contains a mix of the original participants in the Multilateral Working Group on Water Resources in the 1990s. Some states with a diplomatic focus on water diplomacy as well as states with an expertise in stabilization have subsequently joined.[39]

Establishing the Institution

Institutions are more stable and resilient than frameworks, networks, or contact groups. In environmental peacebuilding, joint institutions are acknowledged channels of communication and conflict resolution.[40] In the wider area of conflict prevention there is a recognized clear need for the institutionalization of preventative policies and strategies.[41] There are two main actions here to institutionalize the model:

(i) The establishment agreement: this international agreement provides the legal structure for the multilateral center. It sets out its independent juridical status and its diplomatic status as an international organization. It should set out the high-level mandate to assist the peace process. It should also establish a governing executive council of member state diplomats that links the center to the broader peace process and international system.

(ii) The headquarters agreement: this agreement sets out the diplomatic status and protections afforded the organization and its headquarters seat in the host country. For particularly sensitive matters, this is crucial because it establishes the practical reality of the center's independence and separation from the host country.

In Strategy, Tactics, and Operations being a Resilient Channel in Balance

Again, analogous with the *falaj* approach, the center is the channel; it is the system in balance. The political environment will define the flow of peacebuilding activities. In time of kinetic war, there will be only the diplomatic precedent of multilateral equality. In a slightly improved scenario, there will be equal status contact. Leading up to a process, there will be confidence building measures and in the context of a political track there can be a broad array of peace building activities. The practical institutional characteristics underpinning this approach are the following:

- **A Coequal Partnership**: All member states, including core parties to the conflict and supporting states, are joint owners, joint guarantors, and coequal partners in the institution and its processes.

- **A Diplomatic Structure**: Diplomatic status, inviolability of the headquarters seat and status of center director as head of mission underpin the insistence on diplomatic norms, independence, and respect.

- **Independence:** The independence of the center is paramount and stated in the establishment agreement. While an executive council approves strategic plans, the center is wholly independent, tactically and operationally. It does not seek agreement of all parties on minutiae but rather consults with all and decides on a balanced approach that should be equally agreeable or disagreeable to all.

- **A Clear Mandate**: A broad, clear mandate principally to assist the peace process is preferable. This will empower the center to respond to the external political environment and follow an iterative approach. A frequent issue with treaty-based transboundary water organizations is narrowness of the mandate, which can limit broader peacebuilding activities.[42]

- **Working Primarily With Government Officials**: As a multilateral organization linked to the core parties of the conflict, the center can engage with and feed into deliberations of diplomats and government officials. MEDRC categorizes these as follows.

  - Track I activities involve officials from line departments.
  - Track I+ activities involve officials from line departments and diplomats.
  - Track I++ activities involve officials from line departments and diplomats in a normative process based on equality and balance.

Ideally, there should be a focus on Track I++, which is exceptionally difficult to achieve. A governing executive council of member state diplomats should underpin the Track I nature of the organization.

- **Addressing Capacity Disparities**: In addition to peacebuilding activities that involve core party contact, the center should engage in bilateral activities to address disparities in technical, institutional, or negotiations capacity in the mandate area.[43] Asymmetry and capacity disparities between core parties are harmful to building a sustainable peace. An imbalanced negotiation is less likely to produce an equitable agreement. This is particularly relevant in MEDRC's work; the asymmetry between Palestine and Israel is severe, playing a highly decisive role in peace process failure.[44]

Using the Model for Conflict Resolution

Breaking the cycle of intractable conflict demands societal change and a new repertoire that enables reaching agreement with a past rival.[45] The model is designed to support the entire repertoire. At a minimum, it institutionalizes the contact hypothesis, where equal status contact, sanctioned by institutional supports focused on common interests and common humanity, can minimize prejudice.[46]

Depending on flow, or degree of political will, the model, as a resilient channel, should be able to enact the complete array of technical and political peacebuilding initiatives including design and delivery of confidence building measures, contact groups, joint monitoring and evaluation, negotiations, track three, two, and one activities, joint gap-analysis, and final status negotiation support.

The Model in Practice

Since 2014 MEDRC has conducted its activities, from diplomatic executive council meetings to micro-initiatives such as one-person research projects, on the basis of this approach. The activities are presented below in a reductive form and are limited to activities pursued in the period immediately prior to the current Israel-Hamas war.

They comprise a Trilateral Program that is peace process focused and two bilateral programs focused primarily on Palestinian development assistance and state building support.

Trilateral Program

The MEDRC Trilateral Program was, in past years, the last formal process involving Palestinian and Israeli officials. The program is multilateral and engages Palestine, Jordan, and Israel in a MEDRC chaired process around transboundary environmental issues. The process involves diplomats and officials from line ministries. It is normative because it is multilateral and based on equality and balance. All activities take place in neutral locations, predominantly outside of the region. The program has been supported by the Swedish International Development Cooperation Agency (SIDA), the Netherlands Ministry of Foreign Affairs, and the German Federal Foreign Office. The activities are reviewed by the MEDRC Executive Council.

Under this program, MEDRC convenes an annual Trilateral Coordination Meeting comprising senior officials of Palestine, Jordan, and Israel. The parties meet in the MEDRC framework as joint owners, joint guarantors, and coequal partners in a process chaired by MEDRC. Each of the three member states makes a presentation on pressing environmental issues. The meeting then conducts a joint gap-analysis of environmental issues of concern or interest. Typically, areas of focus might include climate change, models of regional cooperation, or the water-energy nexus.

The meeting agrees on four or five areas of joint concern. These form the focus for four or five trilateral workshops held at neutral venues in Europe in the following year. Each member state is requested to nominate five delegates at the principal officer/director level or above. Again, these meetings are multilateral and members meet as equal parties. All activities are reported to the MEDRC Executive Council by means of a memorandum for information.

Such activities create a cohort of civil servants in key position across the core parties' administrative systems who have engaged in structured and repeated official contact based on equality. This is only feasible in a political framework around equality and multilateralism.

MEDRC also provides regular written briefings for officials of core party countries on issues around transboundary environmental issues, environmental peacebuilding, and public management.

Bilateral Program

The MEDRC bilateral program contains two streams of activity, focusing on Palestine and Jordan respectively. These member states are on the Organisation for Economic

Co-operation and Development (OECD) Development Assistance Committee (DAC) list and are thus entitled to direct bilateral support from international donors through MEDRC in areas where the organization has specific technical expertise.

These programs function as confidence building measures, underlining the ownership role of these states in MEDRC and the investment MEDRC makes in state and capacity building by working through local ministries and agencies. They also seek to equalize imbalance in capacity between core parties that may hinder future negotiations. Finally, they serve as a model for the delivery of development capacity support effectively and efficiently in the context of ongoing conflict.

These activities have been funded by the Qatar Fund for Development, SIDA, German Federal Foreign Office, and Netherlands Ministry of Foreign Affairs. The partners are the ministries in Palestine and Jordan that are also members of the MEDRC Executive Council.

Regarding bilateral activities in Palestine, for more than a decade, MEDRC has supported a fellowship program that supports environmental research in Palestine and Jordan. Activities are conducted in Palestine, in cooperation with the Palestinian Water Authority (PWA), the Ministry of Foreign Affairs and Expatriates, and Palestinian universities. All research is conducted at Palestinian universities under the supervision of Palestinian academics. Under this program, a biannual call for proposals is issued through the PWA for research in areas of national priority set by the PWA. Final selection is done through a joint committee of MEDRC, the PWA, and universities. MEDRC contracts the research activities directly with the researchers.

Since 2011 more than five hundred research projects have been supported in this way. MEDRC also supports a PhD program in water science in cooperation with the Islamic University of Gaza and the Al-Azahar University of Gaza. It has supported the capital costs for laboratory and testing equipment at the universities.

A continuous multiannual training program for officials and practitioners in desalination, wastewater, and non-revenue water, selected by the PWA, systematically builds and maintains a cohort of national experts trained to a high international standard. These are conducted in Palestine and at MEDRC headquarters in Muscat.

As a result of these activities, prior to the current war, MEDRC considered the capacity gap between Palestine and Israel in seawater desalination, non-revenue water, and waste water treatment to be closed. Huge disparities persisted in access to materials, fuel, and technology but they are a function of politics, not technical capacity.

The MEDRC Conflict Resolution Process Guidelines

All MEDRC conflict resolution activities above comply with the MEDRC Model approach. In designing and delivering these activities, MEDRC uses its own Conflict Resolution Process Guidelines that are designed to ensure that the peacebuilding activities operationally and tactically stay true to the model strategy and the commitment to achieving an overtly balanced outcome. They are designed to be transferable and are set out below.

The Rational-Reality Gap—The Test for Inclusion

A rational-reality gap occurs where a policy, project, or process is ineffective because it does not sufficiently account for realities, power-structures, or imbalances on the ground. This can occur when program or process design is conducted at a geographic or cultural distance or without balanced local input or understanding. In the peacebuilding field, this has been evident in recent decades in ineffective programmatic interventions designed to cure conflicts by creating liberal Western systems, in Iraq and Afghanistan especially but also across the Middle East, Balkans, and Africa.[47]

In response, MEDRC activities and processes should ensure that all conflict resolution activities and processes are owned by and co-developed with relevant core parties on the basis of strict equality and balance.

The Solution Looking for a Problem—The Test for Resilience

Peace processes are messy interactions of people, personalities, systems, and cultures. In all such complex human endeavors, people and organizations can be solutions or choices looking for problems.[48] In peace process practice this can lead to a short-term or risky focus on high-profile mediation and back-channel activities by individuals in place of longer-term, resilient, normative and institutional approaches. Conflicts attract all manner of interveners: activists, advocates, mediators, researchers, and enforcers.[49] The system of intervention is more important than the individual.

In response, MEDRC's activities and processes should

- Fit into the strategy to be a replicable model organization.
- Prioritize resilient systems not individual initiatives.
- Prioritize bureaucratic not charismatic leadership.

Transboundary Cooperation is Not Peace—The Test for Equality

Cooperation across borders or between warring factions is not necessarily synonymous with peace. In certain conditions, cooperation can embed neo-colonialism, dependency, or occupation. Broadly, environmental cooperation or joint management may create isolated islands of technical cooperation or symbolic rapprochement with little spillover into actual peace.[50] In conditions of conflict asymmetry, traditional problem-solving techniques such as cooperation can reinforce the relative power of the hegemon.[51] This is especially the case in a situation of profound power imbalances, where proposing 'confidence building' measures and mediation strategies may not only be inappropriate but also ineffective.[52]

In a violent or intractable conflict, the existence of a credible peace process or a political track is the difference between possible cooperation with a partner and impossible collaboration with an enemy.

In response MEDRC activities and processes should

- Utilize the equalizing political framework of joint and equal ownership and a commitment to an overtly balanced outcome.
- Insist on tactical and operational independence by management to secure balanced outcomes on the basis of dialogue with all.

Government is the Operating System—The Test for Multilateral Diplomacy

The Middle East peace process, like most major peace processes, involves multilateral tracks and issues around state recognition, rights, and obligations. States will be signatories, partners, and guarantors. Conflict resolution processes linked to, involving, and feeding into government efforts are especially valuable. In a world of declining multilateralism there is a responsibility to maintain and showcase its effectiveness.

In response, MEDRC activities and processes should

- Feed into diplomatic peace process efforts via the MEDRC Executive Council and briefings to member state foreign ministries.
- Prioritize Track I++ initiatives.
- In bilateral processes, prioritize delivery through state partners and agencies.
- Showcase positive normative effects of the MEDRC model to government systems through their involvement.

Ignoring Politics is Political—The Test for Impartiality

Politics is the ghost in the machine of transboundary dialogue and cooperation. In the peacebuilding field, there is significant acceptance now that peacebuilding is essentially political, not technical and programmatic.[53] Similarly, international deals on shared water resources are always linked with other issues.[54] Water development management or use cannot be purely technical and apolitical.[55]

In response, MEDRC processes should

- Adhere to the equalizing political framework around the joint owner, joint guarantor, coequal partner approach.
- Ensure that all processes, by adhering to this approach, are positively normative, supporting equalizing contact, and further embedding multilateral precedents around balance and equality.
- Be non-aligned and impartial in delivering the mandate, though not necessarily neutral which is non-political.[56]

The Academy is Not Society—The Test for Impact

Academic cooperation around narrow technical issues can be straightforward but often has little read-across to a peace process and conflict resolution. Linking such cooperation and broader political and diplomatic processes is important.

In response, MEDRC activities and processes should

- Engage in bilateral academic projects that are conducted though state partners as part of state capacity building.
- Ensure any trilateral academic processes, if possible, feed into and are part of a political process.

The Institutional and Agency Lacuna—The Test for Best Practice

There is an absence of internationally mandated institutions or actors in this field. There is also no formal peace process or political track between Palestine and Israel. Against that backdrop MEDRC processes need to be taken from universal best practice that is onward transferable to other conflicts and also to other parts of a future Middle East peace process.

In response, MEDRC activities and processes should

- Aim for international best practice and be transferable.
- Be capable of dissemination as part of the MEDRC Model.

Ideally then, for researchers and practitioners of environmental diplomacy, the MEDRC Model and associated Conflict Resolution Process Guidelines can provide greater insight and inspiration on new potential links between environment-related projects and peace. For states, it can provide a proven path to support international relations through joint action on areas like climate, water, and desertification.

Its most urgent and practical benefits are in the precedent is has set and its potential to play a role as part of a revived and reformed Middle East peace process.

Implications of the MEDRC Approach: Middle East Peace Process

The MEDRC capacity to operationalize balance, which elsewhere might be seen as unremarkable, is potentially transformative in the context of a revived Middle East peace process.

The most effective way to end the conflict in Palestine and Israel is through a balanced process that equalizes Palestinian and Israeli agency. That means a commitment to delivering an overtly balanced outcome that contains equal degrees of self-determination, security, and statehood for Palestinian and Israeli people alike. Past efforts failed because, ultimately, the Palestinian side was not offered actual statehood and self-determination. In the aftermath of the current war in Gaza, a reversion to the imbalanced approach is not tenable.

Based on the MEDRC approach, the following measures would indicate a level of seriousness and commitment that could help restore confidence and provide a framework for peace, reconstruction, and reconciliation.

Commit to a Revived Process Based on an Overtly Balanced Outcome

 a. The asymmetry and imbalance in the process over four decades is not a foundation for actual positive peace.

b. An agreement promising a Palestinian state in name only will not work. The usual process ending in last minute high-stakes pressure on the Palestinian side to accept an agreement that delivers unbalanced rights to security, water, economy, or borders will fail.

c. The revived process must be normative and balanced, based on equal status contact with institutional support and balanced international pressure.

d. It must be clear at the outset that a Palestinian state must have the same freedoms, powers, and responsibilities as Israel. It must have the power to guarantee its territorial integrity in the event of a change of Israeli government or future rejection of the peace agreement on the part of Israel.

e. Any legitimate security concerns on either side must be met through joint multilateral structures involving Palestine, Israel, and guarantor states and the UN as joint guarantors and coequal partners.

f. If two equal states are not delivered, the same equality and rights must be shared in one. Inequality on the grounds of religion or race is intolerable.

g. The people of Palestine and Israel must see equal degrees of gain and loss in any final text. This balance was the key reason the Irish peace process worked.

Normalization with Palestine

a. Credibly initiating a revived and balanced peace process requires recognition of a Palestinian state on the 1967 lines at the outset by all who recognize Israel.

b. Where that is not immediately politically possible by all, the imbalance brought about by the Abraham Accords should be reversed. Several Arab states normalized with Israel in the hopes that their actions would progress the peace process. This has not come to pass. To rebalance the process it is the turn of a similar number of Western states that do not recognize Palestine, but want to, to normalize now.

c. These Western states that normalize now with Palestine should do so with the public non-opposition of the US and the EU. This will provide a strong signal that the international commitment to self-determination and statehood for Palestinians is real.

Launch a Multilateral Peace Conference

a. It is appropriate to launch a revived peace process through a multilateral peace conference that would agree on a joint declaration committing to an overtly balanced outcome and equality of the parties to the process.

b. As envisaged in the EU peace conference concept, in the event that Palestine or Israel are not present at the initial phases, it is important that the international community progress and establish the normative framework of balance and begin work.

The New Track

a. The traditional Middle East peace process design included two supporting tracks: Israel-Palestine and Israel-Arab region. This approach is out of date.

b. A revived process requires a new, third US-EU–Palestine track to balance the Israel-Arab track and should include supports for state building, Gaza reconstruction, and long-term development cooperation elements of the settlement and statehood for Palestine.

c. This track implicitly recognizes the responsibility of the West toward Palestine while balancing the responsibility of the Arab nations toward Israel in the context of a final status agreement as envisaged in the Arab Peace Initiative.

New Multilateral Centers

a. A multilateral peace conference should establish or lend support to a series of resilient multilateral working groups based on the MEDRC approach.

b. In time, multilateral centers based on the MEDRC Model could be established, on each of these negotiation tracks or working group areas initially, or possibly on final status issues later on.

c. These would institutionalize progress and establish the new norm of balance.

Communicating the New Reality

a. In South Africa and Northern Ireland the truth that the status quo could no longer hold was a powerful precursor to compromise on the part of the dominant community.[57]

b. Continued settlement expansion, structural and kinetic violence, and what many consider a one-state reality means, already, that a two-state solution will be exceptionally difficult to secure.

c. In that context, it must be abundantly made clear that the focus on balance and equal degrees of self-determination works for two states or one. Failure to deliver equal degrees of self-determination in two states will inevitably lead to the establishment of equality in one state.

Conclusion

The shape of the Middle East peace process has not significantly changed in more than four decades. Since 1976, when the PLO first supported a draft United Nations Security Council Resolution on two states, the weaker Palestinian side has offered essentially the same concrete outcome; a state on the 1967 lines in return for peace and Arab recognition.[58] The stronger Israeli side has offered a staged process based around variations on the Palestinian autonomy approach contained in the 1978 Camp David Accords, autonomy of inhabitants in a state-minus, in a smaller territory.

The significance of MEDRC is its demonstration that another approach is possible. In a revived Middle East peace process, it is a model based on balance, parity of esteem, and multilateralism. Globally, in the area of environmental peacebuilding it is a model for states seeking to use transboundary environmental issues in the service of a peace process.

However, such models and systems are empty vessels without human agency and political will. The *falaj* is not the flow. The process is not the peace. A peaceful settlement to an intractable conflict requires that the majority of society members who participated in the conflict see the settlement as providing a fair and just solution.[59] In the context of the Middle East peace process, that means communities and leaders globally and locally uniting around the reality that for peace to exist there can be no hierarchy of humanity in the Holy Land.

Notes

1   Established formally in 1996 as the Middle East Desalination Research Centre (MEDRC), by virtue of its significantly altered area of focus and mandate, the organization today uses only the original abbreviation MEDRC. In branding the organization uses 'MEDRC: Water – Environment – Peace.'

2   Florian Krampe, Farah Hegazi, and Stacy D. VanDeveer, "Sustaining Peace through Better Resource Governance: Three Potential Mechanisms for Environmental Peacebuilding," *World Development* 144 (2021): 105508, 2, https://doi.org/10.1016/j.worlddev.2021.105508.

3   James Worrall, "'Switzerland of Arabia': Omani Foreign Policy and Mediation Efforts in the Middle East," *The International Spectator* 56, no. 4 (October 2, 2021): 142, https://doi.org/10.1080/03932729.2021.1996004.

4   Jeffrey A. Lefebvre, "Oman's Foreign Policy in the Twenty-First Century," *Middle East Policy Council*, March 22, 2010, https://mepc.org/journal/omans-foreign-policy-twenty-first-century.

5   Valeria Fiorani Piancentini, "The Growth of the Relationships between Oman, the Gulf and the Western Waters of the Indian Ocean. Oman: the Corner-Stone of a Maritime History," in *Oman and Overseas*, ed. Michaela Hoffmann-Ruf and Abdulrahman Al Salimi (Hildesheim: Georg Olms Verlag, 2013), 143.

6   Aman N. Ghazal, "Oman: The Arab View," in *Oman and Overseas*, ed. Michaela Hoffmann-Ruf and Abdulrahman Al Salimi (Hildesheim: Georg Olms Verlag, 2013), 342; Douglas Leonard, "Oman's Unique Approach to Mediation: A Solution for Sunni-Shia Conflicts?," The Centre for Security Studies at ETH Zurich, April 4, 2017, https://isnblog.ethz.ch/uncategorized/omans-unique-approach-to-mediation-a-solution-for-sunni-shia-conflicts; Hussein Ghubash, Oman – The Islamic Democratic Tradition (London: Routledge, 2006), 206.

7   Abdullah S. Al Ghafri et al., "Towards Sustainability and Equity in Access to Water: Design and Practices for *Aflāj* in Oman," *The Journal of Oman Studies* 18 (2014): 28, https://www.academia.edu/13597984/Towards_Sustainability_and_Equity_in_Access_to_Water_Design_and_Practices_for_Afl%C4%81j_in_Oman.

8   Zaher bin Khalid Al Sulaimani, Tariq Helmi, and Harriet Nash, "The Social Importance and Continuity of *Falaj* Use in Northern Oman," *International History Seminar on Irrigation and Drainage* (Tehran, May 2–5, 2007), 7, https://ore.exeter.ac.uk/repository/bitstream/handle/10036/15174/Iran%202007.pdf.

9   Tarek Majzoub, "Water Laws and Customary Water Arrangements," in *Arab Environment: Water; Sustainable Management of a Scarce Resource*, ed. Mohamed El-Ashry, Najib Saab, and Bashar Zeitoon (Beirut: Arab Forum for Environment and Development: 2010), 139, http://www.afedonline.org/en/reports/details/water.

10 Jeremy Jones and Nicholas Ridout, *Oman, Culture and Diplomacy* (Edinburgh, Edinburgh University Press, 2012), 55.

11 Joseph A. Kechichian, "Oman: A Unique Foreign Policy Produces a Key Player in Middle Eastern and Global Diplomacy," RAND Corporation, 1995, 1, https://www.rand.org/pubs/research_briefs/RB2501.html.

12 Benjamin Barthe, "Oman Acts as a Discreet Architect of Peace in the Middle East," *Le Monde in English*, July 13, 2023, https://www.lemonde.fr/en/international/article/2023/07/13/oman-a-discreet-architect-of-peace-in-the-middle-east_6052064_4.html.

13 Barney Afako, *A Field of Dilemmas: Managing Transitional Justice in Peace Processes* (New York: United Nations, 2010), 15, https://peacemaker.un.org/sites/peacemaker.un.org/files/SG-GuidanceNote-Brief-Field-Dilemmas-digital.pdf.

14 Simon Thompson, "Parity of Esteem and the Politics of Recognition," *Contemporary Political Theory* 1, no. 2 (2002): 203–20.

15 Johan Galtung, "Violence, Peace, and Peace Research," *Journal of Peace Research* 6, no. 3 (1969): 167–91.

16 Ghubash, *Oman – The Islamic Democratic Tradition*, 202.

17 Katariina Simonen, *Ancient Water Agreements, Tribal Law and Ibadism: Sources of Inspiration for the Middle East Desalination Research Centre – and Beyond?* (Cham, Switzerland: Springer, 2021), 182, https://doi.org/10.1007/978-3-030-85218-4.

18 Simonen, *Ancient Water Agreements*; Chapters 6 and 7 provide a detailed background.

19 Avi Schlaim, "Prelude to the Accord: Likud, Labour and the Palestinians," *Journal of Palestine Studies* 23, no. 2 (1994): 5–19, https://users.ox.ac.uk/~ssfc0005/Prelude%20to%20the%20Accord%20Likud,%20Labour%20and%20the%20Palestinians.html.

20 Abdel Monem Said Aly, Shai Feldman, and Khalil Shikaki, *Arabs and Israelis: Conflict and Peacemaking in the Middle East*, 2nd ed. (London: Bloomsbury Academic, 2022), 232.

21 Said Aly, Feldman, and Shikaki, Arabs and Israelis, 225.

22 The Oslo Accords, agreed between the PLO and Israel in 1993 and 1995 respectively, established a limited Palestinian self-governing entity within parts of the occupied territories, which became known as the Palestinian Authority. The premise of the Accords was that final status issues would be resolved within five years during which time the PLO would gain administrative experience and both sides would prove good faith. Though silent on the core issues of borders, settlements, the right of return, and the status of Jerusalem, it held out the potential of ending Israeli rule over the Palestinians living in the West Bank and Jordan and to pave the way to a two-state solution.

23 Etel Solingen, "The Multilateral Arab-Israeli Negotiations: Genesis, Institutionalization, Pause, Future," *Journal of Peace Research* 37, no. 2 (March 2000): 170, https://doi.org/10.1177/0022343300037002004.

24 Solingen, "The Multilateral Arab-Israeli Negotiations," 171.

25 Jones and Ridout, *Oman, Culture and Diplomacy*, 243.

26 Simonen, *Ancient Water Agreements*, 179.

27 "Middle East Peace Process Multilateral Working Groups on Water Resources and the Environment, Amman, Jordan, June 22, 1995, Press Statement of the Gavelholders," accessed March 14, 2024, https://1997-2001.state.gov/regions/nea/ppmwg2.html.

28 Amnon Aran, *Israeli Foreign Policy since the End of the Cold War* (Cambridge: Cambridge University Press, 2021), 85.

29 Aran, *Israeli Foreign Policy*, 163.

30 "Press Statement of the Gavelholder, Middle East Peace Process Multilateral Working Group on Water Resources, Hammamet, Tunisia, May 16th, 1996," accessed March 15, 2024, https://1997-2001.state.gov/regions/nea/ppmwg1.html.

31 Mark Zeitoun, *Power and Water in the Middle East: The Hidden Politics of the Palestinian–Israeli Water Conflict* (London: I.B. Tauris, 2012), 63.

32 Jan Selby, Gabrielle Daoust, and Clemens Hoffmann, *Divided Environments: An International Political Ecology of Climate Change, Water and Security* (Cambridge: Cambridge University Press, 2022), 254–55.

33 Jan Selby, "Joint Mismanagement: Reappraising the Oslo Water Regime," in *Water Resources in the Middle East: Israel-Palestinian Water Issues – From Conflict to Cooperation*, ed. Hillel Shuval and Hassan Dweik (Cham: Switzerland: Springer, 2007), 4.

34 Selby, Daoust, and Hoffman, Divided Environments, 254.

35 MEDRC, "The MEDRC Conflict Resolution Model," 2023, 1, https://medrcstabilization.org/wp-content/uploads/2024/05/MEDRC-INTRO-PAMPHLET-6.pdf.

36 Dané Smith and Kirsten Winterman, "Models and Mandates in Transboundary Waters: Institutional Mechanisms in Water Diplomacy," *Water* 14, no. 17 (August 2022): 2662, 4, https://doi.org/10.3390/w14172662.

37 A detailed discussion on the MEDRC Model is in Smith and Winterman, "Models and Mandates in Transboundary Waters."

38 Marko Keskinen, Erik Salminen, and Juho Haapala, "Water Diplomacy Paths – An Approach to Recognise Water Diplomacy Actions in Shared Waters," *Journal of Hydrology* 602 (November 2021): 126737, 3, https://doi.org/10.1016/j.jhydrol.2021.126737.

39 MEDRC Member States are the United States, Oman, Japan, Korea, Qatar, Palestine, Israel, Jordan, Germany, the Netherlands, and Spain.

40 Tobias Ide, "Environmental Peacebuilding," *Capaz Working Papers* 2021, no. 1 (2021): 12, https://usercontent.one/wp/www.instituto-capaz.org/wp-content/uploads/2021/03/DT-2-2021-Ingles-V3.pdf.

41 Alice Ackermann, "The Idea and Practice of Conflict Prevention," *Journal of Peace Research* 40, no. 3 (May 2003): 344, https://doi.org/10.1177/0022343303040003006.

42 Smith and Winterman, "Models and Mandates in Transboundary Waters," 15.

43 Mark Zeitoun et al., "Transboundary Water Interaction III: Contest and Compliance," *International Environmental Agreements: Politics, Law and Economics* 17, no. 2 (May 2016): 280, https://doi.org/10.1007/s10784-016-9325-x.

44 Alpaslan Özerdem and Roger Mac Ginty, "Conclusion: What Have We Learned," in *Comparing Peace Processes*, ed. Alpaslan Özerdem and Roger Mac Ginty (London: Routledge, 2019), 344.

45 Daniel Bar-Tal, *Intractable Conflicts: Socio-Psychological Foundations and Dynamics* (New York: Cambridge University Press, 2013), 323.

46 Krampe, Hegazi, and VanDeveer, "Sustaining Peace through Better Resource Governance," 5.

47 For a more detailed critique: Cedric de Coning, "Adaptive Peacebuilding," *International Affairs* 94, no. 2 (February 2018): 301–17, https://doi.org/10.1093/ia/iix251.

48 Michael D. Cohen, James G. March, and Johan P. Olsen, "A Garbage Can Model of Organizational Choice," *Administrative Science Quarterly* 17, no. 1 (1972): 1–25, https://doi.org/10.2307/2392088.

49 Tom Woodhouse et al., eds., *The Contemporary Conflict Resolution Reader* (Cambridge: Polity, 2015), 376.

50 Ide, "Environmental Peacebuilding," 17.

51 Woodhouse et al., *The Contemporary Conflict Resolution Reader*, 63.

52 Mandy Turner, "Israel and the Palestinians," in *Comparing Peace Processes*, ed. Alpaslan Özerdem and Roger Mac Ginty (London: Routledge, 2019), 250.

53 De Coning, "Adaptive Peacebuilding," 303.

54 Tony Allan, *The Middle East Water Question* (London: Bloomsbury, 2012), 253.

55 Clemens Messerschmid and Jan Selby, "Misrepresenting the Jordan River Basin," *Water Alternatives* 8, no. 2 (2015): 274, https://www.water-alternatives.org/index.php/alldoc/articles/vol8/v8issue2/290-a8-2-13/file.

56 Woodhouse et al., *The Contemporary Conflict Resolution Reader*, 379.

57 Daniel Bar-Tal, *Intractable Conflicts*, 337.

58 Colter Louwerse, "'Tyranny of the Veto': PLO Diplomacy and the January 1976 United Nations Security Council Resolution," *Diplomacy & Statecraft* 33, no. 2 (April 2022): 303–29, https://doi.org/10.1080/09592296.2022.2062127.

59 Bar-Tal, *Intractable Conflicts*, 336.

THE MIDDLE EAST: FROM AN INFLAMMABLE REGION TO A RESILIENT LAND OF OPPORTUNITIES

A CASE STUDY OF ECOPEACE MIDDLE EAST'S UNIQUE APPROACH TO CONFLICT AND ENVIRONMENTAL ACTION

Yana Abu Taleb

EcoPeace Middle East Jordan

Thalsa-Thiziri Mekaouche

EcoPeace Middle East, Yale University

ABSTRACT

The Middle East is an inflammable region on multiple levels. The ongoing war between Israel and Hamas, with its overwhelming loss of human lives, has further disrupted the already fragile prospect of peace in the region. It is also 'inflammable' from an environmental perspective, insofar as it is considered the most climate vulnerable region on Earth, with an expected 4°C increase in average temperature over the next

Yana Abu Taleb is the Jordanian Director of EcoPeace Middle East. She has been a part of EcoPeace for two decades and acting director since 2018. A committed environmental advocate and peacebuilder, she manages national and regional projects, acts as a liaison for environmental protection and water issues, and engages with government and private sectors.

Thalsa-Thiziri Mekaouche is a student at Yale University. She serves on the secretariat of the Centre for International Sustainable Development Law and is Programme Assistant to the Democratising Education for Global Sustainability and Justice program, an initiative by the University of Cambridge. She interned with EcoPeace Middle East in 2023 and 2024. Her work is supported by the Global Food Fellowship, the Henry Hart Rice Foreign Residence Fellowship, the Libby Rouse Fund for Peace, and the Ganzfried Family Travel Fellowship.

decades. Yet, through the example of EcoPeace Middle East, an environmental and peacebuilding regional organization working in Jordan, Israel, and Palestine, this article sheds light on a theory of change that seeks to transform the Middle East into a climate-resilient and peaceful region.

Ongoing Conflict and the Triple Planetary Crisis: the Middle East at a Crossroads

The world is facing a triple planetary crisis: climate change, pollution, and biodiversity loss. These three interlinked issues threaten human livelihoods.[1] It is estimated that over the next fifty years, one to three billion people will live in extreme climate conditions, which will significantly impact health, food security, and migration trajectories.[2] Pollution creates significant health hazards for vulnerable communities while the unprecedented rate of biodiversity loss has been described as a biological annihilation or sixth mass extinction.[3]

The Middle East is one of the most climate vulnerable regions on Earth. While the rest of the world is seeking to avoid a 1.5°C increase in temperature, the Middle East is forecast to see a 4°C increase.[4] Large parts of the region will simply become unlivable during the long summer months. This climate vulnerability is further exacerbated by underlying dependencies on food imports and reliance on fossil fuels. The Middle East is also the world's most water-scarce region, which stresses ecosystems, economies, and population health.

In recent years, growing attention has been paid to the nexus between climate and political stability, giving rise to the concept of climate security, that is, "the impacts of climate change on peace and security, particularly in fragile and conflict-affected settings."[5] In its Sixth Assessment Report, the Intergovernmental Panel on Climate Change concludes "that risks to peace will increase with warming, with the largest impacts expected in weather-sensitive communities with low resilience to climate extremes and high prevalence of underlying risk factors."[6] The acknowledgment of a nexus between climate adaptation and peacebuilding was further highlighted when the COP27 Presidency launched the Climate Responses for Sustaining Peace Initiative, to "ensure that integrated climate responses contribute to sustainable peace and development in line with national ownership and context specificity."[7]

Beyond the risks to the region's stability posed by the triple planetary crisis, the Middle East is already experiencing high levels of conflict and violence. Before the start of the Israel-Hamas war, the region had the world's highest number of battle-related deaths (26,270 in 2021), primarily due to the escalation of the conflict in Yemen.[8] Since October 7, 2023, the region has been plunged further into the horrors of high intensity conflict, and 36,000 have been killed in the first seven months of the war.

Despite this convergence of crises, EcoPeace Middle East, nominee for the 2024 Nobel Peace Prize, has developed a theory of change that seeks to simultaneously address climate change and conflict resolution in Jordan, Israel, and Palestine. This article focuses on this unique paradigm in the region and gives insights into the prospects of reversing the narrative attached to the Middle East: from a climate vulnerable and conflict-prone region to a resilient and peaceful land of opportunities.

EcoPeace Middle East: Born at a Time of Hope and Resilient in Conflict

EcoPeace Middle East was born out of a paradox: because climate change is fundamentally threatening all aspects of human livelihood, it can act as the ultimate trigger for a peace process in seemingly intractable situations. For three decades, the non-profit organization has advocated, and acted on the ground, to demonstrate that climate action, and more broadly environmental stewardship, can serve as a pathway toward peace instead of a trigger for conflict.

At a December 7, 1994 meeting of environmental non-governmental organizations in Taba, Egypt, EcoPeace Middle East was founded to foster sustainable development across the region. In the first stages of its existence, EcoPeace Middle East sought to protect the environment, which was endangered because of a lack of cross border cooperation related to the underlying Israeli-Palestinian conflict and its ramifications in neighboring Jordan. Until 2001, EcoPeace acted from a rational, single-minded focus on the environment, considering the political situation in the region to be a detrimental backdrop that had to be dealt with separately. But soon, when it became obvious that the Oslo Accords had failed to attain their objectives, EcoPeace Middle East started to develop what has become its landmark vision: building peace through environmental action.[9] The organization committed itself to an integrated approach that bridges political and interpersonal gaps between Jordanians, Israelis, and Palestinians by addressing shared challenges.

Prior to the emergence of this new paradigm, peacebuilding had been approached as a lose-lose game in the Israeli-Palestinian conflict. The traditional approach to peace was a story of who would lose territory, identity, or means toward sustainable development. EcoPeace transformed that narrative. Instead of focusing on what could be lost, it focuses on what can be gained, such as a healthy Jordan River Valley, to provide economic and social benefits to all three countries, improved access to high quality water resources, and a vast range of educational opportunities across Jordan, Israel, and Palestine.

At a time when the current crisis seems to have ended all prospects of stability and peace, EcoPeace Middle East is demonstrating a high level of organizational resilience. Throughout its thirty years of existence, it has overcome many acute eruptions of violence. Its flagship project, the Good Water Neighbors (GWN) initiative, was born at a time when no one believed peace was possible, at the start of the Second Intifada in 2001. The Good Water Neighbors project, which involves communities on either side of the border, brought the environmental issues of saving the Dead Sea and rehabilitating the River Jordan to the regional decision-making table, making it a model for educational and community programs in other regions of conflict. EcoPeace Middle East's organizational resilience also springs from its focus on two issues that cannot be sidelined: human prosperity and the environmental crisis. Despite the humanitarian tragedy currently unfolding, and perhaps because of the level of destruction, these two concerns will remain at the forefront of today and tomorrow's policy agenda.

EcoPeace Middle East's Theory of Change

A theory of change is a method that explains how a given intervention, or set of interventions, are expected to lead to a specific development change, drawing on a causal analysis based on available evidence.[10] It is grounded in the local context. It helps to identify solutions that address the underlying causes that hinder progress toward a goal and can help develop and manage partnerships with a variety of stakeholders.

EcoPeace Middle East is uniquely positioned, with its three offices and multi-stakeholder approach, to develop an effective theory of change to advance its vision in Jordan, Israel, and Palestine. Over the last three decades, it has articulated a three-step theory of change.

Increasing Knowledge, Developing Awareness of Climate Change and Environmental Degradation

Jordanians, Israelis, and Palestinians are experiencing conflict on all levels, each with their own narrative, from the most intimate circles to the global political stage. These competing visions and 'narrative landscapes' have become dominated by a few simplified representations of the conflict, which have deepened the polarization of societies.[11] EcoPeace Middle East has long understood that seeking to complexify narratives, while it is an indispensable step in building long-lasting coexistence, can be premature and trigger rejection from local communities and authorities. Thus, it has identified regional climate security and environmental protection as a point of entry for change. EcoPeace first raises awareness of the impacts of these crises at the national level, for instance, how Jordanians are impacted by water scarcity. Then, this national understanding of an acute environmental crisis is broadened through a regional lens, which leads interlocutors into realizing that regional cooperation is necessary to effectively address the environmental crisis.

Positioning

Once a satisfying level of public awareness is reached on climate change and environmental degradation, EcoPeace Middle East works on positioning. Positioning is understood as the realization by an individual or a collective that they must take action regarding the aforementioned issues. In other words, it is the step where the knowledge that there is a crisis becomes an imperative to take personal or collective action. One positions oneself as a doer rather than a disempowered victim.

Behavioral Change

After positioning comes the necessity to seek behavioral change. This 'how to' question arises, i.e., how to take action against what has been identified as a tangible existential threat. At this stage, EcoPeace Middle East utilizes its multi-stakeholder approach to create the enabling environment that will allow individuals, communities, and officials to take effective action against climate change and environmental degradation. At this point, when locals are empowered, they can turn to regional cooperation, understanding that their action alone will not be sufficient to build sustainability.

This theory of change has been adapted to match EcoPeace Middle East's expanded scope of action. Since its founding, the organization gradually moved from community action to a basin-wide approach and later started operating at the national level. In the past decade, EcoPeace built credibility at the regional and international levels by engaging in high-level political forums, for instance the United Nations Security Council where the leadership briefed the Council on urgent steps needed to secure climate resilience and advance peace in the Middle East.[12]

Within this framework of change, EcoPeace Middle East combines two types of approaches, top-down and bottom-up, to bridge the gap between communities, decision-makers, and the urgent actions required to tackle both the environmental crisis and the conflict.

Top-Down Approach

In intractable conflicts, reasons for disagreements and confrontations are endless. Trying to diagnose and resolve each is a daunting task whose potential successful outcomes are doubtful. The Israeli-Palestinian conflict is one of those situations where the number of disputes and psychological barriers is such that traditional approaches to peacebuilding, which typically try to address each dispute separately, has led to repeated failures over the decades.

This is where climate change becomes an opportunity. Never was humanity threatened by such a multidimensional phenomenon. Climate change is a challenge shared by Jordan, Israel, and Palestine, regardless of their political disputes. It is thus the only potential uniting factor to push governments to cooperate. Already, when water resources were at risk during drought periods throughout the 1950s, Jordanian and Israeli officials met at the border in spite of their two countries being at war.[13] EcoPeace Middle East has leveraged the urgency of the climate crisis to advocate for regional cooperation and integration.

A case study of this top-down approach is EcoPeace's flagship strategy: the Green Blue Deal for the Middle East. Inspired by the Green New Deal in the US, the European Green Deal, and the individual nationwide commitments made by Jordan, Israel, and Palestine in their respective climate action plans, EcoPeace Middle East has used its experience in transboundary cooperation to elaborate a vision of regional climate security and integration. The Green Blue Deal for the Middle East is a practical, feasible, and effective policy approach to an urgent challenge, and one that can address conflict drivers, advance a two state solution based on 1967 borders, and promote trust-building and cooperation in a conflict-mired region.[14]

A flagship component of the proposed Green Blue Deal is the Water-Energy Nexus: the vision that a healthy interdependency with regards to water and renewable energy between Israel, Jordan, and Palestine would help advance lasting peace between the three countries.[15] Informed by European history, where agreements over steel and coal were the backbone of the creation of a more peaceful Europe and led to the formation of the European Union, EcoPeace envisions a partnership in which Palestine and Israel would supply desalinated water to Jordan and in turn, Jordan would sell solar-generated electricity to the two countries. With these new arrangements Israel would make significant progress to meet its commitments for renewable energy under the Paris Agreement and Jordan would be able to meet its basic water needs.[16]

After years of advocacy for this transboundary water-energy economy, Jordan and Israel signed a declaration of intent to materialize this exchange of resources. A 600-megawatt (MW) solar farm is to be built by 2026 in Jordan, financed by the UAE's private sector, and will produce energy that will be sent to Israel in exchange for 200 million m³ of water annually from a new coastal desalination facility near Nahariya, Israel.[17] While the current Israel-Hamas war has resulted in uncertainty regarding immediate future prospects for the Green Blue Deal, EcoPeace maintains that achieving regional economic integration by leveraging economically sound comparative advantages on water and energy, will be a key step in building regional resilience.[18] In parallel to advancing the Jordan-Israel deal on water and energy, EcoPeace is working to build upon the existing Palestinian-Jordanian energy bilateral agreements (whereby Jordan supplies electricity from a power station in the Jordan valley to a Palestinian power grid) by advancing dialogue on expanding the existing transmission line to a higher capacity to receive renewable energy. In addition, it has proposed Palestinian-Israeli renewable energy cooperation, whereby a 200 MW solar facility would be built by the Palestinian private sector in Area C of the West Bank to be used there and/or to be transferred through Israel to power wastewater and desalination facilities in Gaza. The climate crisis and its impacts on water and national security are well recognized by all sides. This security interdependence will remain a powerful force to repair and rebuild relations as the climate crisis becomes more and more exacerbated.

Bottom-Up Approach

Political leaders can be reluctant to take bold initiatives, such as the ones proposed in the Green Blue Deal, when they are afraid of popular discontent. For instance, the Palestinian 'anti-normalization' movement opposes any cooperation with Israel and affects political buy-in, from decision-makers and the private sector, to engage in regional cooperation. Hence it is important to work with communities to create acceptance at the grassroots level. Since its creation, EcoPeace Middle East has invested considerably into education to this end.

As mentioned earlier, even when conflict reached a climax in the early 2000s, EcoPeace Middle East committed itself to cross-border education. It developed a community-based awareness program called Good Water Neighbors. In 2001, when it was launched, convincing the eleven original participating communities that they would benefit from the program proved difficult. Today, there are more communities seeking to join the project than the available funds can enable to participate. Jenin and Yatta in the Hebron Governorate, joined the program with concrete cross-border projects they seek to implement with the support of their neighboring community. In fact, EcoPeace believes that instead of 'good fences' creating good neighborly relations, security barriers dividing communities not only contribute to ecological demise but are often the source of attitudes that blame the other side for all of the problems and behaviors that contribute to environmental degradation. EcoPeace's bottom-up education and public awareness programs have therefore focused on the shared interest in good water for all, as the entry point for mainstreaming peace and sustainability issues into education programs.

The Good Water Neighbors project has encouraged young people for nearly two decades to support concrete environmental solutions and become agents of change for regional cooperation. It includes two main components: school programs and young professional programs. The school programs target youth (ages 16 to 18) in Jordanian, Palestinian, and Israeli high schools. EcoPeace helps to develop lesson plans that either expand existing official school curricula or introduce new curriculum, and provide national and regional teacher training, site tours, summit days, and support for student-led projects. Young professional programs include two tracks: Climate Diplomacy for Young Professionals, which allows young leaders from Palestine, Israel, and Jordan to build their knowledge and skills related to climate change and regional cooperation, and the Green Social Entrepreneurship track where young entrepreneurs from the three countries are provided with technical and financial support to set up their own business for their innovative projects with a strong sustainable component.

Through this focus on education, EcoPeace Middle East has trained current and future community leaders in its innovative approach to peacebuilding. This granular work, adapted to local needs and contexts, is key to achieving lasting peace.

Beyond Top-Down and Bottom-Up Approaches: Creating a Space for Psychological Relief and Imagination

Throughout its existence, EcoPeace Middle East leveraged millions of dollars in physical infrastructure investments, in education programs, and in advocacy efforts that have led to promising transboundary cooperation on key environmental and social issues. But perhaps one of its most innovative remedies to conflict in the region has been its focus on helping individuals and communities address the traumas they have experienced. The Jordan EcoPark, an area of biodiversity conservation and green tourism managed by EcoPeace in the Jordan Valley, has been the catalyst of this emphasis on creating a peacebuilding 'mindset' or readiness.[19] When Israelis, Jordanians, and Palestinians gather at the EcoPark to participate in the organization's regional programming, fences and barriers, both physical and mental, eventually fall. For a few hours, or a few days, visitors understand that they belong to the same territory: the Jordan River Basin, with its incredible religious significance for half of the world's population and its unique biodiversity. In other words, the EcoPark represents everything that lasting peace between the three populations could look like. It is a place for exchanging knowledge and letting go of what appears to be intractable in this conflict. This psychological space for a creative approach to peacebuilding is essential, especially in this time of crises.

Finally, the leadership of the EcoPeace organization has engaged in a unique experiment, aimed at building internal resilience. Since October 7, 2023, all staff members have been undergoing mindfulness training under the supervision of a neutral third party to process the impacts of the war on their colleagues and themselves. This illustrates once more that creating dialogue opportunities where psychological barriers previously seemed insurmountable, is key to peacebuilding in the region.

Conclusion

The Middle East is, more than ever, described by observers around the world as an inflammable region, almost doomed to chaos and bloodshed. In this context of destruction and loss of human lives, discussions of climate change and environmental stewardship have been sidelined, despite the fact that every year, more socioeconomic losses are caused by the exacerbation of the triple planetary crisis. War has also created urgent humanitarian needs. This ocean of needs, from two particularly complex challenges, may appear overwhelming. However, this article has shown, through the example of EcoPeace Middle East's work, that by addressing both crises together, there is a way forward to a 'day after' with a climate-resilient and peaceful region. This is not wishful thinking; it is happening in the backstage of the war. Determined organizations and communities are ready to own their future; this is why climate and environmental action can be the means to reinvent another Middle East, one that does not evoke chaos or bloodshed, but that strives toward locally adapted and sustainable solutions for a common future.

Notes

[1] United Nations Climate Change, "What is the Triple Planetary Crisis?," April 13, 2022, https://unfccc.int/news/what-is-the-triple-planetary-crisis.

[2] Chi Xu et al., "Future of the Human Climate Niche," *Proceedings of the National Academy of Sciences* 117, no. 21 (May 2020): 11350–55, https://doi.org/10.1073/pnas.1910114117.

[3] Gerardo Ceballos, Paul R. Ehrlich, and Rodolfo Dirzo, "Biological Annihilation via the Ongoing Sixth Mass Extinction Signaled by Vertebrate Population Losses and Decline," *Proceedings of the National Academy of Sciences* 114, no. 30 (July 2017), E6089–E6096, https://doi.org/10.1073/pnas.1704949114.

[4] Gidon Bromberg, Nada Majdalani, and Yana Abu Taleb, "A Green Blue Deal for the Middle East," EcoPeace Middle East, 2020, https://ecopeaceme.org/wp-content/uploads/2021/03/A-Green-Blue-Deal-for-the-Middle-East-EcoPeace.pdf.

[5] UNDP Climate Promise, "What Is Climate Security and Why Is It Important?," September 1, 2023, https://climatepromise.undp.org/news-and-stories/what-climate-security-and-why-it-important.

[6] Intergovernmental Panel on Climate Change (IPCC), "Key Risks across Sectors and Regions," in *Climate Change 2022 – Impacts, Adaptation and Vulnerability: Working Group II Contribution to the Sixth Assessment Report of the Intergovernmental Panel on Climate Change* (Cambridge: Cambridge University Press, 2023), 2411–538.

7   United Nations Development Programme (UNDP), "First Consultation Meeting of the COP27 Presidency Initiative 'Climate Responses for Sustaining Peace (CRSP)' Sets Roadmap for Implementation," March 12, 2023, https://www.undp.org/egypt/press-releases/first-consultation-meeting-cop27-presidency-initiative-climate-responses-sustaining-peace-crsp-sets-roadmap-implementation.

8   Júlia Palik, Anna Marie Obermeier, and Siri Aas Rustad, "Conflict Trends in the Middle East, 1989–2021," Peace Research Institute Oslo (PRIO), 2022, https://www.prio.org/publications/13298.

9   Gidon Bromberg, "Reflections Paper," accessed February 18, 2024, https://ecopeaceme.org/reflections-paper-gidon-bromberg/.

10 United Nations Sustainable Development Group (UNSDG), "UNDAF – Guidance on Theory of Change," February 2016, https://unsdg.un.org/resources/undaf-guidance-theory-change.

11 Institute for Integrated Transitions (IFIT), "The Role of Narrative in Managing Conflict and Supporting Peace," February 2021, https://ifit-transitions.org/publications/the-role-of-narrative-in-managing-conflict-and-supporting-peace/.

12 EcoPeace Middle East, "EcoPeace Briefs the UNSC on Urgent Steps Needed to Secure Climate Resilience & Advance Peace," YouTube video, January 27, 2022, 16:39, https://www.youtube.com/watch?v=2AFFBpqOSoQ.

13 Yumiko Yasuda et al., "Transboundary Water Cooperation over the Lower Part of the Jordan River Basin: Legal Political Economy Analysis of Current and Future Potential Cooperation," The Hague Institute for Global Justice, August 2017, https://climate-diplomacy.org/sites/default/files/2020-10/Water Diplomacy_Making Water Cooperation Work_Jordan River.pdf.

14 Jessye B. Waxman et al., "A Water and Energy Nexus as a Catalyst for Middle East Peace," *International Journal of Water Governance* 3, no. 1 (2015): 71–92, https://journals.open.tudelft.nl/ijwg/article/view/5893.

15 David Katz and Arkady Shafran, "Water Energy Nexus: A Prefeasibility Study for Mid-East Water-Renewable Energy Exchanges," EcoPeace Middle East / Konrad-Adenauer-Stiftung, 2017, https://reliefweb.int/report/jordan/water-energy-nexus-pre-feasibility-study-mid-east-water-renewable-energy-exchanges; Mohammad Bundokji, "Water-Energy Nexus: An Innovative Approach to Peacebuilding," Climate Diplomacy, March 14, 2017, https://climate-diplomacy.org/magazine/environment/water-energy-nexus-innovative-approach-peacebuilding.

16 "EcoPeace at the UNSC," accessed February 17, 2024, https://ecopeaceme.org/2022/02/06/ecopeace-at-the-unsc/.

17 Al Jazeera, "Israel Advances Water-for-Energy Deal with Jordan, UAE," September 26, 2023, https://www.aljazeera.com/news/2023/9/26/israel-advances-water-for-energy-deal-with-jordan-uae.

18 "EcoPeace at the UNSC."

19 Gabrielle Rifkind and Nita Yawanarajah, "Preparing the Psychological Space for Peacemaking," *New England Journal of Public Policy* 31, no. 1, article 7, https://scholarworks.umb.edu/nejpp/vol31/iss1/7.

PIONEERING THE DIGITAL FRONTIER: CMI'S APPROACH TO FORWARD-LOOKING DIALOGUES

Johanna Poutanen

CMI – Martti Ahtisaari Peace Foundation

Felix Kufus

CMI – Martti Ahtisaari Peace Foundation

ABSTRACT

As contemporary conflicts grow increasingly complex, new approaches to peacemaking are needed. This article outlines how CMI – Martti Ahtisaari Peace Foundation (CMI) incorporates technology-enhanced foresight methodologies into its dialogue and mediation work. Digital tools, such as software dedicated to data analysis and visualization, play a key role in CMI's foresight approach by facilitating broad-based data collection and participatory analysis. Interactive visual aids foster collective sense-making and help challenge entrenched mindsets of conflict stakeholders. The article illustrates how foresight approaches can be used to develop shared future visions and facilitate collaboration even in the context of stalled peace processes.

Johanna Poutanen is CMI's Head for Digital Peacemaking and Women in Peacemaking. She has over two decades of professional experience in peace mediation, having advised and led inclusive dialogue processes in several conflict-affected contexts.

Felix Kufus is a consultant with CMI's Digital Peacemaking Team, focusing on the use of digital tools for inclusion and foresight.

The Changing Nature of Conflict and the Need for Foresight in Peacemaking

As the nature and dynamics of violent conflict evolve, both peace practitioners and policymakers find themselves at a critical juncture. We are witnessing an era of hybrid conflicts, where conventional and unconventional warfare blend with cyber and disinformation campaigns, creating complex and volatile dynamics.[1] The urgent climate crisis introduces another layer of instability, exacerbating resource scarcity and displacing populations, thus becoming a catalyst for conflicts.[2] Growing geopolitical tensions are influencing regional security dynamics and bringing new dimensions to peacemaking efforts. Altogether, the shifting landscape of global peace and security demands more than reactive strategies—it requires a framework that fosters a multidimensional understanding of the underlying causes of conflict and enables the identification of ways forward.[3] To this end, the application of foresight approaches presents significant potential to strengthen peacemaking praxis.

Foresight is understood as the systematic exploration of alternative futures using a variety of methods such as horizon scanning to identify emerging trends and disruptions as well as scenario planning, which entails constructing alternative futures to test and enhance present-day decision-making and policy development.[4] In the context of peacemaking, foresight methodologies are used to aid conflict parties look beyond their current positions and consider wider conflict drivers, such as economic and demographic trends, impacts of climate change, or global political developments.[5] At the same time, foresight methodologies enable conflict stakeholders to imagine alternative futures.[6]

CMI – Martti Ahtisaari Peace Foundation (CMI) is an independent Finnish organization that works to prevent and resolve violent conflicts through dialogue and mediation. Founded in 2000 by Nobel Peace Prize laureate and former president of Finland Martti Ahtisaari, the organization is focused on facilitating track 1.5 and track 2 dialogues that engage a broad spectrum of stakeholders, including political party leaders, civil society actors, and representatives from marginalized groups, often to complement and strengthen formal peacemaking processes.

Over the past decade, CMI has pioneered a digitally enhanced foresight methodology in future-oriented dialogue processes across countries such as Yemen, Libya, Palestine, and Armenia. Fundamental to this approach is the use of software dedicated to data analysis and visualization. CMI's tool of choice has been Inclus, a software solution provided by a Finnish company of the same name.

In practical terms, the forward-looking dialogue process typically starts by jointly analyzing the present state of affairs. Conflict stakeholders are first invited to engage with the factual realities of the conflict by gathering and examining data about past events, current conditions, and views of different groups. The software, coupled with expert facilitation, aids in mapping and displaying the diverse positions of participants. This ensures a comprehensive consideration of various stakeholder perspectives, thereby grounding discussions in the "world as it is."[7] The primary objective of this fact-based approach is to establish a clear and shared understanding of the current state of the conflict. Once key political, social, and economic indicators have been collaboratively examined, the group commonly transitions into the scenario-building phase, crafting alternative futures of the "world as it could or should be" based on the previously established facts and figures.[8] Active facilitation of the process, combined with the use of the Inclus software, provides a structured framework for participatory conflict analysis, scenario building, and enhanced policy planning.

The following sections present two case studies that illustrate CMI's use of digitally augmented foresight in dialogue processes in Armenia and Libya. Drawing on CMI's past experiences, this article suggests some of the key benefits, limitations, and broader potential of foresight and accompanying digital approaches for peacemaking.

CMI's Forward-Looking Dialogue Processes in Armenia and Libya

The conflict between Armenia and Azerbaijan over Nagorno-Karabakh is a long-standing ethnic and territorial dispute that has its roots in the early twentieth century. Nagorno-Karabakh is a region in southwestern Azerbaijan (see Figure 1) that has a majority ethnic Armenian population. The conflict began when the ethnic Armenian population of Nagorno-Karabakh sought to secede from Azerbaijan and join Armenia after the fall of the Soviet Union. A full-scale war in the early 1990s, resulting in significant human suffering, displacement, and economic devastation, ended with a ceasefire between Armenia and Azerbaijan in 1994. Tensions between Armenia and Azerbaijan have continued to simmer, with a major escalation of the conflict in 2020 that resulted in significant losses on both sides and the capture of key territories by

Azerbaijan. A ceasefire agreement was brokered by Russia and led to the deployment of Russian peacekeepers in the region. In 2023, Azerbaijan launched a lightning offensive in Nagorno-Karabakh, which led to the takeover of the region and the official dissolution of the ethnic Armenian enclave on January 1, 2024. The conflict resulted in the displacement of more than 100,500 people to Armenia.[9]

Figure 1. Nagorno-Karabakh region as depicted in December 2020. Nicole Thomas et al., "What the United States Military Can Learn from the Nagorno-Karabakh War."[10]

Shortly before the latest escalation of conflict in September 2023, CMI facilitated a series of dialogue workshops with Armenian stakeholders, including parliamentarians, government officials, and members of civil society, to explore the future trajectories of the country's development and the Armenian-Azerbaijani peace process. The process began by jointly analyzing the present state of affairs in Armenia by gathering and discussing data about past events, current conditions, and views of different groups, to establish a shared understanding of the conflict. Using the Inclus software, stakeholders identified and assessed indicators that could determine Armenia's future political trajectory, either leaning toward liberal or authoritarian directions. These indicators, such as "#25 Armenia becomes a global transit zone," "#49 Azerbaijan again attacks the international border," and "#61 Pro-Russian Armenian oligarchs becomes instrumental in decision-making process in the country," were visualized on a scatter plot, which illuminated the complex interplay of factors driving Armenia's potential path (see Figure 2). After developing the scenario narratives, participants presented and reflected on the implications of each scenario. They ranged from a future Armenia close to Russia to one close to the West and they were characterized by civic polarization or public harmony. Last, participants from each stakeholder group selected key indicators responsible for Armenia's political trajectory in liberal or authoritarian directions and developed concrete actions to achieve or improve those indicators. This exercise fostered a strong sense of ownership and agency among participants, as reflected in one participant's statement: "When thinking about the Future of Armenia, especially when it comes to conflict resolution, we never speak about the agency Armenia has but treat it more as subject to other powers."[11]

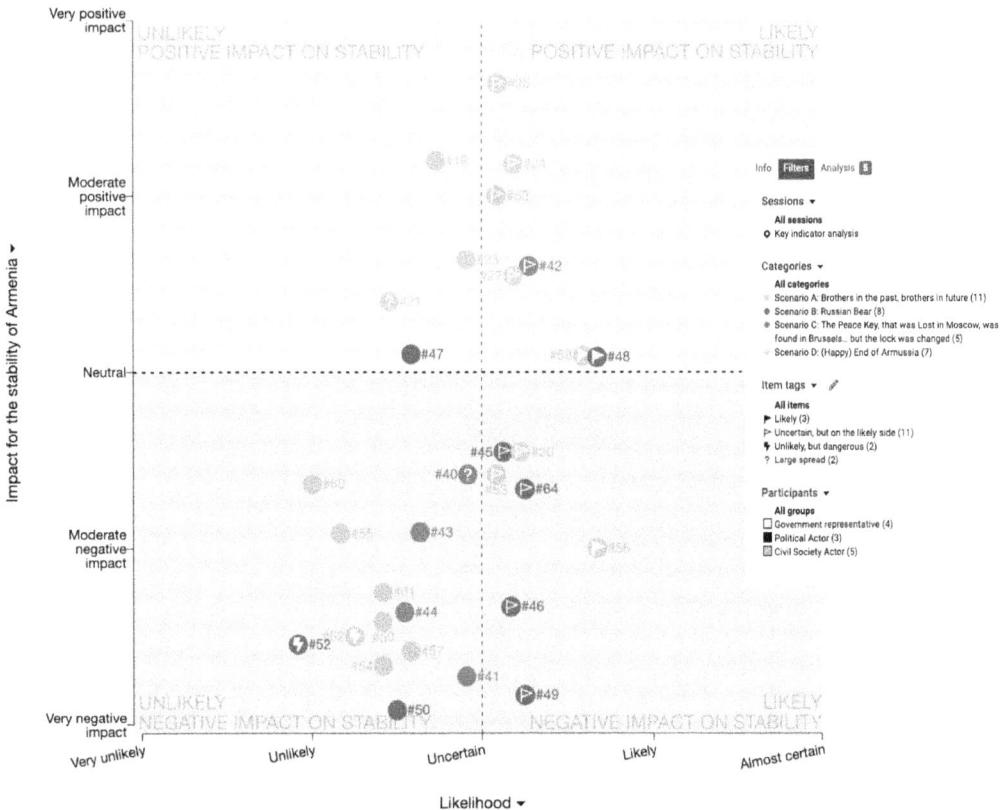

Figure 2. Example of a joint impact analysis generated using Inclus software during the Armenia workshop.

The second phase of the process focused on understanding the current trends of the Armenian-Azerbaijani peace process and possible futures deriving from it. After highlighting around forty conflict-relevant indicators, the participants used the Inclus tool to rank the indicators based on their relevance and impact on the peace process. As a result, the increasing Western mediation in the process and worsening security situation in the Nagorno-Karabakh region were highlighted as the most impactful indicator.

Using these trends, two axes were chosen as a basis for the development of the scenarios: the vertical axis highlighting the failure or success of Western mediation, and the horizontal axis highlighting the problem of human rights and security guarantees for the Armenian population in Nagorno-Karabakh. Four scenarios were developed based on these axes, with the most likely scenario being failed mediation and military escalation in Nagorno-Karabakh, resulting in the exodus of the Armenian population—a scenario that became reality shortly after.

Another example of CMI's forward-looking dialogue is the process conducted in Libya in 2021 as part of efforts to establish a shared vision for the country's political future termed 'Vision 2040 for Libya.'

Since the overthrow of Muammar Gaddafi in 2011, Libya has been engulfed in a state of profound instability marked by the fall of a centralized authority and the rise of multiple armed factions (see Figure 3). The political vacuum has led to severe conflicts, especially since 2014, as two principal factions emerged: the General National Congress (GNC) in Tripoli, and an eastern-based government allied with General Khalifa Haftar. This division has been exacerbated by various regional and international actors, each pushing their agendas through political and military support, further polarizing the nation. Despite a ceasefire deal agreed upon in October 2020, stability remains weak due to the ongoing presence of foreign mercenaries and the deadlock between forces loyal to Haftar and those controlling Western Libya. These complications hinder the UN-led initiatives aimed at unifying the nation through national elections, which are further undermined by repeated delays.[12] Concurrently, the conflict continues to severely impact human rights and gender equality, disproportionately affecting internally displaced persons, migrants, and women. The future development of the conflict and trajectory of the Libyan state is characterized by deep uncertainties intertwined with broader socio-political issues, including the struggle for rule of law and functional governance, and escalating environmental challenges due to climate change.

Against this backdrop of a complex conflict dynamic in Libya, the foresight process facilitated by CMI, and aided again by the data mapping software Inclus, gathered Libyan stakeholders from various political factions to discuss key conflict drivers and to explore potential pathways toward peace and stability. Themes such as national unity, governance models, and the role of external influences on the conflict were central to the discussions.

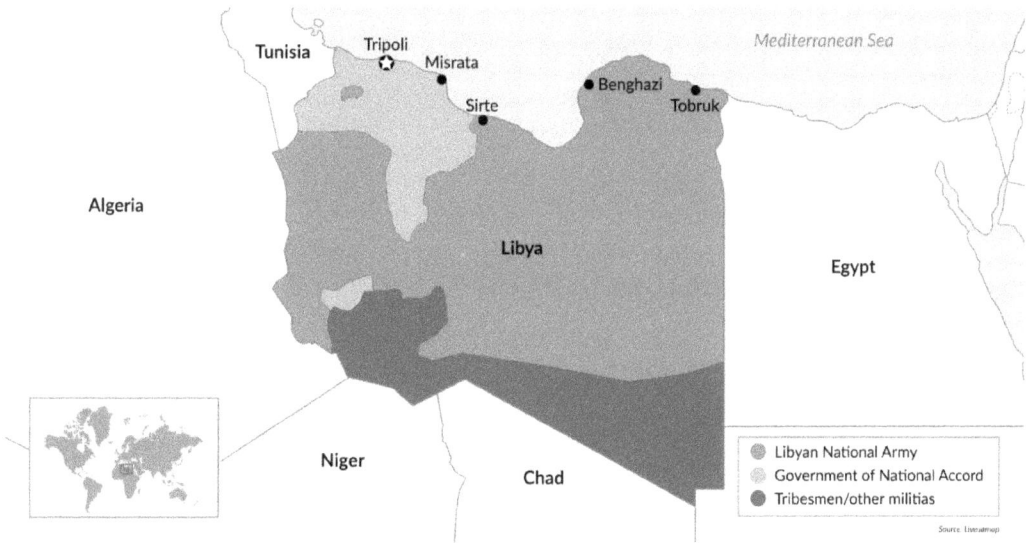

Figure 3. Years of civil war has left Libya torn between the UN-recognized Government of National Accord, based in Tripoli, and the Libyan National Army, based in Tobruk and backed by Russia, Egypt, and the UAE. Federica Saini Fasanotti, "Europe's Mistakes in Libya."[13]

The CMI foresight process aimed to foster dialogue among diverse Libyan stakeholders. The process started with crafting a broad, yet deliberately ambiguous, vision statement that could accommodate the diverse perspectives of all involved parties: "Libya 2040 is a one, civil, democratic, and sovereign state built on fair partnership and citizens' rights, based on decentralization, institutions, the rule of law, and the right to act in political parties." This vision built on a "Charter of Principles" that was previously developed by Libyan political factions with CMI's support. Once participants achieved a consensus on the vision statement, the facilitators shifted the dialogue to operationalizing the vision. This phase of the dialogue necessitated a greater level of detail and engagement from the participants, moving from abstract ideas to specific strategies for future governance and societal structure (see Figure 4). The process culminated in a participatory prioritization exercise where stakeholders assessed the urgency and feasibility of the identified goals, again using the data management and visualization tool to prioritize initiatives that were both urgent and feasible, setting a practical roadmap for immediate action.

The systematic prioritization not only grounded the vision in actionable steps but also ensured that the roadmap had the credibility and commitment among participants necessary for implementation. By balancing abstract visioning with detailed operational planning, CMI's foresight process in Libya bridged ideological divides and laid the groundwork for a shared future, fostering a sense of collective responsibility and forward-thinking among the participants and their respective political parties.

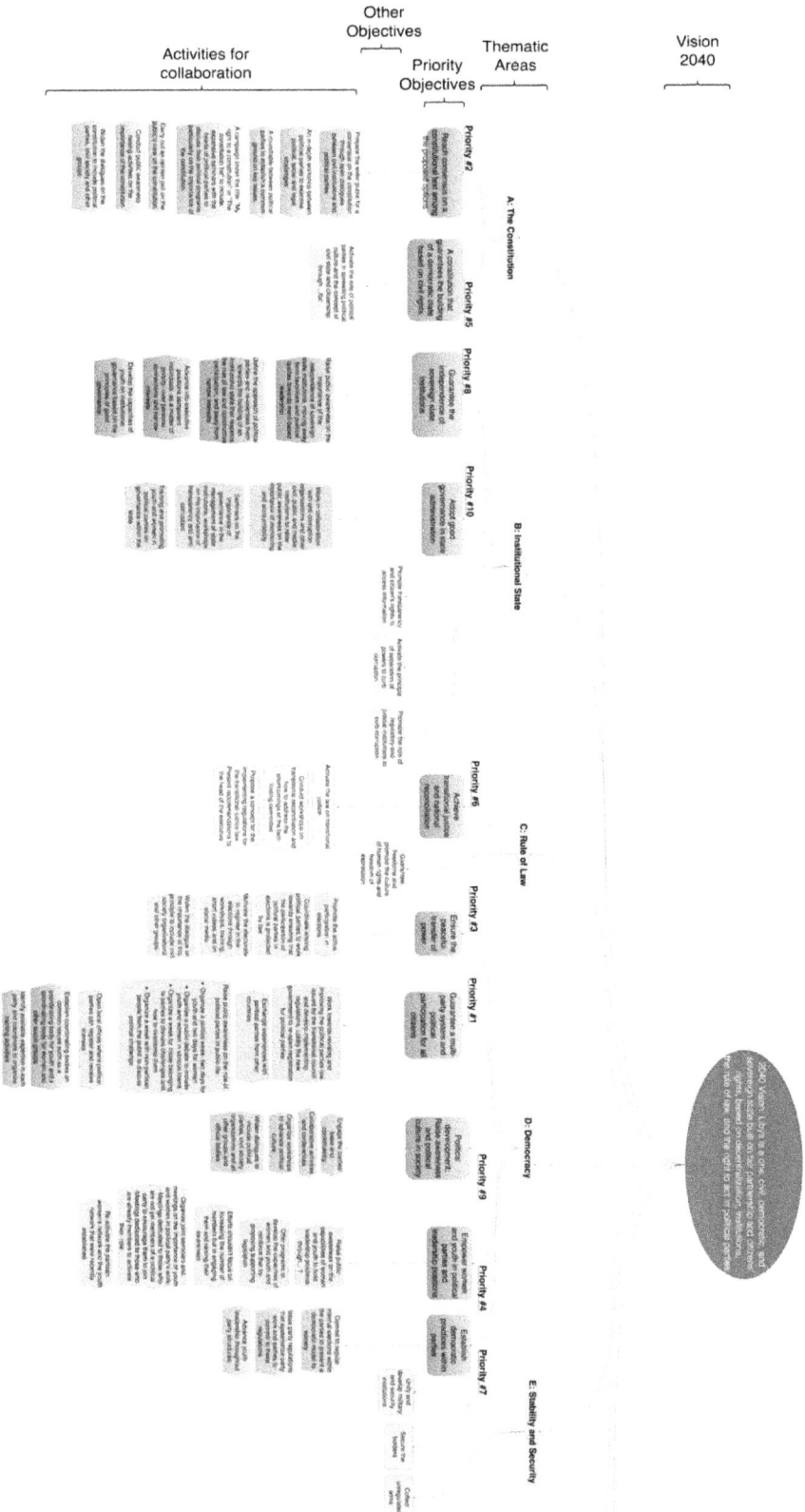

Figure 4. Illustrative example of the results of the road mapping exercise conducted in one of the Libya dialogue sessions, generated with Mindomo software.

The Value of Technology-Enhanced Foresight in Dialogue Processes

CMI's work in these two contexts illustrates how the application of foresight methods, such as scenario planning and horizon scanning, can be used in multi-stakeholder dialogue processes to develop shared visions and roadmaps in regions characterized by prolonged conflict. By operationalizing their shared vision into concrete goals and roadmaps, stakeholders move beyond mere brainstorming and transform foresight into a means for collaborative strategy development. Through such a process, it is possible to empower conflict stakeholders to align around a jointly crafted vision and path forward, enabling the development of longer-term strategies for sustainable peacebuilding in the context in question.[14] Instead of directly addressing contentious issues that can further entrench positions, foresight methods guide participants to move beyond immediate concerns and focus on shared interests and long-term goals. Through participatory exploration of multiple plausible futures, stakeholders can better understand the potential ramifications of their actions and prepare for previously unforeseen developments.[15] CMI's work in Libya and Armenia illustrates these benefits.

The process of considering numerous alternative futures also prompts parties to identify potential risks and opportunities and to develop strategies to address them proactively. This fosters an environment where informed decision-making can take place, empowering stakeholders to shape the future in a positive way. Enabling groups with varying amounts of power and diverse interests to grasp each other's needs, priorities, and the rationale behind their positions builds mutual understanding. Above all, this can nurture trust and confidence in the peacemaking process and in a shared future beyond the conflict.

Challenges for Foresight Practice in Peacemaking

While foresight holds significant potential for peacemaking, it is by no means a silver bullet for conflict resolution, nor does it replace traditional mediation methodologies. Rather, it serves as a useful approach that enhances the set of tools at the disposal of dialogue practitioners.

At the same time, foresight comes with its own set of challenges, many of which are rooted in the intrinsic nature of conflicts and the dynamics between the conflicting parties.[16] At its core, the reluctance of some conflict stakeholders to engage in futures thinking generally stems from fixed positions, a deep-seated fear of considering alternative futures, and the defensive stances that parties often adopt to protect their interests.

In conflict settings, the discourse between parties is often at a standstill, with little shared vision for the future. This impasse is further complicated by past grievances and a general lack of trust, making any discussion of future possibilities a daunting task. Discussions about the future necessitate a willingness to question existing beliefs and entertain the idea of alternative relationships, which is often a significant hurdle to overcome.[17] The key players may be resistant due to fears of undermining their current positions or because they stand to lose from a change in the status quo. Power imbalances, particularly in asymmetrical conflicts, add another layer of complexity, with dominant parties being particularly hesitant to engage in processes that could in any way challenge their superiority.

Implementing a futures thinking process is also challenged by practical considerations such as the inclusion of key actors, securing the necessary time and resources, and ensuring participants' safety. These challenges are also present in online or hybrid settings, where sustaining collaboration and group ownership becomes even more difficult.[18] In summary, while promising, the effective use of foresight approaches in peacemaking is often undermined by challenges that stem from the nature of conflict itself, resistance to change, and the practicalities of implementing such processes in a conflict-affected context.

Conclusion: New Frontiers for Peacemaking

As modern conflicts intensify in complexity, driven by hybrid threats, the climate crisis, and shifting geopolitics, traditional peacemaking approaches face unprecedented tests. Reactive strategies that merely address surface-level symptoms inevitably fall short against these multifaceted drivers of conflict.

Foresight approaches hold clear potential to strengthen peacemaking by fostering understanding of underlying conflict causes while enabling the identification of broader risks and opportunities. Through structured methods like scenario planning, diverse conflict stakeholders can collectively explore alternative futures and uncover fresh perspectives. For actors such as CMI, foresight approaches have been a relevant way to engage otherwise marginalized voices such as those of women, youth, and civil society.

Finally, the strategic use of foresight approaches can also enable practitioners and policymakers to anticipate crises more proactively. They can examine trends and possible future scenarios to enable them to help address root causes of conflict before violent escalation. Where dialogues stall, foresight can help to facilitate collaboration and trust by shifting focus from immediate concerns to shared long-term goals. While it is not a panacea, foresight serves as a powerful complementary approach that expands the toolkit available to peacemakers. CMI's pioneering methodologies that integrate foresight into dialogues yield promising results: proactive engagement, inclusive decision-making, and participants' ownership. Faced with escalating global complexities, the utility of these results has never been greater.

Notes

[1] Conciliation Resources, "Looking Forward: Connecting Futures Thinking, Mediation, and Reconciliation," Briefing Paper, 2022.

[2] United Nations Development Programme Regional Bureau for Asia and the Pacific, "Foresight Playbook," 2022.

[3] Andreas T. Hirblinger, Ville Brummer, and Felix Kufus, "Leveraging Digital Methods in the Quest for Peaceful Futures: The Interplay of Sincere and Subjunctive Technology Affordances in Peace Mediation," *Information, Communication & Society* (2023), https://doi.org/10.1080/1369118X.2023.2247070.

[4] Denis Loveridge, Foresight: The Art and Science of Anticipating the Future (New York: Routledge, 2009).

[5] CMI Insight, "Pioneering the Digital Frontier: CMI's Approach to Future-Oriented Dialogues," CMI – Martti Ahtisaari Peace Foundation, December 2023, https://cmi.fi/2023/12/19/cmi-insight-pioneering-the-digital-frontier/.

[6] Conciliation Resources, "Looking Forward."

[7] Hirblinger, Brummer, and Kufus, "Leveraging Digital Methods."

[8] Ibid.

[9] Council on Foreign Relations, "Nagorno-Karabakh Conflict," Global Conflict Tracker, October 21, 2023, https://www.cfr.org/global-conflict-tracker/conflict/nagorno-karabakh-conflict.

[10] Nicole Thomas et al., "What the United States Military Can Learn from the Nagorno-Karabakh War," Small Wars Journal, April 4, 2021, https://smallwarsjournal.com/jrnl/art/what-united-states-military-can-learn-nagorno-karabakh-war.

[11] Translated from Armenian by the author.

[12] Hatem Ben Salem et al., "Conflict in Libya: A Multidimensional Crisis: State of Play and Paths towards a Sustainable Peace," IEMed, October 16, 2017, https://www.iemed.org/publication/conflict-in-libya-a-multidimensional-crisis-state-of-play-and-paths-towards-a-sustainable-peace/.

13 Federica Saini Fasanotti, "Europe's Mistakes in Libya," GIS, May 8, 2023, https://www.gisreportsonline.com/r/europe-mistakes-libya/.

14 Hirblinger, Brummer, and Kufus, "Leveraging Digital Methods."

15 CMI Insight, "Pioneering the Digital Frontier."

16 Hirblinger, Brummer, and Kufus, "Leveraging Digital Methods."

17 Conciliation Resources, "Looking Forward."

18 Ibid.

SCALING EXPERTISE: A NOTE ON HOMOPHILY IN ONLINE DISCOURSE AND CONTENT MODERATION

Dylan Weber

Changing Character of War Centre, Pembroke College, University of Oxford; Artis International

ABSTRACT

It is now empirically clear that the structure of online discourse tends toward homophily; users strongly prefer to interact with content and other users that are similar to them. I review the evidence for the ubiquity of homophily in discourse and highlight some of its worst effects including narrowed information landscape for users and increased spread of misinformation. I then discuss the current state of moderation frameworks at large social media platforms and how they are ill-equipped to deal with structural trends in discourse such as homophily. Finally, I sketch a moderation framework based on a principal of "scaling expertise" that I believe can contend with the scale of online discourse while maintaining sensitivity to context and culture.

Dr. Dylan Weber is a fellow of the Changing Character of War Centre at Pembroke College and of Artis International where he additionally serves as the director of artificial intelligence and deputy chief technology officer. He is a mathematician whose interests lie mainly in the dynamics of online discourse. This intersects several areas including statistical physics, modeling of self-organized behavior, and data science, and artificial intelligence.

The internet was and continues to be lauded by many for its role in improving discourse and democratizing information by allowing for more direct discussion among the populace and by greatly enhancing access to information generally.[1] However, at its advent and throughout its history, some have cautioned that due to well-established psychological tendencies (such as confirmation bias and selective exposure), discourse on the internet would actually result in a narrowing of the information landscape of its users. This view predicted that, given the freedom to select information from the virtually infinite array that the internet provides, users would spend their time on the internet interacting with those who they already agreed with and consuming information from sources that confirmed their prior views. In other words, this view predicted that the structure of online discourse would tend toward "echo chambers" or *homophily*.[2]

The 2016 United States presidential election prompted many empirical studies that leverage large social media data sets to look into the extent to which homophily presents on social media and what effects it might have on its users. Despite the large variety of methods across this body of work, it is largely unified in its findings; social media has a strongly homophilic structure (see, for example, Figure 1) and this structure contributes to multiple undesirable effects including the narrowing of user information landscapes, enhanced spread of misinformation in homophilic clusters, and increased ideological polarization.[3]

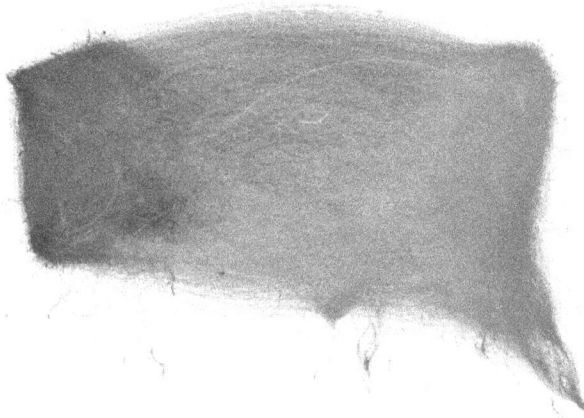

Figure 1. Visualization of the Twitter conversation from May 2023 surrounding the Black Lives Matter movement. Nodes in the network are users, edges represent aggregated interactions between users over the data collection period. Nodes are colored according to their support for or opposition to the Black Lives Matter movement: red indicates support, blue indicates opposition. Edges are directed and are colored according to the color of the source node. The network illustrates a strongly homophilic structure.

The ubiquity of homophily in online discourse and its ill effects has been largely acknowledged (usually under different names) by academia and policy makers, and to a lesser extent by social media platforms themselves. This has prompted a meta-discussion concerning mitigation of these undesirable effects through different strategies to mediate online discourse. All of the methods that have been actually implemented have been devised by social media platforms, resulting in an explosion of controversy surrounding the ethics of mediating speech in online discourse to the point that this has become a political issue itself.[4] Additionally, the implementation of moderation strategies by social media platforms has resulted in data that has allowed for an early foray into empirical measurement of the implemented strategies' effectiveness. Ethical and political discussions aside, I argue that none of these methods have been especially effective, as evidenced by the continued existence of strongly homophilic structures in online discourse and the balance of the research into implemented moderation strategies.

In the first section of the article I review the evidence for the strong tendency toward homophily in online discourse and discuss possible mechanisms for that tendency and its myriad ill effects on discourse. In the second section we discuss the current practice of content moderation on large social media platforms and some of its challenges. In the last section, I present a moderation framework that centers transparency, data, and scaled expertise.

Homophily in Online Discourse

Since the early days of social media, and indeed, the internet, there has been a vocal minority in academia warning that the disintermediated nature of online discourse could result in the formation of "echo chambers."[5] However, until the 2016 United States presidential election, there was a sparse amount of empirical investigation into whether such communities were actually emerging. In the years since, there has been an explosion of research into this question. Given the variation in methods and in the definition of "echo chamber" across these studies, we will first offer some definitions to put all the findings on common ground.

Definition 1. A network is a collection of nodes and a collection of edges that connect the nodes.

Definition 2. Given a network and a quantity defined on its nodes that is a priori independent of the network edge structure, we say that the network is homophilic with respect to the quantity if nodes are more likely to be connected in the network if they have a similar value of the quantity.

In short, a network is homophilic if "users of a feather connect together." It is important to consider that given a network, it may be homophilic with respect to one quantity and not another. For example, if we consider a network of users engaging in a debate about two political candidates we would expect that network to be homophilic with respect to support for the candidates but not with respect to support for various sports teams or food preferences. All online discourse can be viewed through the lens of network structure where users are represented by nodes of the network and edges represent their interactions online. All research about the existence of echo chambers in online discourse can be viewed as an investigation into homophily within the user interaction networks with respect to some measure of the users' ideology. From this point of view, there is a meta-methodology employed by researchers to investigate homophily within online discourse (though there is much variation in specific methodologies to accomplish each step). First, researchers collect a large social media data set on an issue or collection of issues. Next, they define a methodology for quantifying a user's ideology on the issue in question. Then, a scheme is defined for structuring the data set into a network and a metric for quantifying homophily on the resulting network with respect to the defined ideology measure. This methodology has produced a stark answer: the structure of social media tends strongly toward homophily.

Early forays into the use of this methodology identified homophilic structures in conversations surrounding the 2012 presidential election and other political issues in the United States including the 2013 government shutdown, minimum wage, and marriage equality.[6] The presence of strong homophily within networks pertaining to specific political conversations was confirmed by Kiran Garimella et al. through an investigation of the conversations surrounding gun control, Obamacare, and abortion, and by Bjarke Mønsted and Ana Lucía Schmidt through an examination of the Twitter and Facebook conversations surrounding vaccines.[7] Several years later, Matteo Cinelli et al. looked into the abortion, gun control, and vaccine conversations using more sophisticated metrics for ideology and homophily and again found that strong homophily presented on

Facebook and Twitter. Through leveraging their more sophisticated ideology measure and examining the same conversations on Reddit and Gab, they were also able to show that entire social platforms can be echo chambers with respect to certain issues.[8] However, homophily is not limited to conversations surrounding a single topic. Robert Bond and Solomon Messing, and Eytan Bakshy et al. conducted investigations of the US political conversation on Facebook writ large.[9] All three studies identify pronounced homophily using various ideology metrics. Nor is homophily restricted to political conversation; Walter Quattrociocchi et al., Alessandro Bessi et al., and Fabiana Zollo et al. examined Facebook discussion driven by either science backed information or conspiracy backed information and find homophily within the Facebook friendship network.[10] Those who consumed information from conspiracy groups were very unlikely to be friends with those who consumed information from groups centered on science and vice versa. A similar pattern was found in news consumption on Facebook by Schmidt; users tend to only interact with a small group of similarly aligned outlets in lieu of all other news sources. Users who consume the same group of news sources are much more likely to interact with each other.[11]

Though there is strong consensus on the existence of strong homophily within online discourse, the work on mechanisms that drive this effect is in early stages. Many originally pointed to the algorithmic curation of content as a likely primary driver. Proponents of this theory pointed out that algorithmic curation of content could place users in a "filter bubble" where they are mainly exposed to content for which they have previously demonstrated preference.[12] However it seems that this effect is less pronounced than feared and that homophily is more likely driven by a natural tendency to self-select aligned content and place oneself in an "engagement echo chamber."[13] Indeed in a study of political cross-cutting content, which is content that disagrees with the political ideology of the user viewing it, Bakshy et al. found that the filter bubble effect was small; "there is on average slightly less cross-cutting content: conservatives see approximately 5% less cross-cutting content compared to what friends share, while liberals see about 8% less ideologically diverse content." However, they also confirmed that individuals engage with cross-cutting content at much lower rates than ideologically aligned content.[14] Indeed, despite the evidence that the filter bubble effect is small, there is much evidence that the dynamic of selective exposure is large and is a primary driver of the observed tendency toward homophily. For example, Schmidt et al. find that Facebook users tend to initially engage with a large amount of pages but quickly converge to spending most of their time on a small collection.[15] Additionally, the most active users focused their attention on the fewest number of pages, a finding confirmed by Cinelli et al.[16]

These studies by Schmidt and Cinelli et al. demonstrate a worrying effect of homophily in online discourse; the information landscape of the average social media user is greatly diminished. This effect is also confirmed by Dimitar Nikolav et al.[17] More worrying, homophilic clusters are very susceptible to the spread of misinformation. Michela Del Vicario et al. find that a certain degree of homophily within the user interaction network is necessary for a viral cascade to occur and that the more homophilic a network is, the larger the size of the cascades it can facilitate. Additionally, they find that content must be sufficiently aligned with the ideology of a homophilic component in order to initiate a viral cascade.[18] Indeed, Aris Anagnostopoulos et al. find that the main factor in determining virality is "users' aggregation around shared beliefs."[19] This suggests that content could easily spread within a homophilic cluster if it is aligned with the ideology of the cluster regardless of whether the content is factual or not. Because misinformation could be crafted to align with the ideology of a cluster, one could surmise that misinformation actually spreads more effectively than the truth within homophilic network structures. Indeed, a study by Soroush Vosoughi et al. examined the structure of viral cascades that originate from content that has been verified as either true or false and found that false information spreads much more effectively than the truth:

> Whereas the truth rarely diffused to more than 1000 people, the top 1% of false-news cascades routinely diffused to between 1000 and 100,000 people. Falsehood reached more people at every depth of a cascade than the truth, meaning that many more people retweeted falsehood than they did the truth. The spread of falsehood was aided by its virality, meaning that falsehood did not simply spread through broadcast dynamics but rather through peer-to-peer diffusion characterized by a viral branching process. It took the truth about six times as long as falsehood to reach 1500 people and 20 times as long as falsehood to reach a cascade depth of 10. As the truth never diffused beyond a depth of 10, we saw that falsehood reached a depth of 19 nearly 10 times faster than the truth reached a depth of 10. Falsehood also diffused significantly more broadly and was retweeted by more unique users than the truth at every cascade depth.[20]

Current Moderation Strategies

The ill effects of homophily in online discourse are not just well-established in the academy. They have become central to a larger meta-discussion concerning the role of social media platforms in discourse and what the platforms' role should be in moderating discourse within their spheres. There is a general acknowledgment that the fully open and disintermediated discourse provided by social media platforms has had a host of unintended consequences including the emergence of strongly homophilic discourse. This discussion has led to a large and public slew of moderation efforts from the platforms, most visibly Facebook. Indeed, as Evelyn Douek notes:

> Facebook's update to the "values" that inform its Community Standards is perhaps the starkest example of the dominance of this new paradigm. Where once Facebook emphasized connecting people it now acknowledges that voice should be limited for reasons of authenticity, safety, privacy, and dignity.[21]

In my view, these interventions have not been successful, mainly evidenced by the continued existence of strong homophilic clusters and the spread of harmful discourse within them. In this section I discuss the current practice of content moderation on large social media platforms and some of its challenges.

We define *content moderation* generally as efforts to reduce the proliferation of content considered to be harmful, mainly through alteration of the content itself, limitation of its visibility, or ultimately its removal from the platform in question. A general definition is necessary because there is no wide consensus on what constitutes harmful content and the practice of moderating its spread and impact is currently solely in the hands of the social media platforms themselves (though Section 230 of the US Communications Act of 1934, enacted as part of the Communications Decency Act of 1996, guarantees that they have no legal obligation to do so).[22] The modern practice of content moderation is also in its infancy; most major platforms have always had rules forbidding certain classes of exceptional content (e.g., illegal activity, copyrighted material, or extremist content) but most consider its modern practice as beginning in earnest in 2016 when Facebook began working with third party fact checking organizations in response to the Cambridge Analytica scandal. By 2018, Facebook had more than 20,000 people working in content moderation.[23]

At "industrial" scale platforms (e.g., Facebook, Twitter, and YouTube) the general approach to content moderation follows the same model. A public facing set of "standards" or "guidelines" is published; the public goal of content moderation is to ostensibly ensure that all content on the platform is within these standards. However, the language in these standards is general and vague; it is not always possible to directly infer from them when a particular piece of content is in violation. The rules that are actually enforced in practice are written by a policy team that works under the umbrella of the larger apparatus responsible for content moderation. These rules are often opaque to the public. In the words of Robyn Caplan, "most platform companies keep their content moderation policies partially, if not mostly, hidden."[24] These policies are then operationalized into the actual practices of the content moderation teams. Content moderation teams are tasked with making the ultimate moderation decision on pieces of content served to them by both artificial intelligence (AI) detection capabilities and user reports. By all accounts the goal of this operationalization is to disambiguate complex concepts such as hate speech and disinformation into a discrete set of practices that could be applied consistently by moderation teams in order to deal with the huge scale of the task. In the words of one Facebook employee anonymously interviewed by Caplan, the goal is to create a "decision factory."[25] The end result is that it seems that much of content moderation is reduced to a mechanical process that is not considerate of the larger context from which content originates.[26] This can have disastrous outcomes, evidenced clearly, for example, by widespread political violence in Myanmar in 2018, which Facebook admits was driven by discourse on its platform.[27] Mark Zuckerberg further commented that its moderation teams lacked the proper cultural context to effectively identify the fomenting content.[28] In this sense, the lack of transparency into content moderation policies is particularly problematic because it is impossible for society to evaluate whether platforms are leveraging the best state of empirical knowledge to inform the goals of content moderation, the crafting of the related policies, and ultimately the operationalization of these policies into practice for the moderation teams.

There is a young but increasingly robust literature that generally proposes content moderation strategies based on foundational psychological literature and then measures their effectiveness in labs and survey settings. For example, in the arena of approaches for debunking misinformation, there is clear enough consensus on empirically-motivated best practices to allow for a distillation of the literature by Stephan Lewandowsky et al. into a *Debunking Handbook*.[29] (See "The emerging science of content labeling: Contextualizing social media content moderation" by Garrett Morrow et al. for a good review of similar work.[30]) One would hope that social media platforms are leveraging this type of information to inform their content moderation policies, but in the current state of play, that is impossible to know. A main takeaway from this body of literature is that there are replicable, significant effects of content moderation that have been identified in lab settings but it is unclear how these effects will scale on the platforms. As an example, Gordon Pennycook et al. showed that Facebook's work with third party fact checking organizations to assign warning labels to news stories identified as false resulted in stories lacking a label to be perceived as more likely to be true, regardless of whether the unlabeled stories had been fact checked or not.[31] To investigate the effects that "local" phenomena like this so-called "implied truth effect" have on global features of the structure of discourse like homophily would require an investigation that leverages the full scale of platform data and necessarily more transparency from the platforms.

Indeed, scale seems to be the most problematic aspect of content moderation. In the words of the same anonymously interviewed Facebook employee, even in Facebook's earlier days when the user base was only around seventy million users, "you would have to hire everybody in India to look at all the content that was uploaded, and you still wouldn't be able to do it."[32] Even if content moderation policies and their operationalizations into the practices of content moderators are transparent and informed by empirical best practice this only serves to improve the moderation of content when the final moderation decision falls into the hands of a human moderator. The massive speed and scale of information on large social media platforms makes this completely intractable. Automation must be brought to bear on the problem. Facebook has acknowledged for years that AI systems play a major role in flagging content for review by its moderation teams and as early as 2018 acknowledged that these systems participate in the automatic removal of content in the previously mentioned exceptional classes.[33] The extent to which AI systems participate in automatic removal versus referral to the moderation queue remains unclear. In 2020 Facebook acknowledged that in response to pressures on its moderation workforce caused by the COVID-19 pandemic it would increasingly rely on AI to make content moderation decisions.[34] It seems that the work force was never fully replenished—users continue to receive messages that their reports will not be processed by content moderators due to a "high volume of reports."[35] Generally it seems that platforms originally used AI for automatic removal of unambiguously objectionable content while relegating more context dependent moderation decisions to humans and that this balance has increasingly shifted toward the use of AI systems as time has gone on. Recently, Facebook announced that it would investigate the use of large language models (LLMs) to allow for more use of context in automated moderation decisions.[36]

Regardless of where the current balance between human moderation and automated moderation stands, it has long been stated that the actions of human moderators are used as training data to improve the performance of the AI capabilities.[37] While on the surface this would seem to be in line with AI alignment best practices, it is concerning, given the current practice of content moderation, for several reasons. Fundamentally, the goal of such a system is to scale the decision-making power of the human moderators to the models. However, as noted, the goals of moderation policies are opaque outside of published community guidelines, the policies themselves similarly lack transparency, and the evidence we do have about how they are operationalized points to a system that prioritizes scalability of human decision-making over the nuances of context that content moderation requires. Additionally, human moderators are largely not Facebook employees and do not have any expertise in conflict reduction or psychology. There have been many whistleblowers' reports to the media and governments about working conditions and adverse mental effects from doing the job.[38] Said shortly, it seems that the decision-making process that is being scaled to automated AI capabilities, and used to intermediate the largest discourse platforms ever created, is based on objectives and policy that society is ignorant of, is operationalized in a manner that prioritizes scalable process over contextual and cultural understanding, and is ultimately carried out by a workforce that has no expertise, is overworked, and has no hope of confronting the scale of the task. This does not bode well for the function of these systems at scale.

Scaling Expertise

So what is to be done? It is clear from the prevalence of homophily in the structure of online discourse, the frequency of large misinformation spreading events within homophilic clusters, and high levels of affective polarization between homophilic clusters, that current moderation policies used by large social media platforms are not effective at mitigating the worst effects of homophily. It is also clear from the sheer scale of discourse on these platforms that any attempt at effective moderation of this tendency must leverage automation to scale moderation strategies, likely in the form of AI-powered capabilities. A good initial step would be for platforms to make transparent the goals of content moderation and the specific moderation policies that attempt to accomplish these goals. This transparency would allow independent experts and researchers to have a voice in what best practices should look like and to publish suggestions as to how the policy should evolve and be tested by the platforms.

More importantly, the problem of access to platform data needs to be addressed. Currently, virtually all of the data needed to effectively measure online discourse, and necessarily the effectiveness of moderation strategies is wholly controlled by the platforms themselves and disseminated to independent researchers at their discretion and at great cost. Additionally, the methods by which the data is sampled for clients who purchase it are opaque. For example, Facebook recently announced that it would close CrowdTangle, its research data application programming interface (API), in August of 2024 and announced plans for a replacement but, at the time of writing, has provided little documentation as to the reasons for the change or what changes in functionality will occur. As previously noted, research into effective forms of content moderation is at the stage where there are plenty of theoretically motivated ideas, some of which have been tested in lab settings and have significant and replicable effects. Access to platform data would allow these strategies to be investigated at their intended scale. Moderation approaches should be evaluated on their effects on global platform phenomena such as homophily and viral misinformation spread. Greater access to platform data would also allow for more investigation into methods of measuring discourse and the dynamics of platform structure and content. Better understanding of the dynamics of global platform structure could be used to better inform the specific goals of moderation policies.

Finally, given a content policy that is grounded in empirical best practice, the job of content moderators should be viewed by the platforms as a role that requires expertise. Instead of relying on third party contractors, platforms should be thoughtful about crafting their moderation workforce and hire for skills relevant for the task such as conflict resolution and media literacy. Steps should be taken to ensure that moderators have a good cultural understanding of the content they interact with, ideally by hiring from a variety of geographies, and moderators should be deeply trained in the theory that grounds moderation policies. Content should be served to moderators with as much of its originating context as possible so that these skills can be effectively leveraged.

A content moderation framework that can confront structural problems in online discourse such as homophily should focus on a principle of "scaling expertise." This requires two main elements. First it requires a moderation policy with goals and techniques informed by empirical best practice and a measurement capability that can capture the global structure of the platform and its dynamics to assess the effectiveness of moderation and inform its further iteration. Second it requires a workforce of human moderators that have deep expertise in the moderation policy and have a cultural understanding of the content they are moderating. With these elements in place it is feasible to create a virtuous cycle for the creation of an automated moderation capability that can scale and augment the decision-making of the human moderators so that they can confront the massive scale of online discourse. Careful measurement of the online information environment (including current moderation activity) and testing of moderation strategies is translated into thoughtful and empirically informed moderation policies. These policies are deeply understood by moderators with cultural knowledge whose decisions are scaled to an automated capability which is then, of course, measured for effectiveness relative to the goals of the moderation policy and so on. Many of the problems with online discourse can be understood as a scaling of our own worst tendencies. Likewise, solutions to these problems demand similar scale but with greater consideration. In the words of Lewandowsky, "if technology can facilitate such epistemic fractionation in the first place, then it stands to reason that it might also contribute to the solution."[39]

Notes

Endnotes

1   Howard Rheingold, *The Virtual Community, Revised Edition: Homesteading on the Electronic Frontier* (Cambridge, MA: MIT Press, 2000); Robert H. Anderson et al., "Universal Access to Email: Feasibility and Societal Implications," in *The Digital Divide: Facing a Crisis or Creating a Myth?*, ed. Benjamin M. Compaine (Cambridge, MA: MIT Press, 2001), 243–62; James S. Fishkin, "Virtual Democratic Possibilities: Prospects for Internet Democracy" (paper presented at Internet, Democracy, and Public Goods, Belo Horizonte, Brazil, November 2000); Vincent Price and Joseph N. Cappella, "Online Deliberation and Its Influence: The Electronic Dialogue Project in Campaign 2000," *IT & Society* 1, no. 1 (2002): 303–29.

2   Jodi Dean, "Why the Net Is Not a Public Sphere," *Constellations* 10, no. 1 (2003): 95–112; Lincoln Dahlberg, "Cyberspace and the Public Sphere: Exploring the Democratic Potential of the Net," *Convergence* 4, no. 1 (1998): 70–84; Hubertus Buchstein, "Bytes That Bite: The Internet and Deliberative Democracy," *Constellations* 4, no. 2 (1997): 248–63; Eli Pariser, *The*

Filter Bubble: How the New Personalized Web Is Changing What We Read and How We Think (New York: Penguin, 2011); John Kelly, Danyel Fisher, and Marc Smith, "Debate, Division, and Diversity: Political Discourse Networks in USENET Newsgroups" (paper presented at the Online Deliberation Conference 2005, Stanford University, May 2005), 3; Cass R. Sunstein, "Democracy and Filtering," *Communications of the ACM* 47, no. 12 (2004): 57–59; Cass R. Sunstein, *Republic. Com* (Princeton, NJ: Princeton University Press, 2001).

3   Kiran Garimella et al., "The Effect of Collective Attention on Controversial Debates on Social Media," in *Proceedings of the 2017 ACM on Web Science Conference* (Troy, NY: ACM, 2017), 43–52, https://doi.org/10.1145/3091478.3091486; Matteo Cinelli et al., "The Echo Chamber Effect on Social Media," *Proceedings of the National Academy of Sciences* 118, no. 9 (March 2021), https://doi.org/10.1073/pnas.2023301118; Bjarke Mønsted and Sune Lehmann, "Characterizing Polarization in Online Vaccine Discourse—A Large-Scale Study," *PLOS ONE* 17, no. 2 (February 2022): e0263746, https://doi.org/10.1371/journal.pone.0263746; Ana Lucía Schmidt et al., "Polarization of the Vaccination Debate on Facebook," *Vaccine* 36, no. 25 (June 2018): 3606–12, https://doi.org/10.1016/j.vaccine.2018.05.040; Matteo Cinelli et al., "Selective Exposure Shapes the Facebook News Diet," *PLOS ONE* 15, no. 3 (March 2020): e0229129, https://doi.org/10.1371/journal.pone.0229129; Michela Del Vicario et al., "The Spreading of Misinformation Online," *Proceedings of the National Academy of Sciences* 113, no. 3 (January 2016): 554–59, https://doi.org/10.1073/pnas.1517441113; Soroush Vosoughi, Deb Roy, and Sinan Aral, "The Spread of True and False News Online," *Science* 359, no. 6380 (March 2018): 1146–51, https://doi.org/10.1126/science.aap9559.

4   Meysam Alizadeh et al., "Content Moderation as a Political Issue: The Twitter Discourse around Trump's Ban," *Journal of Quantitative Description: Digital Media* 2 (October 2022), https://doi.org/10.51685/jqd.2022.023; Samuel Mayworm et al., "Content Moderation Folk Theories and Perceptions of Platform Spirit among Marginalized Social Media Users," *ACM Transactions on Social Computing* 7, no. 1 (March 2024): 1:1–1:27, https://doi.org/10.1145/3632741; Ángel Díaz and Laura Hecht-Felella, "Double Standards in Social Media Content Moderation," Brennan Center for Justice, 2021, https://www.brennancenter.org/sites/default/files/2021-08/Double_Standards_Content_Moderation.pdf.

5   Kelly, Fisher, and Smith, "Debate, Division, and Diversity"; Sunstein, "Democracy and Filtering"; Sunstein, *Republic.Com.*

6   Pablo Barberá, "Birds of the Same Feather Tweet Together: Bayesian Ideal Point Estimation Using Twitter Data," *Political Analysis* 23, no. 1 (2015): 76–91, https://doi.org/10.1093/pan/mpu011; Pablo Barberá et al., "Tweeting From Left to Right: Is Online Political Communication More Than an Echo Chamber?," *Psychological Science* 26, no. 10 (October 2015): 1531–42, https://doi.org/10.1177/0956797615594620.

7   Garimella et al., "The Effect of Collective Attention"; Kiran Garimella et al., "Political Discourse on Social Media: Echo Chambers, Gatekeepers, and the Price of Bipartisanship," in *Proceedings of the 2018 World Wide Web Conference, WWW '18* (Geneva: International World Wide Web Conferences Steering Committee, April 2018), 913–22, https://doi.org/10.1145/3178876.3186139; Mønsted and Lehmann, "Characterizing Polarization in Online Vaccine Discourse"; Schmidt et al., "Polarization of the Vaccination Debate on Facebook."

8   Cinelli et al., "The Echo Chamber Effect on Social Media."

9   Robert Bond and Solomon Messing, "Quantifying Social Media's Political Space: Estimating Ideology from Publicly Revealed Preferences on Facebook," *American Political Science Review* 109, no. 1 (2015): 62–78, https://www.doi.org/10.1017/S0003055414000525.

10 Alessandro Bessi et al., "Science vs Conspiracy: Collective Narratives in the Age of Misinformation," *PLOS ONE* 10, no. 2 (2015): e0118093, https://doi.org/10.1371/journal. pone.0118093; Fabiana Zollo et al., "Debunking in a World of Tribes," *PLOS ONE* 12, no. 7 (2017): e0181821, https://doi.org/10.1371/journal.pone.0181821.

11 Ana Lucía Schmidt et al., "Anatomy of News Consumption on Facebook," *Proceedings of the National Academy of Sciences* 114, no. 12 (March 2017): 3035–39, https://doi.org/10.1073/ pnas.1617052114; Schmidt et al., "Polarization of the Vaccination Debate on Facebook."

12 Dominic Spohr, "Fake News and Ideological Polarization: Filter Bubbles and Selective Exposure on Social Media," *Business Information Review* 34, no. 3 (September 2017): 150–60, https://doi. org/10.1177/0266382117722446; Pariser, *The Filter Bubble.*

13 R. Kelly Garrett, "The 'Echo Chamber' Distraction: Disinformation Campaigns Are the Problem, Not Audience Fragmentation," *Journal of Applied Research in Memory and Cognition* 6, no. 4 (December 2017): 370–76, https://doi.org/10.1016/j.jarmac.2017.09.011.

14 Eytan Bakshy, Solomon Messing, and Lada A. Adamic, "Exposure to Ideologically Diverse News and Opinion on Facebook," *Science* 348, no. 6239 (June 2015): 1130–32, https://doi.org/10.1126/ science.aaa1160.

15 Schmidt et al., "Anatomy of News Consumption on Facebook"; Schmidt et al., "Polarization of the Vaccination Debate on Facebook."

16 Cinelli et al., "Selective Exposure Shapes the Facebook News Diet."

17 Dimitar Nikolov et al., "Measuring Online Social Bubbles," *PeerJ Computer Science* 1 (December 2015): e38, https://doi.org/10.7717/peerj-cs.38.

18 Del Vicario et al., "The Spreading of Misinformation Online."

19 Aris Anagnostopoulos et al., "Viral Misinformation: The Role of Homophily and Polarization," preprint, submitted November 2014, https://doi.org/10.48550/arXiv.1411.2893.

20 Vosoughi, Roy, and Aral, "The Spread of True and False News Online."

21 Evelyn Douek, "Governing Online Speech: From 'Posts-As-Trumps' to Proportionality and Probability," *Columbia Law Review* 121, no. 3 (2021), https://doi.org/10.2139/ssrn.3679607.

22 Tanner Mirrlees, "GAFAM and Hate Content Moderation: Deplatforming and Deleting the Alt-Right," in *Media and Law: Between Free Speech and Censorship*, ed. Mathieu Deflem and Derek M. D. Silva, Sociology of Crime, Law and Deviance, vol. 26 (Leeds, UK: Emerald Publishing Limited, 2021), 81–97, https://doi.org/10.1108/S1521-613620210000026006.

23 Robyn Caplan, "Content or Context Moderation? Artisanal, Community-Reliant, and Industrial Approaches," Data & Society Research Institute, November 2018, https://apo.org.au/ node/203666.

24 Caplan.

25 Caplan.

26 Tomas Apodaca and Natasha Uzcátegui-Liggett, "How Automated Content Moderation Works (Even When It Doesn't)," *The Markup*, March 1, 2024, https://themarkup.org/automated-censorship/2024/03/01/ how-automated-content-moderation-works-even-when-it-doesnt-work.

27 Alexandra Stevenson, "Facebook Admits It Was Used to Incite Violence in Myanmar," *New York Times*, November 6, 2018, https://www.nytimes.com/2018/11/06/technology/myanmar-facebook.html.

28 Steve Stecklow, "Why Facebook Is Losing the War on Hate Speech in Myanmar," *The Wire*, August 16, 2018, https://thewire.in/tech/why-facebook-is-losing-the-war-on-hate-speech-in-myanmar.

29 Stephan Lewandowsky, John Cook, and Doug Lombardi, *Debunking Handbook 2020*, 2020, https://doi.org/10.17910/B7.1182.

30 Garrett Morrow et al., "The Emerging Science of Content Labeling: Contextualizing Social Media Content Moderation," *Journal of the Association for Information Science and Technology* 73, no. 10 (2022): 1365–86, https://doi.org/10.1002/asi.24637.

31 Gordon Pennycook et al., "The Implied Truth Effect: Attaching Warnings to a Subset of Fake News Headlines Increases Perceived Accuracy of Headlines Without Warnings," *Management Science* 66, no. 11 (November 2020): 4944–57, https://doi.org/10.1287/mnsc.2019.3478.

32 Caplan.

33 "How Does Facebook Use Artificial Intelligence to Moderate Content?," Facebook Help Center, accessed May 20, 2024, https://www.facebook.com/help/1584908458516247; Caplan, "Content or Context Moderation?"

34 Kang-Xing Jin, "Keeping People Safe and Informed about the Coronavirus," Meta Newsroom, December 18, 2020, https://about.fb.com/news/2020/12/coronavirus/.

35 Ina Fried, "Facebook's Content-Review Black Hole: The Flagged Posts That Never Get Read by a Human," Axios, June 22, 2023, https://www.axios.com/2023/06/22/facebook-content-moderation-black-hole-human-review.

36 Nick Clegg, "Labeling AI-Generated Images on Facebook, Instagram and Threads," Meta Newsroom, February 6, 2024, https://about.fb.com/news/2024/02/labeling-ai-generated-images-on-facebook-instagram-and-threads/.

37 "How Does Facebook Use Artificial Intelligence to Moderate Content?"

38 Cristina Criddle, "Facebook Moderator: 'Every Day Was a Nightmare,'" BBC, May 12, 2021, https://www.bbc.com/news/technology-57088382; David Pilling and Madhumita Murgia, "'You Can't Unsee It': The Content Moderators Taking on Facebook," *Financial Times*, May 2023, https://www.ft.com/content/afeb56f2-9ba5-4103-890d-91291aea4caa; Casey Newton, "The Trauma Floor: The Secret Lives of Facebook Moderators in America," *The Verge*, February 25, 2019, https://www.theverge.com/2019/2/25/18229714/cognizant-facebook-content-moderator-interviews-trauma-working-conditions-arizona.

39 Stephan Lewandowsky, Ullrich K. H. Ecker, and John Cook, "Beyond Misinformation: Understanding and Coping with the 'Post-Truth' Era," *Journal of Applied Research in Memory and Cognition* 6, no. 4 (December 2017): 353–69, https://doi.org/10.1016/j.jarmac.2017.07.008.

PERSONAL REFLECTIONS FROM A GRASSROOTS PEACEBUILDING JOURNEY

Mark Clark

Saïd Business School, University of Oxford

ABSTRACT

This article presents the author's personal reflections from experiences over the past thirty years, working at the intersection of leadership development, complexity, and conflict: a journey from corporate law, the British Army, and armed conflict, through the British Foreign & Commonwealth Office and the US-led coalition's intervention in Iraq, emergency humanitarian response in the Democratic Republic of the Congo, and violence reduction and post-conflict reconciliation in Papua New Guinea, to a Jordan-based international peacebuilding organization that supports grassroots peacebuilding efforts in fifty-two countries, and finally a return home to Scotland. It is a journey of naïveté, hubris, curiosity, and an attempt at sense-making. It describes the application of peacebuilding theories in practice in diverse contexts. Although it does not purport to offer any solutions, it concludes that courageous leadership is needed: to embrace conflict as a source of energy for positive, constructive, generative development; to resist the seductive drama and hero-leadership of focusing only on present crises; and to focus more investment on upstream prevention.

Mark Clark MBE, is an associate fellow at Saïd Business School, University of Oxford, and co-founder and CEO of Transformational Ltd., working at the intersection of leadership, complexity, and conflict. He began his career as a corporate lawyer in the UK and India, served as a British Army officer and with the British Foreign & Commonwealth Office, and was CEO of Generations For Peace in Jordan for twelve years, 2011-2023. This article was developed from a presentation given at the annual conference of the Centre for the Resolution of Intractable Conflict at University of Oxford Harris Manchester College in September 2023.

did not start out as a peacebuilder. Nor was it really planned. Rather, my journey into peacebuilding and conflict transformation was a nonlinear series of moments when I said "yes" to emergent opportunities as they popped up. Over the past thirty years, it is a journey from corporate law, the British Army, and armed conflict, through the British Foreign & Commonwealth Office and the US-led coalition's intervention in Iraq, emergency humanitarian response in the Democratic Republic of the Congo, and violence reduction and post-conflict reconciliation in Papua New Guinea, to a Jordan-based international peacebuilding organization that supports grassroots peacebuilding efforts in fifty-two countries, and finally a return home to Scotland. It is a journey of naïveté, hubris, curiosity, and an attempt at sense-making. Along the way I learned to let go of many preconceptions I had about how the world works and how change happens, and tested the application of peacebuilding theories in diverse conflict contexts.

I grew up during the last decade of the Cold War and my father was in the British Army, so as a family we moved back and forth between the UK and different postings in Germany. When I started university in 1992, studying law at the University of Edinburgh, the quick succession of events—from the fall of the Berlin Wall and the dissolution of the Soviet Union in 1989, to the signing of the 1992 Maastricht Treaty that created EU citizenship and paved the way for the Euro—all seemed to be an affirmation of Western liberal democracy and what Francis Fukuyama called "the end of history."[1] I had no doubts that conflicts would continue to arise, but I believed that the age of conventional wars, at least in Europe, was indeed over.

That was relevant to me because, in parallel with my career as a corporate lawyer working in the UK and in India, I was also serving in the British Army as an officer in a reconnaissance unit. I found the juxtaposition of those two lives extremely valuable, and I benefited greatly, in different ways, from experiences in each. The difference around leadership was stark. In my corporate law firm, at least at my relatively junior level, leadership seemed rather invisible and was neither spoken about nor explicitly developed, while in the army almost every waking moment was spent thinking and talking about leadership, developing and practicing leadership at every level—not in a rigid hierarchical sense, which may be the stereotypical view of military culture, but striving to develop at every level effective capabilities to take initiative, responsibility, and accountability for rapid assessment of fast-changing situations and adapting a course of action to pursue a mission objective. But one key aspect in common between those legal and military worlds was the importance of a rules-based order and the idea of creating, imposing, and protecting order, especially in the face of chaos and kinetic violence. I felt there was a larger system at play, with clearly established rules of the game that everyone broadly followed, and which supported a trend toward positive progress.

My time in India, working with a law firm in Mumbai, immersed me in a context of contrasts: rich and poor, Bollywood and super-rich tech company elites and those in extreme poverty, vibrant modern digital innovation and a robust traditional caste system, and an Anglo-Saxon legal system overlaid upon the diverse traditional cultures of a subcontinent. I moved there soon after the September 11, 2001 terrorist attacks, and I felt that there was a growing uneasy sense that the United States' strength and pride had been hurt significantly and that the reaction to those attacks would be felt worldwide, far beyond neighboring Pakistan and Afghanistan.

A decade after *The End of History and the Last Man*, and after the lessons and relative successes of interventions in Bosnia and Herzegovina, Kosovo, and Sierra Leone, the acutely felt need for robust revenge for 9/11 coincided with strategic interests in Iraqi oil and the height of Western interventionist hubris. When the US-led coalition invaded Iraq and deposed Saddam Hussein, I served as a British Army officer on Operation Telic in Iraq in early 2003 then stayed on in Iraq through 2003 and 2004 in a role with the British Foreign & Commonwealth Office (Foreign Office), serving in the Coalition Provisional Authority (CPA), the temporary government.

The absurdity and chaos of that chapter in Iraq is immediately apparent from the fact that, for a short time, I was the acting Minister for Youth and Sports for Iraq, with few relevant qualifications for the role other than being available on the ground, expressing an interest in youth and sport, and recognizing their importance both in terms of grassroots youth engagement and high-level national identity. I was one of three "Brits" sitting around the table in L. Paul Bremer III's CPA cabinet meetings as he appeared to seek to govern Iraq's transition by spreadsheet. To be fair, the story of the CPA is a mixed bag of successes and failures, and many of the failures were not in Bremer's control, but some were, including the disastrous first two executive orders he promulgated: CPA Order 1 on "De-Baʿathification of Iraqi Society," prohibiting any person affiliated to the Baʿath Party from any role in the top three layers of management of any national government ministry, affiliated corporations, or other government institutions; and CPA Order 2 on "Dissolution of Entities," disbanding the Iraqi military, security, and intelligence infrastructure of President Saddam Hussein. Ultimately, Bremer was given an impossible mission: a maximalist reform agenda to stand up a model democracy that would serve as a beacon for the entire region, but with a minimalist application of money and people. For me, it was a massive awakening—a Wizard of Oz moment. I saw behind the facade of order and glimpsed, with horror, the catastrophic assumptions and lack of planning laid bare, as the political infighting between Colin Powell's Department of Defense and Donald Rumsfeld's State Department played out on the ground with momentous consequences for people's lives. My hope is that the story of intervention in Iraq may provide an object lesson of the costs and consequences of unprepared intervention and naive attempts at nation-building.

From my military experience (at least from my junior perspective), it also seemed that the US-led coalition in Iraq failed to adhere to the number one principle of war in the UK Defence Doctrine: "selection and maintenance of the aim," the so-called "master principle." In November 2022 the publication of the sixth edition of the UK Defence Doctrine made two changes to the long-standing list of ten principles of war, following the failures in Iraq, Afghanistan, Libya, and Syria, and Vladimir Putin's annexation of Crimea in 2014 and full-blown invasion of Ukraine in February 2022.[2] Number six, "concentration of force" became "concentration of effects," in recognition of the new significance of cyber warfare. Number nine, "cooperation" became "integration," in recognition that working together while retaining independence (i.e., cooperation) is insufficient, and that much closer linkage of entities and actions into a unified system (i.e., integration) is required. Where the doctrine previously characterized three instruments of national power—diplomatic, military, and economic—information was added as an important fourth instrument. As the updated doctrine notes, "The character of warfare is changing rapidly, driven by the pace and pervasiveness of information and technological change, not least in terms of space and cyber, and in emerging and disruptive technologies. Distinctions between public and private, foreign and domestic, state and non-state, and virtual and physical are blurred."

At the same time, certainly, my ego was seduced by the sense of adventure and drama in Iraq, the urgency of the mission, and the power to influence things. With a small but dedicated team working out of an office in Saddam Hussein's Republican Palace in Baghdad, we worked to get all of the Ministry of Youth and Sports staff verified and back to work, and 161 youth center facilities rehabilitated and cleared of debris and military ordnance, so that positive sport, arts, and education programs for male and female youths could be reactivated nationwide.

On the non-governmental side of sport, we were confronted with the history of the National Olympic Committee of Iraq (NOCI), which Uday Hussein (Saddam Hussein's eldest son) had, as its president, run as his own fiefdom. We received delegations with box files of evidence alleging the NOCI's involvement in abuses, from money-laundering and smuggling, to unlawful imprisonment and torture of sportsmen and women, and the sexual abuse of female athletes. Discussing these allegations with the International Olympic Committee (IOC) in Lausanne, Switzerland, it became clear that they had received the same evidence over several years but had neither investigated nor suspended NOCI for abuses of the Olympic Charter. With some persuasion, the IOC eventually voted to suspend Iraq on May 17, 2003. Soon afterward, on July 22, 2003, Uday Hussein and his brother Qusay Hussein were killed in a four-hour firefight. The question arose: how to get Iraq back into the Olympic Movement? The answer was to go back to the grassroots of sport structures nationwide, and to conduct a series of democratic elections for sports clubs then national federations for each sport, creating a general assembly for the election of a new NOCI. Led by the Interim Committee to Administer Sport in Iraq, with support from the CPA, the IOC, and the Olympic Council of Asia, more than 600 elections were conducted, for each sports club in each district and each governorate, and then for the national federation for each sport, over five months of an extremely hot summer in 2003 (temperatures exceeded 50°C / 122°F). With the national federation senior office holders forming a general assembly, the final election of a new NOCI was held at Lake Dukan, in Sulaymaniyah Governorate, in the Kurdish north of Iraq, on January 29, 2004 in the presence of IOC observers, leading to the lifting of NOCI's suspension by the IOC on February 27, 2004.

The new NOCI comprised Sunni and Shia Muslims, Christians, Arabs, and Kurds, eleven men and one woman. It caught media attention beyond the sports pages as an example that a democratic process in the "new Iraq" could produce a secular and (relatively, except for gender balance) representative outcome. The successful election triggered the next challenge: with just six months until the Athens Olympic Games, what sort of team would Iraq be able to mobilize to represent that "Iraq is back" on the world stage? A rapid talent identification process produced a list of athletes and their coaches in different sports. Armed with this list, I contacted each of the coalition countries' foreign ministries in turn, seeking their support to host the Iraqi athletes and their coaches for a selected sport in a sport training camp in their country until the Olympics. Fast, positive responses enabled us to get all of the individual athletes and their coaches out of the country on sport scholarships in host countries. The soccer team, however, remained in Iraq, being too large as a squad to be hosted for six months at the expense of another country, but with a remarkable German coach, Bernd Stange, they progressed through their qualification matches.

Because other teams considered it too dangerous to come to Baghdad, the Iraqi Olympic soccer team ended up playing all of their "home" matches in neighboring Jordan, with significant support from the Jordanian Olympic Committee under its president, His Royal Highness Prince Feisal Al Hussein. We flew in and out of Iraq in military C130 "Hercules" aircraft, seated in body armor and helmets on the red canvas webbing seats in rows down the length of the fuselage. Despite the context of chaos and insecurity, power cuts, and increasing lawlessness growing in Iraq, the young, talented team kept their focus, and kept winning. On those occasions when I remained in Baghdad instead of traveling with the team, it became clear how the team was becoming a powerful symbol of a united Iraq. Standing on a rooftop in Baghdad each evening, one could listen to sporadic gunfire and watch green and red tracer fire being exchanged in horizontal arcs in different neighborhoods across the city. But when the Iraqi Olympic soccer team's match started on TV, the shooting ceased: everyone was watching the match and united in cheering for the Iraqi team. Each time, of course, Iraq won; and each time, their victory was hailed with celebratory gunfire across the city, with the red and green tracer fire shooting vertically into the night sky for twenty minutes or so, until eventually it reverted to the customary horizontal exchanges.

The security situation deteriorated progressively month by month. There were numerous improvised explosive device attacks—mainly car and truck bombs—attempted on the Green Zone or targeting high profile convoys. I was uncomfortably close to the receiving end of AK47 gunfire on one occasion (although not, I think, personally targeting me), and frequent mortar attacks into the Green Zone, where I worked in the palace and where I slept in a trailer in the palace grounds. One mortar round exploded on the roof of our office in the palace, with remarkably little structural damage to the solid concrete roof, but blasting in all of the windows and sending shattered glass across our office, fortunately an hour before our working day started. With each mortar attack, we came to expect that there would be four or five shells at most before those firing would need to move, knowing that the coalition forces had the capability to identify mortar firing positions and have a helicopter and vehicle rapid reaction force on location within minutes. Typically, one would hear the whistle of the first mortar shell coming in, hit the deck on the spot, and count the blasts. After a longer pause following a fourth or fifth round, one judged that the attack was over and would get up, dust oneself off, and resume one's routine. About thirty seconds later the security loudspeakers across the palace complex would broadcast a loud, rather belated, "Take cover! Take cover!" message. I was also sleeping in the Al Rasheed Hotel on October 26, 2003, when it was hit early in the morning by six rocket propelled grenades in quick succession, killing one person and inflicting life-changing injuries on fifteen others. Amid these different attacks, I felt a mix of things. First, that I deployed initially on a military tour and that such risks should not be unexpected; second, that the probabilities of being impacted were something of a roll of the dice and that while the consequences of impact could be extremely serious indeed, the overall probability was still very low; and that it was a question of following training and maintaining situational awareness and vigilance, focusing on measures within one's control without becoming paralyzed into inaction.

In my role with the CPA, I was expected to follow Foreign Office security protocols. For any meetings outside the protected Green Zone, this required me to book in advance and travel in a two-vehicle convoy, with each vehicle being a shiny new white armored Toyota Land Cruiser, each with two ex-military security contractors, two of whom would then be my close protection bodyguards attending meetings with me. In addition, I was to travel wearing body armor and a helmet. I quickly discovered that arriving to any meeting with external stakeholders in such a manner prevented me from making progress. The physical security measures presented significant barriers to nurturing the relationships I was seeking to establish. The conspicuous three-vehicle convoy also projected me as a much more high-value VIP target than I felt I deserved. On one occasion, at a symbolic tree-planting ceremony for the new National Olympic Committee of Iraq, a single rifle shot rang out and my bodyguard leapt on me and bundled me into an adjacent bush. I felt grateful for his instinctive reactions to protect my safety, but embarrassed that none of my Iraqi colleagues had given the shot as much attention. I asked him to get off me, dusted myself off, and we carried on with planting the tree and envisioning what the future of Iraq might be as the tree grew taller.

I decided something had to give. I saw others in CPA roles restricting their movements to the Green Zone and avoiding any external meetings entirely, thereby placing on their Iraqi counterparts and stakeholders the sole risk and significant inconvenience of queuing to go through the security procedures to enter the Green

Zone. I chose a different strategy. I bought a discrete but solid saloon car and drove myself around. I felt much less conspicuous and like less of a target. The relationships with my Iraqi counterparts changed visibly, as they understood the risks I was taking and my commitment to make progress together with them. They, in turn, began to show a sense of responsibility for my security, and I found their intelligence and assessment of the security situation and risks related to particular locations or events to be more timely and precise than the security assessments I received through official coalition channels. A lingering question in my mind is whether anyone in the Foreign Office noticed that my requests for official security for moves outside the Green Zone dropped to zero, and if so, whether a blind eye was turned without raising the subject with me, perhaps because they saw that I was making some progress.

Far worse were the daily risks taken by Iraqis. Many of the improvised explosive device (IED) bombings targeted main roads used by coalition forces, from the airport into the city, and especially around entrances to the Green Zone. These attacks inflicted far more deaths and life-changing injuries on Iraqi civilians than on coalition personnel. Iraqis working in the CPA faced a growing risk of being identified and targeted as coalition sympathizers. It remains deeply distressing to me that our small CPA Youth and Sports team was not immune from this. One morning Ahmad Hassan, one of our four young Iraqi colleagues, was shot dead in a targeted assassination: a single shot to the back of the head as he left his home to make his way to the Green Zone to work in our office. I received the news via a call from Ahmad's mobile later that afternoon, from a French journalist at a local hospital writing a story about victims of an unrelated IED attack close to the Green Zone that day. Because he spoke English, the journalist had been asked by the hospital staff to call my number, because my name showed up on Ahmad's phone's most recent missed calls list. I alerted the CPA authorities of the news and then, in breach of a security lock-down due to the IED, I drove out of the Green Zone to the hospital to locate and identify Ahmad's body. I wanted to be absolutely sure, before informing his family and his Iraqi colleagues in our team at the CPA. The scene of carnage in the hospital morgue—an overflow morgue improvised from a shipping container and without any refrigeration—was gruesome, with Ahmad lying alongside so many bodies and parts of bodies from the IED explosion.

In this context, we kept chipping away at our work with the ministry and its programs in youth centers nationwide, until the June 30, 2004 official handover to a new Iraqi government and a new Minister for Youth and Sports. On the Olympic side, following the handover, I stayed on in Iraq to support the new NOCI to prepare for the Athens 2004 Olympic Games. It was an extraordinary, good news story that at those Olympic Games, Iraq was represented by twenty-five athletes in seven sports, including men's soccer, and I was so proud to travel with the team to the Olympics and support their management. More extraordinary still: the soccer team continued their winning form in Athens, eventually coming fourth after losing 2 to 1 to Italy in the play-off match for the bronze medal. That was undoubtedly a high point for me, both personally and professionally. After the Olympics, I continued to work with the NOCI in a private consulting capacity, now living outside the Green Zone, advising on their strategy and sponsorship deals, before eventually leaving Iraq amid a worsening security situation that was sliding rapidly into open anarchy, lawlessness, and civil war. As one example, amid the many stories of kidnappings for extortion, which were generally not of foreign officials but any Iraqi considered affluent—doctors, lawyers, and businessmen—came a story in which a militia group at a checkpoint near Sadr City had brazenly "kidnapped" a coffin from the roof of a car, when the family inside was on its way to bury their loved one killed earlier that day, and extorted a ransom for return of the coffin.

After Iraq, while decompressing, I spent time completing an Executive Masters in Management at Université Claude Bernard Lyon 1, basing myself in Chamonix, France to alternate my studies with paragliding, climbing, and skiing. After what I felt were unique contextual conditions in Iraq, I was keen to learn about more typical, mainstream, international development and started job hunting. I was still unmarried and mobile, and deliberately identified South Sudan and the Democratic Republic of the Congo (DRC) as contexts with intense challenges where I could learn a lot. I was offered jobs in each and chose a role in the DRC with an Irish non-governmental organization (NGO) called GOAL, based in Goma in Eastern DRC on the border with Rwanda, and working from there in remote communities in Lulingu, South Kivu and Manono, Katanga.

While I had spent time traveling in Egypt, Morocco, and South Africa, for me, flying to Kigali in Rwanda in 2005 then entering the DRC through the border crossing at Gisenyi, and later traveling from Goma to Lulingu and Manono, felt like a journey into the heart of the African continent. I was acutely aware that I was carrying with me on this journey my white, male, privileged, middle class, colonial legacy, including my most recent identities related to my roles with the British Army and Foreign Office in Iraq. The prevailing winds of intractable conflict and violence in the DRC, sustained by systemic forces within and beyond its borders, made it difficult for me to resist associations with Joseph Conrad's *Heart of Darkness*.[3] The humanitarian emergency response work was intoxicating in its intensity, its drama and tragedy, its daily heroism and relentless dynamism. But it was also soul-destroying, when reflecting that such an emergency had been going on for decades (and, sadly, has continued for decades after I left).

We worked in response to the ebbs and flows of fighting, providing emergency food and shelter to people fleeing for their lives, carrying what little they could as they fled their villages into the jungle. The most heart-breaking of all was the emergency therapeutic feeding stations for starving babies and their mothers. In between the emergency work, we developed a network of health extension workers and medical supply chains for each community, rolled out vaccination programs, drilled water wells and introduced sanitation programs, and provided support for agriculture projects for local food production and other sustainable livelihoods for income generation. A key channel for awareness programs was sport activities, which for me echoed the way that grassroots sport-based approaches had proved useful in Iraq. Also echoing my experience in Iraq, I found that our security came far more from building trust and relationships with the local community, who valued our presence, felt responsibility for our safety, and provided far more timely and precise knowledge of security threats than the international NGO community or local United Nations agencies.

The remote communities that we served in Lulingu, South Kivu, were accessible from Goma only by air. The old road connections to Goma were completely impassable: long-neglected and consumed by the jungle. But within each location there were some rough tracks passable on motorbikes and quad bikes pulling small trailers. The local airstrip, cut from the jungle, was short and limited incoming aircraft to the size of a Cessna Grand Caravan, with a small payload capacity of only 1,400 kg. These factors presented a major constraint on the overall capacity of our aid operation to support supply chains for emergency food and shelter, medicines and vaccines, and equipment for water and agriculture projects. I wondered whether we could re-examine the parameters and explore the art of the possible. I asked: "Would a four-wheel drive vehicle, like a Toyota Land Cruiser, be useful in Lulingu, if we could get it there?" The answer was "yes, but of course such a vehicle would not fit in a Cessna Grand Caravan." But it would if we took it apart. And so, we dismantled a brand-new Toyota Land

Cruiser and sent the pieces into Lulingu's tiny airstrip on three consecutive flights, with our mechanic on the third flight and people placing bets on whether he would manage successfully to piece the vehicle back together again. After twenty-four hours the vehicle was operational, and with a larger trailer also flown in, it expanded the load-carrying capacity ten-fold overnight.

While that felt like a success and I was learning a lot, and the daily aid we were providing was certainly saving lives, I still felt grossly inadequate to really make a significant difference. While I was pondering this, a scorpion's tail in Iraq came back to sting.

On July 15, 2006, the NOCI held its annual general meeting in Baghdad, attended by all of the officials I had worked with so closely as colleagues, except two committee members who were abroad attending sport events. In the middle of the meeting, about sixty uniformed gunmen stormed the conference venue. After shooting two bodyguards dead, and letting the drivers and junior staff go, they abducted the president, Ahmad Al Samarrai, the secretary general, Amer Jabbar, and all of the other elected committee officials except for the vice president, Bashar Mustafa (local speculation was that this was possibly because of his Kurdish identity). The twenty-four officials abducted have never been seen again, and their bodies never recovered. While no one claimed responsibility for the abduction and murder, most fingers pointed directly to the new Shia government itself.

Reeling from the news, this moment felt like another awakening for me. I glimpsed the bigger forces at play and the horrific audacity of raw power using violence to achieve political objectives. For a brief time, the story of sport-for-development in Iraq had been a good news story, both at grassroots levels in youth centers and at the national level as a symbol of Iraqi national identity and pride. I still believed in the power of sport in both of these domains, but had been chastened to qualify that belief with a deeper appreciation for the bigger forces at work and the lack of limits to their exercise of power. Indeed, this echoed what I was feeling in the DRC, that bigger forces at play were locking the system into intractable violence, with the majority—especially the most poor and most vulnerable—suffering and losing the most, while others were clearly thriving and winning from the status quo. For me, in both Iraq and the DRC, I felt like I was a small pawn on a chess board, without full knowledge of all the pieces or even how big the board was and how many other pieces were in play, out of sight. It made me determined to learn more and to figure out how to have an impact further upstream, on violence reduction and prevention, rather than responding to the downstream effects of violence.

From the DRC, in 2006 I moved to Papua New Guinea (PNG), first to design and then to lead the first four years of a ten-year Sport For Development Initiative—a nationwide grassroots violence reduction program as part of the Australian government's bilateral support to the PNG government. This large and long-term investment was a response to widespread violence in PNG. In Bougainville, one of the largest islands, there had been a decade of civil war from 1988 to 1998, and a lot of work remained to be done on post-conflict reconciliation and peacebuilding. Across the country, urban areas were dominated by criminality, gang violence, and youth violence, fueled by home-brewed alcohol and lack of positive opportunities for youth. At the time, the capital city, Port Moresby, was ranked the most violent city in the world outside of an actual war zone. Up in the highlands, there was significant violence in the form of tribal fighting, often using traditional bows and arrows, knives, and axes, with the more recent appearance of the occasional (and sometimes homemade) firearm. Across all communities there was pervasive violence against women. There was also violence associated with HIV and AIDS and beliefs linking it to sorcery.

It was in the remote, isolated communities of the highlands and islands of PNG, in forests swirling with deep beliefs in spirits and sorcery, that I really began to learn to let go of my Western preconceptions, mental models, heuristics, and assumptions about what is going on. I learned to let go, to slow down, to withhold judgment, and to just be open and curious. "The system makes sense to itself, even if it doesn't yet make sense to me" became my mantra. "Seek first to understand" became my primary task. That mantra and that primary task served me well in PNG and in all my experiences since, when stepping into any new country, community, organization, team, or board room.

In PNG, compared with the urgency and intensity of Iraq and the DRC, I had the luxury of taking time for a thorough six-month design process, traveling the country and engaging with the diverse and unique cultures of isolated communities, which allowed for a truly participatory design. That, in turn, flowed directly into a participatory programming philosophy that embraced that diversity and complexity, and took a strengths-based approach to leverage local resources and capabilities, including the potential of youth-led and women-led initiatives, and the power of sport-based approaches to providing an entry point for community engagement and a vehicle for education and behavior change.

In 2007, while I was in PNG, His Royal Highness Prince Feisal Al Hussein of Jordan founded an international initiative called Peace Through Sport, with a mission to use grassroots sport activities in communities to address local issues of conflict and violence. A year later, the initiative was formally established as Generations For Peace (GFP): the change of name intentionally providing a broader scope for activities such as arts-based and advocacy programs, to complement and reinforce sport-based approaches. I visited Jordan in 2009 to attend a GFP camp for young peacebuilding leaders from around the world. It was inspiring and thought-provoking. I shared some feedback and the approaches we had developed in PNG, but I saw a lot of potential in GFP and a seed was also sown. In January 2011, I moved from PNG to Jordan to take up a role serving as CEO of GFP.

I arrived in Amman just before the Arab Spring and served as CEO for twelve years, through the Syrian refugee crisis, the rise of violent extremism and of the Islamic State in Iraq and Syria (ISIS), also known as Daesh, Vladimir Putin's annexation of Crimea and later full-scale invasion of Ukraine, and the COVID-19 pandemic. During that time, we grew the organization eleven-fold, trained more than 22,000 peacebuilders, and supported their grassroots programs in communities in diverse contexts in fifty-two countries worldwide. The contexts included inter-tribal, inter-ethnic, and inter-religious violence; violent extremism; gender inequality; post-conflict trauma response, reconciliation, and reintegration; exclusion of minorities including internally displaced people (IDPs), refugees, and people with a disability; and challenges of social cohesion and integration in multi-cultural societies. The type of programs also expanded to six "vehicles for peace," used in varying combinations in different communities: sports, arts, advocacy, dialogue, economic empowerment, and media for peace. GFP gained recognition for its impact and was ranked twenty-fifth in the top 200 social good organizations (SGOs) in the world, the number three peacebuilding SGO in the world, and the number one SGO in the Arab world.[4]

GFP identifies itself explicitly as a "peacebuilding" organization, dedicated to sustainable conflict transformation at the grassroots in communities. Although many of the aims of peacebuilding overlap with those of peacemaking, peacekeeping, and conflict resolution, peacebuilding is a distinct idea. Peacemaking involves stopping an ongoing conflict, whereas peacebuilding happens before a conflict starts or once it ends. Peacekeeping prevents the resumption of fighting following a conflict; it does not address the underlying causes of violence or work to create societal change, as peacebuilding does. Peacekeeping also differs from peacebuilding in that it only occurs after conflict ends, not before it begins. Conflict resolution, strictly defined, would not include some components of peacebuilding, such as state building and socioeconomic development.

While some use the term peacebuilding to refer only to post-conflict or post-war contexts, most use the term more broadly to refer to any stage of conflict. Before conflict becomes violent, preventive peacebuilding efforts, such as diplomatic, economic development, social, educational, health, legal, and security sector reform programs, address potential sources of instability and violence. This is also termed conflict prevention. Peacebuilding efforts aim to manage, mitigate, resolve, and transform central aspects of the conflict through official diplomacy as well as through civil society peace processes and informal dialogue, negotiation, and mediation. Peacebuilding addresses economic, social, and political root causes of violence and fosters reconciliation to prevent the return of structural and direct violence. Peacebuilding efforts aim to change beliefs, attitudes, and behaviors to transform the short- and long-term dynamics between individuals and groups toward a more stable, peaceful coexistence. Peacebuilding is an approach to an entire set of interrelated efforts that support peace.

The Norwegian sociologist, Johan Galtung, coined the term peacebuilding in 1975, arguing that "peace has a structure different from, perhaps over and above, peacekeeping and ad hoc peacemaking. [...] The mechanisms that peace is based on should be built into the structure and be present as a reservoir for the system itself to draw up. [...] More specifically, structures must be found that remove causes of wars and offer alternatives to war in situations where wars might occur."[5] Galtung's work emphasized a bottom-up approach that decentralized social and economic structures, amounting to a call for a societal shift from structures of coercion and violence to a culture of peace. John Paul Lederach further developed the model of peacebuilding focused on getting beyond addressing the presenting issues of direct violence (to achieve so-called "negative" peace) to work on the deeper issues of structural violence (to achieve so-called "positive" peace) and cultural violence (to achieve so-called "just" peace).[6]

Cultural violence is manifested in cultural narratives that portray in-group and out-group traits of identity. Such identity differences become cultural violence when referred to as the reason to justify treating a person differently. In this way cultural violence can then legitimize and normalize structural violence and, ultimately, direct violence. In every country I worked in, the cultural, structural, and in some cases direct violence often related to identity divides: inter-tribal violence in Papua New Guinea and Northwest Pakistan; inter-ethnic violence in the Balkans and the Caucasus; inter-religious violence in the Middle East, Nigeria, and Sri Lanka; violence against migrants, internally displaced people, and refugees; violence against those with disabilities; and sexual and gender-based violence absolutely everywhere.

As CEO of GFP, and as a Steering Group member of the global peacebuilding coalition known as +Peace, I was directly involved, with GFP, in the 2018 +Peace campaign to get the word "peacebuilding" into the dictionary. Today, the Oxford Reference Dictionary defines "peacebuilding" as "a variety of measures aimed at solidifying peace and avoiding future conflict in a society, undertaken by actors such as government agencies and civil society organizations. Peacebuilding measures include overseeing the disarmament, demobilization, and reintegration into peaceful society of warring parties, electoral support, rebuilding political and economic institutions, and supporting local capacities to manage differences without turning to violence." Some argue that peacebuilding is a manifestation of liberal internationalism, but I believe properly demand-driven, responsive peacebuilding efforts need not necessarily be directed toward liberal democracy.

The +Peace global peacebuilding coalition also established, as one of its projects, the global Peace in Our Cities campaign, focused on working to halve urban violence by 2030. In 2019, the campaign noted that while more than half a million people die violently every year, only eighteen percent of violent deaths take place in conflict zones; eighty-two percent of victims of lethal violence are killed in homes, towns, cities and countries that are ostensibly "at peace." While conflict deaths increased ninety-five percent during 2021 to 2022, primarily due to wars in Ukraine and Ethiopia, still less than one-third of violent deaths take place in conflict zones. So it is important to understand that we tend to demonstrate a cognitive bias around conflict deaths, causing many to think they are a larger percentage of violent deaths, perhaps fueled by the drama-bias of news media about conflict.

While getting to grips with the new challenge of leading an organization engaged in such complex work, in 2011 and 2012 I completed a Masters in Consulting and Coaching for Change, delivered jointly by University of Oxford's Saïd Business School and HEC Paris. It furnished me with a valuable smorgasbord of theoretical models, academic research, and practitioner experiences—encompassing systems theory, complexity theory, and complex adaptive systems, theories of individual and collective learning, theory of action, psychodynamics, cognitive neuroscience, transitional change, agency, adaptive leadership, and reflection-in-action—which I devoured hungrily, combined with theories of trauma, identity, social capital, international development, conflict transformation and peacebuilding, and contact theory, and synthesized into applications for the peacebuilding mission of GFP.

I saw that the burgeoning field of sport for peace and development, and peacebuilding more broadly, faced a need to close the gap between rhetoric and reality; to connect theory and praxis. A key difficulty in many well-intentioned peacebuilding programs was a lack of precision in the overall theory of change underpinning the intervention. The focus too often seemed immediately to be on the design and implementation of activities, rather than on the analysis of the situation and the choice of an appropriate change strategy. Grassroots peacebuilding practitioners found the theory too complex, too inaccessible, or too distant from their practical concerns. To close the gap between rhetoric and reality, and to connect theory and praxis, requires peacebuilding practitioners to be much more rigorous in the following: devoting sufficient attention to careful analysis and deep understanding of the local context; maintaining a tight focus on particular precise desired outcomes, rather than diluting effort across too many desired outcomes; specifying the theory of change for each intervention, and articulating a strong causal connection between each link in the chain from inputs to outputs to desired outcomes and longer term impacts; and embracing complexity and adopting an adaptive approach toward transformational change.

Viewing peacebuilding essentially as a change process—an adaptive leadership challenge within complex adaptive systems—prompted me to embrace theory as metaphor and explore multiple different theoretical frames to see how they might each provide useful insights into the underlying processes of change in peacebuilding interventions, serving to better inform the diagnosis and analysis of the conflict situation, the most appropriate choice of change strategy, and the design, implementation, and evaluation of such programs.

My masters' thesis research confirmed the challenges peacebuilding practitioners faced in explicitly articulating a theory of change, and their tendency to skip diagnosis and analysis and jump straight into program design and implementation.[7] But their interview responses also identified some common aspects of their programs that appeared to confirm support for many of the theoretical frames discussed in the literature. While seeking to "demystify theory" for easier application by practitioners, I also sought to "re-mystify practice," by showing how use of an organizational toolbox of multiple theoretical frames, to be selected and used in combination, could provide a richer praxis and more flexible, nonlinear, adaptive, context-sensitive approach that avoids "one size fits all" repetition or over-simplification.

In applying this thinking to grassroots peacebuilding work with GFP, in diverse contexts around the world, I recognized the following:

(a) Cultural and structural violence are soft complexity "wicked problems," and conflict transformation requires acting within a complex dynamic system through local action and a nonlinear, flexible and adaptive process.[8]

(b) Much more effort should be dedicated to diagnosis and analysis of the conflict context and the current situation, working back from episodes of conflict to their generative epicenter, in order to understand more deeply the systemic dynamics at play and the underlying personal, relational, cultural, and structural dimensions of the conflict.

(c) In seeking to address deep cultural and structural violence, community programs are most effective when operating on the principle of local action, and seeking to create a social movement for change at the grassroots level within a community, in a manner that demonstrates a deep understanding of the power relations of the local political context and the history and artifacts of local cultural identities.

(d) The type of intervention and the target group must be very carefully selected if the program is to be focused on making the most difference.

(e) The activity must provide a new, neutral "container"—both a transitional space and a transitional object—for facilitating individual and collective behavior change. The space offered can provide an opportunity to interrupt and inhibit negative reinforcing feedback loops that sustain protracted conflict.

(f) Inter-group sport activity, especially if in mixed teams, provides an opportunity for generating task interdependence within which people from different groups can connect and engage and explore "differences" and have new "exchanges" that allow for perspective-taking, perspective-breaking, and perspective-making.

(g) Activities must be fun and must be repeated and regular over a long period of time, supported by coaching and mentoring relationships, to effect real behavior change that will be sustained. Role plays and drills played out in the safe transitional space of the container should rehearse the micro-tactics needed to demonstrate new behavior outside the container.

(h) Above all, sport for peace programs are not simply about playing sport. The characteristics of sport situations provide some peer groups and powerful dynamics for interaction and engagement, but it requires deep understanding of the context, and strong competencies in advocacy and facilitation to create the holding "container," mobilize and attract participants, and regulate the distress at a constructive level for positive learning and attitudinal change.

One particular theoretical frame that I found useful in practical application was the five colors model developed by Leon De Caluwé and Hans Vermaak as an attempt to organize the array of diverse theories of change in a meta-framework.[9] Their effort was focused on theories of organizational change, but I saw an opportunity to apply their meta-framework to grassroots peacebuilding work, as an organizing structure to help peacebuilders to get to grips with different theoretical perspectives and gain different insights. De Caluwé and Vermaak use five colors to distinguish between five different ways of thinking about "change," which in turn drive different paradigms for thinking through five stages of action: analysis and diagnosis; choice of change strategy; actual intervention; and evaluation and reflection. For me, working with grassroots volunteer peacebuilders in diverse communities around the world, the attractiveness of the five colors framework as a meta-theory is in its ability to organize, and thereby make more accessible, a diverse range of approaches. The use of colors and the simplicity of the five colors model provides an intuitive shared language that is visual and carries some immediate warmth. This makes it memorable and accessible, and therefore useful across different language barriers, cultures, backgrounds, and levels of education. I have presented the framework and its application in more detail elsewhere, but in its simplest form the Five Colors Meta-Framework is an accessible, memorable, and practical five-by-five matrix as shown in Figure 1, below.[10]

	Yellow Power and Politics	Blue Rational Mechanical Technical	Red Emotions and Identity	Green Learning Growing Coaching	White Self-Organizing Adaptive Systems
1. Diagnosis/Analysis					
2. Choice of Change Strategy					
3. Intervention Design Process					
4. Intervention Implementation					
5. Evaluation/Reflection					

Figure 1. Five Colors Meta-Framework.[11]

Applying the framework to grassroots peacebuilding, it became clear that (a) it is important to devote time and effort to each one of the five stages of intervention; (b) at each stage, it is useful to gain insights from thinking through all five colors; (c) grassroots peacebuilders need the capacity to react to context and program events and to change the color of their approach in response; and (d) grassroots peacebuilders tend to adopt a variety of roles evolving over time, but perhaps primarily a role as a facilitator or change agent.

Conclusions from my research applying the framework with grassroots peacebuilders across a variety of contexts and programs included the following:[12]

(a) There is generally a mix of two or more colors in each approach, but Blue was perhaps the least dominant. The need to persist and not give up when faced with failure points to White colored experimentation and trial and error (i.e., "You need to be flexible and adapt; there is no one correct way").

(b) Yellow thinking appears to be a success factor; grassroots peacebuilding programs would probably benefit from deeper diagnosis and analysis of the local power relations and politics. Yellow-colored relationships of power and political processes seem likely to be particularly important in conflict contexts, along with Red-colored issues of identity.

(c) Blue thinking seems to be the least appropriate for conflict transformation, and where programs were less successful it could be due to too great an emphasis on a Blue-colored approach. But it is acknowledged that aspects of Blue thinking will still be required in planning and implementing the more "technical" pieces of a program, and in responding to Blue demands from stakeholders, including international development donors.

(d) An adaptive, generative, flexible and incremental process is likely to be more successful than a (Blue) process of planned change. Readiness of the target group and other participants is critical and several program phases may be required to generate readiness for the main intervention and openness to learning.

(e) Grassroots peacebuilders emphasize the importance of engaging with people emotionally and that "seeing is believing," implicitly emphasizing Red thinking and John Kotter and Dan Cohen's "see – feel – change" dynamic.[13]

(f) Where there was evidence of Green double-loop learning, there seemed to be greater program success.

(g) White thinking seem to be underestimated and could be worthy of greater attention by grassroots peacebuilding practitioners. White-colored understanding of systems dynamics and adaptive change processes seems to offer promising possibilities for conflict transformation and Green-colored thinking promises ways for individual and collective learning of new behavior (what Chris Argyris and Donald A. Schön might call Model II behavior) that seems important for sustainability.[14]

These reflections flowed into the new Programming Framework for GFP, introduced across all programs worldwide in 2013. The framework, summarized visually in a grid shown in Figure 2 below, guides the participatory design of a program through initial conflict analysis, construction of a theory of change, and development of a robust program logic, with clearly identified inputs, activities, and outputs, intended to have specific measurable outcomes on the specific target group, and specific impacts on the wider beneficiary community. The framework then supports monitoring, reflection and learning during implementation, and participatory evaluation that captures quantitative and qualitative data at the end of the program period.

At its core are the principles of the participatory approach we had developed and crafted in PNG. GFP facilitators (staff and the more experienced volunteers) train and mentor local peacebuilders (volunteers) to lead participatory processes in their community for conflict analysis, community needs assessment, construction of a theory of change and program logic, and then detailed program design. Importantly, it is the community themselves who identify their priorities for action and articulate indicators of what successful impact would look like. The community also leads evaluation of program activities against the indicators they set. In this way, real ownership of decision-making and sense-making is vested firmly within the community.

In 2018, five years after this Programming Framework was introduced, GFP published a compendium of 114 community-generated participatory indicators of peace, developed and used in GFP programs in twenty-seven countries across three continents.[15] Fourteen percent of the 114 indicators related to aspects of conception of self; fifty-four percent related to knowledge, beliefs and attitudes; eighteen percent related to behavior and practices; and thirteen percent related to community structures.

While GFP's focus was on grassroots peacebuilding activities in communities, over time, as programs succeeded in demonstrating positive impacts, they generated trust, credibility, and more support within a country, and new opportunities emerged and were exploited to connect upward from grassroots to a nationwide scale. For example, in Sri Lanka, GFP's community grassroots people-to-people reconciliation programs connected at the district level with District Inter-Religious Committees, and upward to inform the National Peace Council in its work in driving national truth and reconciliation processes and transitional justice processes. The work on these processes was also passed down to grassroots for consumption in communities, creating a feedback loop between local and national levels.

Generations For Peace (GFP) | M&E Grid | Version 10/04/2013

PROGRAMME INFO:	Country:	City/Town:		Lead Delegate / Pioneer name:	Programme Name:		Baseline Date: / Evaluation Date:

BEFORE

CONFLICT ANALYSIS

Conflict Context:
- What is the issue of conflict/ violence that you want to address?
- Who are the different "sides" to the conflict?

What dimension(s) of conflict are you focused on in this programme?

| Is your focus on Personal dimension? (Consider individual feelings of weakness or empowerment, attitudes and individual behaviour) | Is your focus on Relational dimension? (Consider quality of relationships, interactions, cooperation, and conflict management between people and groups) | Is your focus on Structural dimension? (Consider inequality, unfairness, exclusion, discrimination, lack of transparency or access, or restrictions of rights) | Is your focus on Cultural dimension? (Consider values promoted and demonstrated in a community; what behaviour and language are acceptable or not, what labels are used, what is celebrated, who are role models) |

THEORY OF CHANGE

| If: (we do something...) (eg: if we bring youth from these two communities together for ongoing SPPY activities each week over six months...) | Then: (something will change...) (eg: then we will see reduction in violence between youths from these communities...) | Because: (of something...) (eg: because the SPPY activities will allow them to gain new perspectives of each other, break down stereotypes, build greater understanding and trust.) | Target Group: (the people you want to involve directly in as participants in the Training and the regular Ongoing Activities) | Beneficiary Community: (the people you want to benefit from the change created by the programme) |

PROGRAMME LOGIC

| Key Stakeholders and the Inputs they will provide: | Planned Activities and Dates: (Events: SPE, ADPE; Training: SPT, ARPT, EPT, ADPT, DPT, TTT; Ongoing Activities: SPPC, SPPY, ARPP, EPP, ADPP, DPP) | Planned Outputs: (number of people trained and levels of participation in ongoing regular activities) | Expected Outcomes in the Target Group: (describe expected changes in frequency and quality of interactions; for example, changes in attitude or behaviour) | Expected Impacts in the Beneficiary Community: (describe expected changes in broader relations or reduced violence) |
| Risks and Assumptions: | Risks and Assumptions: | | Evidence Indicator of Outcomes: (What one thing will you measure to show Outcomes and how will get that information?) | Evidence Indicator of Impacts: (What one thing will you measure to show Impacts, and how will get that information?) |

DURING

MONITORING *Gathering evidence of what's happening*

| Learning and Reflection Process:
 • In what ways is learning and reflection happening:
 ○ Amongst the Delegates/ Pioneers?
 ○ Amongst the Target Group?
 • What is the process to ensure lessons-learned are being used? | Total # of volunteers (Delegates & Pioneers) active this year: Male / Female | Total # of hours this year spent volunteering: hours | # of people Trained in this year's programme cycle: Male / Female | Outcomes Indicator Baseline situation and Date measured: (how the indicator looks when you start, and the date you measured it) | Impacts Indicator Baseline situation and Date measured: (how the indicator looks when you start, and the date you measured it) |
| | Ongoing Activities in programme cycle: Total # of sessions / Total # of hours | # of Participants in regular Ongoing Activities this year: Age 6-15 / Age 16-24 / Age 24+ (M F) | Do participants come from all "sides" of the conflict? YES / NO | Change from Baseline at the end of the year, and Date measured: (how the indicator looks at the end of the programme year, and the date you measured it) | Change from Baseline at the end of the year, and Date measured: (how the indicator looks at the end of the programme year, and the date you measured it) |

AFTER

EVALUATION *Understanding what happened and why, then learning and planning improvements*

| (1) Understanding what happened and why:
 • What worked well and why?

 • What didn't work well and why not?

 • What evidence is there to show outcomes/ impacts? | (2) Most Significant Changes:
 • What do people in the Target Group and Beneficiary Community, consider the most important changes over the last year, and why? (note their first response, then prompt to consider personal, relational, structural, cultural dimensions)
 • What do they believe caused these changes?
 • Why are these changes considered the most important? | (3) Unexpected, unwanted, and unconnected changes:
 • Were there any unexpected or unintended outcomes/ impacts?
 • Have there been any negative outcomes/impact?
 • What else was happening that could have caused the changes? | (4) Looking Forward:
 • Are the changes sustainable? (will the changes be lasting or will things return to the way they were)
 • Is the programme cost-effective? (consider time, effort, and resources put in)
 • Should this programme be replicated or scaled-up? (should it be continued, or increased in size, or taken to a new place, or not?) | (5) Action Points:
 • What changes should we make to update our understanding of the Conflict Context?
 • What changes should we make to our Theory of Change?
 • What changes should we make to our Programme Logic or Activities?
 • For Pioneers/Delegates: What changes should we make to improve our indicators and our processes for M&E and Learning? |

Figure 2. Generations For Peace, Program Monitoring and Evaluation Grid. From the Generations For Peace Programming Framework, 2013.

In Jordan, the Nashatati ("Our Activities") Program started as a small pilot in four schools in 2013, but was scaled up over seven years to 1,000 girls' schools and boys' schools in partnership with the Ministry of Education and The United Nations International Children's Emergency Fund (UNICEF). The program transitioned from after-school activities to in-school activities integrated within the official school curriculum, and scaled by training sixty-one teachers as Master Trainers, forty-two Ministry of Education focal points across the country, and 6,931 teachers to lead activities, ultimately providing the capacity to engage more than 150,000 Jordanian and Syrian refugee students each year in thirty hours of high-quality activities within their school year. Nashatati used GFP's Sport For Peace approach to foster life skills, active lifestyles, tolerance, acceptance, and social cohesion in communities across Jordan, including those most heavily impacted by the Syrian refugee crisis. Even prior to the Syrian refugee crisis, UNICEF data in Jordan showed decades of serious levels of systemic violence in public schools, with a widespread culture of violence manifesting itself in physical violence as well as psychological, verbal, and structural violence, perpetrated by teachers or students. These persistent issues were further amplified and exacerbated by the Syrian refugee crisis and the mass influx of refugees, the majority of whom were of school age, which put enormous pressures on host communities. The approach proved to be effective in reducing systemic violence in schools, improving educational performance and school attendance, and strengthening resilience and social cohesion, especially in host communities bearing enormous pressures under the Syrian refugee crisis. The GFP activities helped to transform the engagement and relationship between teachers and students. Among Jordanian and Syrian students, it reduced physical and verbal violence, increased mutual understanding, and enhanced tolerance between the two communities. The program resulted in behavior-change outcomes including a sixty-six percent decrease in youth responding to conflict with physical violence, sixty-three percent of participants expressing increased self-confidence and self-esteem, sixty-three percent of participants reporting improved social cohesion across the participating schools, sixty-one percent of participants reporting improved communication skills helping them in turn to express their thoughts, feelings, and opinions and engage in respectful dialogue, forty-one percent of participants reporting improved problem-solving skills, fifty-one percent of participants reporting increased interaction with peers outside usual everyday social networks, and forty-eight percent of participants reporting improvement in their teamwork skills and generally in attitude toward working in a team.

Ever since its conception in 2007, GFP's focus was predominantly (but not exclusively) on young people and supporting youth leadership to address local issues of conflict and violence in their own communities. Years later, in 2015, following the Global Forum on Youth, Peace and Security, hosted in Amman, Jordan, and the subsequent United Nations Security Council (UNSC) debate chaired by Crown Prince Al Hussein of Jordan (the youngest person ever to have chaired a UNSC session), the UNSC unanimously adopted Resolution 2250 on Youth, Peace and Security. Three years later, in September 2018, the Global Progress Study report back to the UNSC noted the prevalence of "policy panic" and the importance of debunking stereotypes of youth being seen as violent, a problem, or a threat; that efforts must be made to redress "the violence of exclusion" felt by youth, including exclusion from economic participation (youth unemployment in Jordan, for example, was fifty-two percent), political participation, and social and cultural participation; and that young people need to and can show agency, ownership, and leadership in peacebuilding.

I have seen, in communities and societies around the world, youth represent an enormous untapped reservoir of potential, ready to be engaged and supported as partners and leaders in peacebuilding and development. But this opportunity is, too often, being squandered. Too often, youth are instrumentalized, securitized, treated only as economic objects, or seen as a "problem" to be fixed. Too often, government policies and programs set out to do things "to" youth or "for" youth, rather than working "with" youth. Too often, youth are given opportunities to attend trainings and workshops, but without any subsequent programmatic structure to support them afterward to turn what they have learned into effective actions to deliver positive change in their communities. I felt that the inherent and vibrant altruism and energy of youth was being workshopped to death. Following the Arab Spring, for example, I saw that across the Middle East and North Africa so many opportunities were being offered to youth for two- or three-day trainings or workshops in leadership or community projects, without any follow-on programmatic structure to support the application of what they learned and its conversion to meaningful action. I saw how, over time, their hope of receiving such meaningful support to equip them to make positive changes in their communities and society, was gradually being dimmed, and they came to view such opportunities more cynically as a CV-building exercise to help them not to lead change, but rather to find an escape via a scholarship or job abroad. Such tired, traditional approaches seemed to me to be squandered opportunities and a gross failure. The failure fed into political upheavals, violent conflicts, violent crime, and violent extremism.

In contrast, GFP avoided providing a training or workshop in isolation. On GFP's journey, we learned that the best sustainable 'positive peace' impacts for youth empowerment, resilience, social cohesion, conflict transformation, and reduced vulnerability to violent extremism, come from developing positive values and positive peer-group fusion through experiential learning and activities sustained over time, in existing local structures such as schools, youth centers, and community centers. GFP programs provided training and then ongoing mentoring and support through program design, implementation, and participatory evaluation, giving youth opportunities actually to demonstrate their leadership and responsible citizenship through small local actions in their own communities, and to experience—often for the first time—the feeling of being trusted by adults and authority figures, and appreciated for their contribution to their community. Participatory evaluation focus groups then ensured youth inclusion in local sense-making and local ownership, and provided that moment of intergenerational reflection and dialogue in which elders may share how their perspective has shifted from seeing youth as a problem to seeing their positive potential.

In August 2023, after twelve years serving as CEO, I stepped down from GFP to leave Jordan and return home to Scotland after twenty-two years away, in order to be closer my aging parents and to get my young twin children into school. The move provided me with valuable reflective space to consider what I am returning to, what may I find my new purpose to be, and what I have carried back with me that may be useful to serve that purpose.

I revisited once again an extract from Friedrich Nietzsche's *Twilight of the Idols: or How To Philosophize with a Hammer*, which I have kept printed and folded in my wallet since I first discovered it at age eighteen:

> You run *ahead*?—Are you doing it as a shepherd? Or as an exception? A third case would be the fugitive ... *First* question of conscience.
>
> Are you genuine? Or merely an actor? A representative? Or that which is represented?— In the end, perhaps you are merely a copy of an actor ... *Second* question of conscience.
>
> Are you one who looks on? Or one who lends a hand?— Or one who looks away and walks off? ... *Third* question of conscience.
>
> Do you want to walk along? Or walk ahead? Or walk by yourself? ... One must know *what* one wants and *that* one wants. *Fourth* question of conscience.[16]

To me this has always been an exhortation to have the moral courage to make a conscious, clear choice to step up and lead. Regarding purpose, certainly I feel that my return home to Edinburgh is an opportunity to devote myself to some sort of positive impact in Scotland, in Northern Ireland, and in the UK more widely. I also saw, more clearly visible in the rearview mirror than it had been on the journey, a golden thread woven through my different careers, which was a fascination with leadership and leadership development; with processes of change and transformation in individuals, in organizations, and in communities; and with conflict and how it can be leveraged as source of energy for positive, constructive, generative outcomes, rather than negative, destructive, and degenerative outcomes. I saw a rough sense of progression upstream, from unintended complicity in creating chaos and violence in Iraq, to the reactive emergency humanitarian response work in the DRC, through violence reduction and post-conflict reconciliation in PNG, to grassroots peacebuilding and conflict transformation with GFP in fifty-two countries around the world. I realized I wanted to continue to work my way upstream, to find ways to work at the systems level on prevention and on unleashing squandered potential, to reduce violence, to accelerate public value creation, and to accelerate the energy transition to net zero and nature positive solutions.

However, I worry that in our human systems we do not seem very good at focusing our attention and resources upstream. Our relationship with the past and present seems far more powerful than our relationship with the future. While there are clear moral and economic arguments for much greater investments in upstream prevention, we continually fail really to heed them. For example, the global economic cost of direct violence is enormous. In 2022 the annual economic cost of violence was 17.5 trillion USD, or 12.9 percent of global gross domestic product (GDP). In 2022 global military expenditure rose by 16.8 percent to 7.626 trillion USD. Compare this with total global expenditure on peacebuilding, which in 2022 was just 24 billion USD, i.e., 0.3 percent of military spending.[17] And yet there is robust evidence of a compelling return on investment: that 1 USD spent on 'upstream' violence prevention saves 16 USD on 'downstream' costs of violent conflict.[18] Why then, do we spend only 24 billion USD on peacebuilding globally, while spending about 40 billion USD on perfume, about 100 billion USD on makeup, and about 119 billion USD on ice cream each year? What does our spending, our resource allocation decisions, say about our values as a society?

I also see the significant cost of conflict within businesses and public services: high staff turnover, absenteeism, sick leave, mental health crises, and toxic work cultures driven by fear and cultural violence. And the same economic argument applies—that upstream prevention is cheaper than cure. Yet how much do businesses invest in leadership development for conflict transformation? For my work recently with the Black Leadership Group in the UK, I looked into the economic cost of racism. The International Monetary Fund calculates that in the United States the wealth gap between white and black people is projected to cost the US economy between 1 and 1.5 trillion USD in lost consumption and investment between 2019 and 2028.[19] That equates to four to six percent of GDP in 2028. In France, reducing racial gaps in access to employment, work hours, and education could secure an economic bonus of 3.6 billion USD over the next twenty years. That equates to 1.5 percent of GDP. In the UK, Route2.com calculations in 2020 showed that ethnic discrimination in the workplace costs the UK 40 billion GBP annually.[20] That equates to 1.8 percent of GDP. In addition, Route2.com's research to evaluate the economic costs of racial discrimination in the workplace found that persistent experiences of discrimination, racial or otherwise, reduce a person's well-being, estimating that 19.8 percent of cases of mental health disorders among black, Asian, and minority ethnic persons are attributable to experiences of discrimination in the workplace.

The same argument, that in both blood and treasure, prevention is cheaper than cure, applies not only to violence prevention, but also to public health and to the climate emergency and energy transition to net zero. In each case we seem consistently to fail to make sufficient smart investments in upstream prevention. I am curious about this. Why do we seem really to act only when things have become a crisis, when the impacts are already much more costly? What is it about our psychological relationship with the future compared with the present? What is it about the rhythms of our societies, including democratic election cycles, that constrains the horizon in which we really consider and calculate consequences? What is the role of board level governance and professional advisers, in assessing intergenerational fairness and the risks of inaction?

I founded Transformational Ltd. to be a vehicle to continue to work at this intersection of leadership development, complexity, and conflict, and I see these questions as being at the heart of developing the quality of leadership we want and desperately need in every sector. I believe that transformational positive change for greater intergenerational fairness and more effective use of precious resources seems to require at least the following three things:

(a) Data that is good quality, timely, relevant, and well-presented visually. This is essential to reverse the slide toward a post-truth world.

(b) Participatory engagement to connect perspectives of people across the system in generative dialogue, including those most directly impacted and affected.

(c) Accountability and incentive mechanisms to drive the behavior of current leaders.

But a fourth ingredient is also essential, and often seems lacking currently, in my view: courageous leadership. Courageous leadership is needed to transform conflict and also to stand up to the seductive forces that drive attention to the past and present, to focus more attention on the future, and more investment on upstream prevention.

My overall reflection, therefore, is that conflict is normal and exists in every human system, every society, every community, every corporation and organization, and it is precisely conflict that is the arena demanding leadership. Conflict transformation is *the crucial task* of leadership. In our daily work in teams and organizations, that requires us to really think about and work on transforming *inter*-personal conflict, *intra*-group conflict, and *inter*-group conflict. In addition, I would add *intra*-personal conflict— the conflict we have within ourselves and our own self-talk. The key here is that we will not progress *inter*-personal or *inter*-group conflict transformation if we have not first progressed on *intra*-personal and *intra*-group work. And yet I think we see people in so-called leadership positions struggling with conflict, because it is hard. It is hard because it is emotional and requires some vulnerability and risk, and people generally feel unskilled at dealing with the emotions within conflict. This means a lot of leaders are guilty of work avoidance, of side-stepping this emotional labor, and of abdicating this key responsibility of leadership. Courageous leadership is needed, to embrace conflict as a source of energy for positive, constructive, generative development; to resist the seductive drama and hero-leadership of focusing only on present crises; and to focus more investment on upstream prevention.

Notes

1   Francis Fukuyama, *The End of History and the Last Man* (London and New York: Penguin, 1992).

2   Joint Doctrine Publication, *JDP 0-01, UK Defence Doctrine*, 6th ed. (London: Ministry of Defence, 2022).

3   Joseph Conrad, *Heart of Darkness* (Edinburgh and London: Blackwood's Magazine, 1899).

4   Thedotgood, "Welcome to the World 200 Top SGOs," 2023, https://thedotgood.net/ranking/2023-world-200-sgos/.

5   Johan Galtung, "Three Approaches to Peace: Peacekeeping, Peacemaking, and Peacebuilding," in *Peace, War and Defense: Essays in Peace Research*, ed. Johan Galtung (Oslo: PRIO, 1975), 297–98.

6   John Paul Lederach, *Building Peace: Sustainable Reconciliation in Divided Societies* (Washington, DC: United States Institute of Peace, 1997).

7   Mark Clark, "Demystifying Theory and Remystifying Practice: Theoretical Frames for Better Practice of Sport-Based Approaches to Conflict Transformation" (master's thesis, HEC Paris, 2012).

8   For an explanation of "wicked" and "tame" problems, see Horst W. J. Rittel and Melvin M. Webber, "Dilemmas in a General Theory of Planning," *Policy Sciences* 4, no. 2 (June 1973): 155–69.

9   Leon de Caluwé and Hans Vermaak, *Learning to Change: A Guide for Organization Change Agents* (London: Sage, 2003); and "Change Paradigms: An Overview," *Organization Development Journal* 22, no. 4 (Winter 2004): 9–18.

10 Clark, "Demystifying Theory."

11 Clark, "Demystifying Theory."

12 Clark, "Demystifying Theory."

13 John P. Kotter and Dan S. Cohen, *The Heart of Change: Real-Life Stories of How People Change Their Organizations* (Boston: Harvard Business Review Press, 2002).

14 Chris Argyris and Donald A. Schön, *Organizational Learning: A Theory of Action Perspective* (Reading, MA: Addison-Wesley, 1978).

15 Sairah Yusuf and Suna J. Voss, *The Generations For Peace Institute Compendium of Participatory Indicators of Peace* (Amman: Generations For Peace Institute, 2018).

16 Friedrich Nietzsche, *Twilight of the Idols and The Anti-Christ*, trans. R. J. Hollingdale (London: Penguin Books, 1990), 36–37.

17 Institute for Economics and Peace, *Global Peace Index 2023* (Sydney: Vision of Humanity, 2023).

18 Institute for Economics and Peace, *Measuring Peacebuilding Cost-Effectiveness* (Sydney: Vision of Humanity, 2017).

19 Joseph Losavio, *"What Racism Costs Us All,"* International Monetary Fund, September 2020, https://www.imf.org/en/Publications/fandd/issues/2020/09/the-economic-cost-of-racism-losavio.

20 "Workplace Discrimination: The Cost," Route2, July 27, 2020, https://route2.com/workplace-discrimination-the-cost/.